"Nessan is a thorough and gifted scholar, whose grasp of Wilhelm Loehe is not just historic, but lived. Nessan embodies the Loehe legacy, describing its effectiveness for building communities of faith and service today. This book brings to life a tradition that endures and holds great promise for reforming the church and the world."

—LOUISE JOHNSON
President, Wartburg Theological Seminary

"At a time when the struggles, missteps, fresh impulses, and contributions of missionaries and missiological thinkers of earlier times are relegated to quick summaries or tucked away in footnotes, it's gratifying that we have this solid and thorough analysis of the work and witness of Wilhelm Loehe. Dr. Nessan writes with the conviction that amidst the realities of our times, a rediscovery of his legacy will enliven and challenge our thinking as well as energize and kindle our praxis."

—J. JAYAKIRAN SEBASTIAN
Dean and H. George Anderson Professor of Mission and Cultures,
United Lutheran Seminary

"Using original sources, including archival material, Nessan looks at multiple aspects of Loehe's influence on mission, liturgy, and church life in nineteenth-century American Lutheranism. Students of Lutheran history and theology will welcome this well-crafted study of a remarkable pastor and missional leader and the legacy which he left in North America."

—JOHN T. PLESS
Concordia Theological Seminary

"This volume offers us the abundant harvest of Nessan's writing on the impact of Wilhelm Loehe's worship-centered, ecclesial, and missionary theology on Lutherans in North America. Here you will find readable, well-informed history, and illuminating theological discussion of Loehe and those who followed his lead. And more—you will see the impulses from Loehe for imagining the renewal of the church in its life and mission today. Nessan is a superb guide into this territory."

—THOMAS H. SCHATTAUER
Professor of Liturgics and Dean of the Chapel, Wartburg Theological Seminary

"*Wilhelm Loehe and North America* is a must-read narrative of the origins of the Lutheran church in the Midwest. The book is a conversation—using primary sources with a keen hermeneutical eye—where we can dialogue with the protagonists about their struggles and hopes as they mirror many of ours today."

—FRANCISCO JAVIER GOITÍA PADILLA
Program Director for Theological Formation, Seminaries and Schools, Evangelical Lutheran Church in America

Wilhelm Loehe
and North America

Missional Church, Public Theology, World Christianity

Stephen Bevans, Paul S. Chung, Veli-Matti Kärkkäinen,
and Craig L. Nessan, Series Editors

IN THE MIDST OF globalization there is crisis as well as opportunity. A model of God's mission is of special significance for ecclesiology and public theology when explored in diverse perspectives and frameworks in the postcolonial context of World Christianity. In the face of the new, complex global civilization characterized by the Second Axial Age, the theology of mission, missional ecclesiology, and public ethics endeavor to provide a larger framework for missiology. It does so in interaction with our social, multicultural, political, economic, and intercivilizational situation. These fields create ways to refurbish mission as constructive theology in critical and creative engagement with cultural anthropology, world religions, prophetic theology, postcolonial hermeneutics, and contextual theologies of World Christianity. Such endeavors play a critical role in generating theological, missional, social-ethical alternatives to the reality of Empire—a reality characterized by civilizational conflict, and by the complex system of a colonized lifeworld that is embedded within practices of greed, dominion, and ecological devastation. This series—Missional Church, Public Theology, World Christianity—invites scholars to promote alternative church practices for life-enhancing culture and for evangelization as telling the truth in the public sphere, especially in solidarity with those on the margins and in ecological stewardship for the lifeworld.

Wilhelm Loehe and North America

Historical Perspective and Living Legacy

with gratitude!

Shalom,

Craig L. Nessan

Craig L. Nessan

Foreword by
Kathryn A. Kleinhans

PICKWICK *Publications* · Eugene, Oregon

WILHELM LOEHE AND NORTH AMERICA
Historical Perspective and Living Legacy

Missional Church, Public Theology, World Christianity 10

Pickwick Publications
An Imprint of Wipf and Stock Publishers
199 W. 8th Ave., Suite 3
Eugene, OR 97401

www.wipfandstock.com

PAPERBACK ISBN: 978-1-5326-8656-6
HARDCOVER ISBN: 978-1-5326-8657-3
EBOOK ISBN: 978-1-5326-8658-0

Cataloguing-in-Publication data:

Names: Nessana, Craig L., author. | Kleinhans, Kathryn A., foreword.

Title: Wilhelm Loehe and North America : historical perspective and living legacy / Craig L. Nessan ; foreword by Kathryn A. Kleinhans.

Description: Eugene, OR: Pickwick Publications, 2020. | Missional Church, Public Theology, World Christianity. | Includes bibliographical references and index.

Identifiers: ISBN 978-1-5326-8656-6 (paperback). | ISBN 978-1-5326-8657-3 (hardcover). | ISBN 978-1-5326-8658-0 (ebook).

Subjects: LCSH: Loehe, Wilhelm, 1808–1872. | Wartburg Theological Seminary. | Lutheran church—Doctrines.

Classification: BX8080 2020 (print). | BX8080 (ebook).

Manufactured in the U.S.A.   06/17/20

"I shall not cease from mental fight
Nor shall my sword sleep in my hand
till we have built Jerusalem
in England's green and pleasant land."

—WILLIAM BLAKE

Contents

Foreword

Imagine a context where the church struggles both to minister faithfully to its long-time members and to reach out to those who have never heard the Gospel.

Imagine a context where technological innovation and increasing urbanization disrupt traditional social patterns.

Imagine a context where social needs outweigh the ability of governmental and family structures to meet them, leaving the church to fill the gap.

Imagine a context where unemployment rates are high, with employers and economic systems unable to ensure that all have a livable wage.

Imagine a context where young people delay marriage because of the uncertainty of being able to establish and support a family under current conditions.

Imagine a context without enough seminary-trained candidates to serve as congregational pastors.

Imagine a context where the challenges faced in ministry go well beyond one's seminary preparation.

Imagine a context where church members and church leaders alike disagree on the role of the Lutheran Confessions, personal piety, and the appropriate use of reason and critical thinking in the Christian faith.

Imagine a context where the church wrestles with how to honor the pastoral ministry of Word and Sacrament and a diaconal ministry of Word and Service.

What context, what church are you imagining? Did you think first of the church in our own context in the first quarter of the twenty-first century?

If so, you are correct. You would also be correct if you imagine the Lutheran church in the German region of Franconia in the mid-nineteenth century.

Johann Conrad Wilhelm Loehe (1808–1872) was a missionary who never left home. He served for most of his life as the pastor in the Bavarian village of Neuendettelsau. Still today, in the courtyard of the *Mission EineWelt* (Mission One World) complex in Neuendettelsau, stands a signpost with wooden panels pointing to locations around the world that were—and continue to be—touched by Loehe's ministry: Mozambique, Congo, Malaysia, the Philippines, Papua New Guinea, Brazil, the United States, and more.

Loehe's faithful commitment to ministry led him to pay careful attention to his context. He worked creatively and faithfully to meet not only the spiritual needs but also the material and physical needs of the community to which he had been called. Starting a brick factory provided employment and made it possible for the residents of Neuendettelsau to build better housing than the mud huts in which most of them lived when Loehe was called to the village in 1837. Starting a deaconess training program provide meaningful work for women and a servant corps for meeting social needs in the community.

Loehe's sense of call extended far beyond the village boundaries. Attentive to the needs of German emigrant communities, he provided basic ministerial training for young men willing to emigrate themselves and to serve among German settlers in other lands. The "emergency helpers" Loehe sent to the United States influenced both the formation of the Lutheran Church—Missouri Synod and the Iowa Synod (one of the regional church bodies that eventually became part of the Evangelical Lutheran Church in America).

Although it has been almost 150 years since Loehe's death, his legacy lives on. Neuendettelsau continues to be a center of global mission. Although the number of actual deaconesses is small, the ministry of Word and Service continues through the work of *Diakonie Neuendettelsau,* the largest social ministry organization in Bavaria, providing education, health care, and services for the elderly and the mentally and physically challenged. One backwater pastor's faithful ministry and creative, entrepreneurial vision launched ministries that have influenced —and continue to influence—hundreds of thousands of people around the world.

Until now, Loehe's life and legacy have been known primarily to those affiliated with Wartburg College (Waverly, Iowa), Wartburg Theological Seminary (Dubuque, Iowa), and Concordia Theological Seminary (Fort Wayne, Indiana). In 2005, representatives of these institutions, together with representatives of *Diakonie Neuendettelsau, Mission Eine Welt*, and the *Gesellschaft für Innere und Äußere Mission* (Society for Inner and Outer Mission), founded the International Loehe Society "to promote study of the life, theology, and work of Wilhelm Loehe (1808–1872) in historical context and to explore Loehe's continuing significance for the church in its life and mission today."

In this book, Craig Nessan brings Loehe's history and legacy to a wider audience. While following the historical and institutional development of Loehe's various ministry activities, Nessan lifts up key themes and insights that are valuable for anyone doing ministry in a context of great change and great need—that is, for anyone doing ministry. In Nessan's words, Loehe brings together "liturgical worship and passion for mission, confessional orthodoxy and pietistic devotion, evangelical proclamation and diaconal servanthood, theological imagination and pragmatic skills in administration and financial management." May learning more about Loehe's life and legacy empower others to do likewise in our own contexts!

Kathryn A. Kleinhans
Dean, Trinity Lutheran Seminary at Capital University
Columbus, Ohio

Introduction

What Does Wilhelm Loehe Mean to Me?

"WHAT DOES LOEHE MEAN to me?" I was first asked to reflect on this question when Stefan Bär posed it to me in 2009.[1] He is a member of the St. Michaels parish in Fürth, Germany, whose family purchased and renovated the house nearby the church where Loehe was born on February 21, 1808. Today the bedroom, in which he was likely not only born but baptized, is dedicated to an exhibition about Loehe's life and legacy.

The name of Wilhelm Loehe first became known to me when I was a young seminarian at Wartburg Theological Seminary in Dubuque, Iowa in the mid-1970s. The centrally located worship space at the seminary is named Loehe Chapel. Although during my years of study I became familiar with the name of Loehe as the founder of our seminary and regularly attended daily worship services in that chapel, at that time I really did not learn much more about him.

When twenty years later I returned to Wartburg Theological Seminary as a member of the faculty, I began intentional research on the history of our school, including learning more about Loehe as the founder. In the meantime, President William Weiblen had written a history of the seminary, which included information about the relationship of Loehe to the Iowa Synod, to which the seminary originally belonged.[2] Moreover, I began to investigate the various places where the seminary was located for shorter periods of time in the nineteenth century—not only Dubuque but also at St. Sebald in Clayton County, Iowa, and Mendota, Illinois—before returning to its current location at Dubuque in 1889. I also conducted projects in oral history with some of those who carried

1. Bär, ed., *Was mir Loehe bedeutet.*
2. Weiblen, *Life Together.*

xiii

the historical memory of the school, including Weiblen, Edwin Schick, and the widow of William D. Streng, Helen. The conversations with Dr. Weiblen were later transcribed and, together with some of his sermons and writings, published as a book.[3] From this research gradually there emerged a coherent narrative of the history of the seminary that convinced me that the Loehe legacy continues to exert major influence over the character of the school and its graduates many generations later, therefore deserving our ongoing attention.

Loehe's thought has been fittingly described as an "ecclesial theology."[4] While this description identifies the centrality of the church in Loehe's theology, it is even more revealing to distinguish how the church for Loehe was always moving outward in mission. This book demonstrates the decidedly "missionary" character of Loehe's life and legacy. Loehe wrote in *Three Books about the Church*:

> Springing up on Pentecost and Calvary, the church flows through the ages like a river, and that same river and no other will flow unchangingly on through the ages until that great day when it will empty completely into the famed sea of eternal blessedness.[5]

Loehe's ecclesiology imagined and formed a church that flows like a river always in motion, that is, the church in mission.

The theological institute founded by Loehe—and, as we will discover, supported by his colleague, Friedrich Bauer—began to send teachers and pastors to minister to the many German immigrants coming to North America in the mid-nineteenth century. Thereby Loehe was acknowledged as the founder not only of the Iowa Synod in 1853, but also as an organizer of the Lutheran Church-Missouri Synod already in the 1840s. Eventually the Iowa Synod became, through a sequence of mergers, part of the Evangelical Lutheran Church in America (ELCA). Through the heritage of the Iowa Synod, the ELCA inherited a set of ecclesial elements that continue to contribute creatively to the life of the church to this day, including confessionalism, pietism, liturgical renewal, *diakonia*, open questions, and mission. Each of these elements as elaborated in this book, historically and theologically, are dynamic contributions for reinventing ecclesiology in our time.

3. Nessan, *The Air I Breathe Is Wartburg Air.*

4. Ratke, *Confession and Mission, Word and Sacrament.*

5. Loehe, *Three Books about the Church,* 55.

First, the missionary theology of Loehe is *confessional*. As a theologian of his era, he viewed Lutheranism as the epitome of the development of Christian doctrine in contrast to other confessional traditions.

Second, the missionary theology of Loehe is *pietistic*. Loehe was influenced by the pietistic revival of his time. Pietism gave him and the leaders of the Iowa Synod a vivid sense of the living God's activity and involvement in human life.

Third, the missionary theology of Loehe is *liturgical*. Loehe engaged as a scholar in serious study of the liturgical traditions of the early church, retrieving many ancient worship practices for the renewal of worship in his own time. This conviction nourished his imagination that the God who comes to us in Word and Sacrament is the same God who is at work in Christian mission to save the world.

Fourth, the missionary theology of Loehe is *diaconal*. Loehe founded a deaconess order, which led to the formation of the charitable institutions that continue to minister in Germany to this day. Thereby the diaconal ministry of the church was offered in service to many persons in acute need, including sick, dying, poor, disabled, and elderly persons.

Fifth, Loehe allowed for the possibility of "*open questions*." Where there is agreement about the central matters of Christian faith centered in the doctrine of justification by grace through faith in Jesus Christ, there can be unity of faith, even without agreement on secondary matters. This dimension of Loehe's ecclesiology is a special gift for the contemporary church in its ecumenical work and guards against the impulse to schism.

Sixth, combining all these characteristics into his own creative pattern, the theology of Loehe is intentionally *missionary*. The church of God through the ages is a church in motion.

> For mission is nothing but the one church of God in motion, the actualization of the one universal, catholic church . . . Mission is the life of the catholic church. Where it stops, blood and breath stop; where it dies, the love which unites heaven and earth also dies. The catholic church and mission—these two no one can separate without killing both, and that is impossible.[6]

Loehe entertained a profound imagination for the church in mission. All elements of Loehe's theology—confessional, pietistic, liturgical, diaconal, and open questions—finally serve this primary passion for mission.

---

6. Loehe, *Three Books about the Church*, 59.

The book is organized into eight chapters. Chapter 1 introduces the shape of the Loehe legacy and its significance for church and mission in North America. Chapters 2, 3, and 4 document Loehe's relationship to the Iowa Synod through primary source material and contrast the character of his influence in the Iowa and Missouri Synods. Chapters 5 and 6 retrieve the contributions to theological education and theological curriculum by Loehe's colleague, Friedrich Bauer, restoring him to his rightful place as co-worker with Loehe. Chapter 7 focuses on the theology of Wartburg Theological Seminary as it has evolved over the course of its history, from the time of its founders into the twenty-first century. Chapter 8 concludes with the argument that six dimensions of the Loehe legacy remain robust and energetic for the reinvention of the church in our time.

The Loehe legacy gained renewed and vital interest with the founding of the International Loehe Society at Wartburg Theological Seminary at Dubuque in 2005. The publications from this and subsequent meetings—at Neuendettelsau in 2008, Fort Wayne, Indiana and Frankenmuth, Michigan in 2011, and again at Neuendettelsau in 2014—generated new research and significant recovery of the Loehe legacy for the life of the church and mission today. This book gathers and expands upon my own research into "all things Loehe." It is my hope that this history and legacy continue to make a profound contribution not only to those institutions founded by Loehe—Wartburg College and Wartburg Theological Seminary—but to the life of the one holy catholic apostolic church, to whose flourishing Loehe dedicated every measure of his life energy.

While earlier versions of some chapters have appeared previously, these have been entirely revised and integrated into the design of this book. I appreciate the permission of *Lutheran Quarterly* for the use of articles in chapters 2 and 5, *Logia: A Journal of Theology* for chapter 3, *Currents in Theology and Mission* for chapter 4, and the Concordia Historical Institute for the use of material in chapter 2 that was reprinted in *The Pieper Lectures*, Volume 13 (2012). I am also thankful to the editors and publishers who have included my work in volumes documenting the proceedings of meetings about Loehe held in Germany.

I express deep gratitude to my assistants, Tania Schramm, for her excellent copy editing, constructive improvements, and formatting of the text, and Nathaniel Adkins for help with proofreading and indexing. Also, I express my thanks to archivists of the ELCA Region 5/Wartburg Theological Seminary Archives who have supported this work over many years: Robert Wiederaenders, Nancy Carroll, and Suzanne Dodd, together with the volunteer extraordinaire, Jean Peterson. Moreover, I am grateful to Susan Ebertz, Director of the Reu Memorial Library, and its staff.

This book is dedicated to the alumni, students, staff, and faculty of Wartburg Theological Seminary who are among the bearers of the Loehe Legacy in our time. I express special appreciation to Professor Thomas H. Schattauer, cofounder with me of the International Loehe Society. *Soli Deo Gloria*!

Craig L. Nessan,
Dubuque, Iowa
Epiphany 2020

1

Wilhelm Loehe's Significance
for Church and Mission in North America

PASTOR WILHELM LOEHE (1808–1872) had a negative first impression of the obscure Franconian village of Neuendettelsau, Germany, where he was called to serve as pastor in 1837. Yet from this humble, out-of-the-way congregation led by a pastor who did not want to go there arose a mission movement that has changed church and world in remarkable ways, including the church in North America. Wilhelm Loehe held together commitments often seen as contradictory: liturgical worship and passion for mission, confessional orthodoxy and pietistic devotion, evangelical proclamation and diaconal servanthood, theological imagination and pragmatic skills in administration and finance. This chapter introduces these themes. The Loehe legacy is fascinating not only for its historical contributions in the nineteenth century but also for providing a matrix for us to rethink and reconfigure the shape of the church and its mission in our time.

Biographical Orientation

During his lifetime, Loehe's missionary theology acquired ever new accents: God's mission necessitates the church, mission begins at worship, mission entails confessional loyalty, mission involves pastoral care, mission requires leaders prepared through theological education, mission sends ministers to serve overseas, and mission flows into diaconal service. This book explores the historical record regarding the influence of Loehe in North America and draws upon this legacy for constructing

1

vital approaches to ministry and mission for the church in our post-Christian age.

Loehe's biography demonstrates—from his earliest engagement in public ministry to the end of his life—how his pulse beat with a passion for both vital liturgical worship and for sharing the good news of Jesus Christ. Johann Konrad Wilhelm Loehe was born on February 21, 1808, in a room within his family home in Fürth, Germany, the neighbor city to the regional center of Nuremburg.[1] Raised as a child who loved the church and influenced by the devotion of his mother and experiences in his home parish of St. Michael's, Loehe expressed the desire from an early age to become a pastor. As a theological candidate aspiring to a pastoral call in a prominent urban location, he ran into repeated disfavor with judicatory officials, making it difficult for him to land a permanent position of any kind. The combination of an uncompromising zeal about Lutheran confessional identity in opposition to "unionism" with the Reformed tradition and the implementation of pietistic practices into pastoral ministry (such as prayer, Bible study, and hymn singing in private homes) made him suspect.

Consistent with the pietistic leanings of his childhood home, Loehe became notorious for organizing missionary circles and missionary societies during his theological studies.[2] At Erlangen University he was captivated by the pietistic theology of Professor Johann Christian Krafft. After completing his university study in 1830 and his ordination in 1831, Loehe spent seven years serving in temporary positions at several locations in an extended series of vicarages. It was a disquieting period for Loehe, who wanted to establish a settled residence, where he could serve his Lord and Savior as a parish pastor among God's people. Yet conflicts and disappointments seemed to meet him at every turn.

One bright light amid the shadows and turmoil of these years was his engagement and marriage in July 1837 to Helene Andrae, daughter of a merchant family from Frankfurt and his confirmand in 1835. Together the newly married couple buoyed their courage to move into the parsonage in the remote and, to Loehe's eyes, backwards village on August 1, 1837.

---

1. The house, renovated by Stefan Bär and the Wilhelm-Löhe-Gedenkstätte, is located at Königstrasse 27. The room where Loehe was born is now a small museum.

2. Weber, *Missionstheologie bei Wilhelm Loehe*, 44–161.

What did Neuendettelsau look like at this time? The low thatched houses with their dirty window panes, the "disorderly manure piles" in front of every house were not an inspiring sight. Only the baronial mansion, the parsonage, the inn and the homes of wealthy farmers were roofed with expensive tiles. If it rained, one had to wade through the mud of the unpaved village streets, otherwise through dust. Loehe, who was so fussy about cleanliness, could not walk the short way from the parsonage to the church without having his robe splattered with dirt. Therefore he had this way paved during the first year of his ministry—the first paved street in Neuendettelsau.[3]

Based on his earliest encounters with this place, Loehe is purported to have remarked that he would not even want his dog to be buried there. Ironically, Loehe would later purchase property for a town cemetery, where his own grave, together with those of his wife and co-workers, holds a prominent place. During his first ten years in Neuendettelsau, Loehe applied for calls to city parishes four times, none of them successful.[4] So he committed his life and ministry to this isolated place.

The early years of parish ministry were filled with opportunities and challenges for the new pastor. Loehe dedicated himself to restoring the Sunday worship service as the center of parish life. He had great interest in studying historic liturgical forms and sought to introduce the congregation to worship practices that he found especially meaningful; for example, he encouraged congregational participation in the service by saying "Amen" after prayer or kneeling during the Lord's Supper, some of which prompted noticeable resistance. Loehe devoted great attention to the preparation of his sermons, which aimed at faithfulness to God's Word expressed in a form that would communicate effectively with the simple lives of the villagers. In his pastoral visitation, Pastor Loehe recognized the harsh living conditions of the people, overcrowding in many homes, and the lack of adequate care for the aged and persons with disabilities. He became increasingly focused on greater participation by members in the educational and worship life of the congregation, including children and their mothers.

Helene played a significant role as the pastor's wife in the life of the parish, starting a preschool for small children whose mothers had many other responsibilities in the afternoons. Their first child, Johann

3. Geiger, *Wilhelm Loehe*, 69–70.
4. Ottersberg, "Wilhelm Loehe," 172.

Friedrich, was born after a difficult delivery in July 1838. Three more children soon followed at approximately eighteen-month intervals: Marianne, Gottfried, and Philipp. The parsonage was filled with the bustle of a lively and active family. While exercising strict discipline, Loehe also rejoiced in times of daily play with his children. Wilhelm and Helene enjoyed six years of blessed marriage until a tragedy struck the family, one from which Loehe never would recover. Early in 1843 the village was overcome by a series of illnesses, including scarlet fever, whooping cough, and pneumonia. On a visit to help care for the children after the birth of Philipp in January 1843, Helene's mother became sick and soon died.

After a period of acute mourning for her mother, Helene resumed her spirited involvement in her family roles as mother and wife and congregational role as pastor's wife. In the fall of the same year, Loehe was struck with a bad case of influenza. Helene, who nursed him back to health, soon succumbed to the illness herself, which was accompanied by high fever and the onset of typhus. On November 24, after a moving exchange between husband and wife at her bedside, Helene died at the age of 24. Loehe wrote about her death:

> I thanked her for her countless deeds of charity, for her sacrificial love—I became the most miserable person under the sun, while she inherited eternal riches.[5]

The death of his beloved wife forever after diminished Loehe's vitality, challenging his faith in God and complicating his relationship as father to his children. While urged to consider a second marriage for the sake of his family, Loehe decided never to take another wife. His grief for Helene affected him for the remainder of his life.

Loehe's pastoral and missional commitments made him eager to take action when he read an appeal in 1840 by Pastor Friedrich Wyneken for help with the mission in North America. Loehe responded to the plea for financial support and volunteers for mission work among the German immigrants in North America by writing an article: "The Lutheran Emigrants in North America: An Address to the Readers of the *Sonntagsblatt*" ["*Die lutherische Auswanderer in Nordamerika: Eine Ansprache an die Leser des Sonntagsblattes*"].[6] Together with other partners, Loehe

---

5. For more about Helene's death and the quote, see Geiger, *Wilhelm Loehe,* 78.

6. Loehe, "Die lutherische Auswanderer in Nordamerika," 16–19. See also Loehe's sermon comments in *Gesammelte Werke,* 640–41.

took up the task of organizing a strategy for disbursing contributed funds and preparing volunteers, who soon made themselves available for this missionary work in North America. After an initial period of offering support for the work of the Ohio Synod and its seminary at Columbus, Ohio, Loehe turned to the Lutheran Church—Missouri Synod (LCMS) as a mission partner more consistent with his own confessional commitments. In 1849 Loehe founded the Society for Inner Mission in the Spirit of the Lutheran Church [*Gesellschaft für innere Mission im Sinne der Lutherischen Kirche*] to sustain this work among the German immigrants.

Of interest for the history of Wartburg Theological Seminary, Loehe supported the organization of German immigrant colonies in the vicinity of Saginaw, Michigan, sending colonists from Germany to populate them and religious leaders for their spiritual care. Loehe envisioned that these colonies would provide ministry to the German immigrants and also imagined how they would develop missionary work among the Chippewa people, on whose land the villages were being established. Among the religious leaders, Johannes Deindoerfer was sent as pastor to the colony at Frankenhilf in 1851 and Georg Grossmann as director of a teachers seminary at Saginaw in 1852. When conflict ensued over the nature of ordained ministry, Deindoerfer and Grossmann found themselves accused of doctrinal error by the leaders of the LCMS. This conflict prompted those loyal to Loehe to leave behind the work begun in Michigan and seek out a territory not yet under development by the LCMS. That destination was Iowa.

This brief sketch of Loehe's earliest outreach to North America leaves unmentioned other missionary impulses of his work in Neuendettelsau and other parts of the world, most importantly his deaconess initiative. In 1853, the same year that Loehe's emissaries moved from Michigan to the new mission territory in Iowa, he founded the Lutheran Society for the Female Diaconate [*Lutherischer Verein für weibliche Diakonie*]. The organizing of this association for Lutheran deaconesses in Neuendettelsau, with their charitable work focused on marginalized members of society, required an increasing amount of Loehe's attention in subsequent years. Following a path begun by Theodor Fliedner (1800–1864) at Kaiserswerth, Loehe envisioned bringing together the needs of the weakest members of the surrounding community with the desire of women to develop and share their gifts in service to those in need. From modest beginnings of training in the local guest house, *In der Sonne*, a Mother House for deaconesses was constructed in 1854 and a neighboring chapel built in 1858–1859. The deaconesses received a rigorous and thorough training in learning to care appropriately and effectively for the unique needs of each group.[7] The deaconesses also developed a rich spiritual and community life. Some effort was made to send deaconesses from Neuendettelsau to serve in the Iowa Synod as early as 1857–1859; however, the careers of these particular deaconesses led them either to marriage or a return to Germany.[8]

Lively correspondence ensued again in the late 1860s between Loehe and Pastor Johannes Doerfler, who was leading an orphanage sponsored by the Iowa Synod at Toledo, Ohio.[9] Following Loehe's direction, pastors from the Iowa Synod founded a Society for Common Works of Mercy in the Spirit of the Evangelical-Lutheran Church in North America in 1870, in order to establish preconditions for receiving deaconesses to serve at the orphanage. Sister Luise Adelberg was sent to work on this initiative in 1868; however, due to complications, she spent most of her years serving not in Toledo but as a housemother at another institution in Buffalo, New York. She returned to the Mother House in Neuendettelsau in 1879. Deaconess Anna Lutz was sent from North America to Neuendettelsau for training in 1873, a year after Loehe's death, to be prepared for service at the orphanage in Toledo and to establish an independent motherhouse there. These plans also never came to fruition.[10]

The deaconess order was organized and structured by Loehe at Neuendettelsau in the same years as the Iowa Synod was being organized far away. Much of Loehe's attention and effort shifted at this time from North America to the challenges of developing the deaconess work. During the following years his colleague, Friedrich Bauer, took over an increasing portion of the theological education work for the candidates being prepared for service in the Iowa Synod. As we will explore in chapters 5 and 6, Bauer became the primary figure to communicate with the leaders in the Iowa Synod and at Wartburg Seminary. Nevertheless, Loehe himself continued to support the mission work in North America,

---

7. For a description of the training of deaconesses for nursing, see Honold, "Deaconesses in Nursing Care," 65–77.

8. Olson, *Deacons and Deaconesses*, 265.

9. An excellent resource documenting this history and the related correspondence is Liebenberg et al., *Diakonissen fuer Amerika*.

10. For this description of the Neuendettelsau deaconess activity within the Iowa Synod, see Liebenberg et al., *Diakonissen fuer Amerika*, XXXIV–XXXV.

especially through the institutions of the Iowa Synod, until the end of his life in 1872.

The Matrix of the Loehe Legacy and the Mission of the Church Today

During thirty-five years of pastoral ministry in Neuendettelsau (1837–1872), Wilhelm Loehe demonstrated an amazing capacity for a wide range of activities in service of God's mission: serving the local congregation in his daily pastoral duties, encouraging piety, involved as an active clergy colleague, engaging in liturgical research, publishing many volumes of Christian literature in a variety of genres, establishing theological education for teachers and pastors, organizing support for missionary outreach to North America, producing an extensive body of written correspondence, founding the deaconess order with its various forms of diaconal service to neighbors in acute need, and active as an effective administrator on behalf of all these efforts and more.

The Loehe legacy brings together a unique pattern of ecclesial commitments that are often viewed as mutually exclusive or even contradictory: liturgical worship and passion for mission, confessional orthodoxy and pietistic devotion, evangelical proclamation and diaconal servanthood, theological imagination and pragmatic skills in administration and financial management. This configuration of ministry gifts is of historical interest relative to Loehe's own pastoral activity but also because these forms of service constitute a matrix of creative elements much needed for the ministry and mission of the church in our post-Christian age.

Liturgical Worship and Passion for Mission

A missionary theology of worship begins with the conviction that the primary actor at worship is the Triune God. The Three Persons of the Trinity, who constitute the unity of the Godhead, exist in life-giving relationships one with another. The dynamic inter-personal relationships among the Father, Son, and Holy Spirit, named in the doctrinal tradition as *perichoresis*, constitute a divine dance into which the church as *ecclesia* is invited to join.[11] The life-giving relationships among the Divine Persons are extended through the church as a means of grace for the life

---

11. Zizioulas, *Being as Communion*.

of the world. It is at worship, following the pattern of the historic *ordo* as researched and renewed by Loehe for his generation, that the members of the body of Christ are invited to learn the steps of this liturgical dance as a way of life. At worship the Triune God teaches the gathered people of God how to dance! This is what liturgical theologian, Thomas Schattauer, means by turning worship "inside out" for an age of mission.[12]

While liturgy had received decreasing attention in the age of rationalism, Loehe recognized the practices of worship as central to the life and mission of the church.[13] His own study of liturgics seems to have intensified after the death of his wife, starting with an investigation of the oldest Lutheran orders of worship and handbooks; reportedly, he examined about two hundred of these. Loehe next explored worship in the ancient and medieval church, giving particular interest to the rites of the old Eastern churches. "His *Agende* is the product of these studies, designed particularly for the missions in [North] America. It was a handbook, appearing in two editions during his lifetime, which broke ground for a resurgence of interest in liturgics in the Lutheran Church."[14] Loehe was criticized as a "Romanizer," including by colleagues in Bavaria, because of these interests. This did not deter him, however, from restoring and implementing liturgical renewal in his local parish, which was accomplished by carefully instructing the congregation about the meaning of proposed changes to worship practice. For example, Loehe was able to introduce liturgical reform among the deaconesses, and also stimulate interest in the use of paraments and provide training for crafting them.

Loehe understood the relational character of the Triune God, who meets and forms us at worship and sends us forth to the ends of the earth in mission.[15]

> Just as the stars revolve around the sun, so does the congregation in its services, full of loveliness and dignity, revolve around the Lord. In holy, childlike innocence which only a child's innocent heart understands properly, the multitude of redeemed, sanctified children of God dances in worship around the universal Father and the Lamb, and the Spirit of the Lord of lords guide their steps. The spiritual joy and heavenly delight enjoyed by those who take part in this sort of liturgy cannot be described.

12. Schattauer, "Liturgical Assembly as Locus of Mission."

13. Ottersberg, "Wilhelm Loehe," 178–79.

14. Ottersberg, "Wilhelm Loehe," 179.

15. Schattauer, "The Reconstruction of Rite," 249.

> When the liturgy is performed by devout souls it also speaks
> powerfully to those who are less devout, and the pure confession
> has no lovelier or more attractive form than when it is seen in
> the act of prayer and praise.[16]

Loehe's vivid liturgical theology flows seamlessly together with this lively sense of Christian mission, as "the one church of God in motion . . . which flows through time and into which all people pour."[17] The relationship between liturgy and mission is one of the most prominent themes interwoven throughout this book, to which we will especially return in the final chapter.

Confessional Orthodoxy and Pietistic Devotion

Interpretations of Protestantism in the centuries following the Reformation have made a conventional distinction—if not opposition—between "Orthodoxy" and "Pietism." Within Lutheranism this interpretation emphasized how the doctrinal formulations of the Lutheran Confessions became codified through precise dogmatic expression in the post-Reformation era. One fascinating compendium of Orthodoxy was assembled by Heinrich Schmid in his *Doctrinal Theology of the Evangelical Lutheran Church*.[18] This collection of excerpts from the works of orthodox theologians primarily writing in the late sixteenth and seventeenth centuries is organized and systematized in five major parts: part 1 "Of God," part 2 "Of Man," part 3 "Of the Sources of Salvation," part 4 "Of the Means of Grace and the Church," and part 5 "Of the Last Things." The discussion of the "concomitants and consequences of justifying faith" is illustrative of the approach of Lutheran Orthodoxy, which presents and analyzes the following constituent elements: divine call, illumination, regeneration and conversion, mystical union, renovation, and good works.[19] In many respects, this was a return to the theological method of scholasticism, a project consolidating the theological gains of the Reformation in response to the Roman Catholic counter-Reformation.

As a movement in church history, Pietism originated with the work of Philipp Jakob Spener (1635–1705) at Frankfurt, Germany. Influenced

16. Loehe, *Three Books about the Church*, 177.

17. Loehe, *Three Books about the Church*, 59.

18. Schmid, *Doctrinal Theology*.

19. Schmid, *Doctrinal Theology*, 441–99.

by the writings of Johann Arndt and Jean de Labadie, Spener initiated a
renewal movement that emphasized personal devotion, Bible study, and
pious practices by individuals combined with gatherings of the faithful
(conventicles) for prayer, singing, and study of the Christian faith. He
was committed to the spiritual formation of church members, so that
they would live out their faith in all arenas of their lives. In his classic
book, *Pia Desideria* (1675), Spener also advocated for the education of
pastors to be informed by the practice of pious devotion with special
attention in pastoral ministry for developing and deepening the faith
of church members.[20] It was especially due to its criticisms of existing
theological education of pastors and an overly formalized approach to
pastoral ministry, including the preaching of doctrinally weighted sermons, that Pietism became juxtaposed as antithetical to Orthodoxy.
Other major figures in the German Pietist movement of the seventeenth
and eighteenth centuries were August Hermann Francke (1663–1727) at
Halle (noteworthy for the development of educational and social service
outreach) and Count Nikolaus Ludwig von Zinzendorf (1700–1760) at
Herrnhut.

Wilhelm Loehe was influenced by the enduring effects of Pietism
in the nineteenth century in his own Christian formation, approach to
pastoral ministry, support for foreign mission, and administration of
deaconess ministries in service to people in need. German Pietism includes central features that can be readily identified as marking Loehe's
life and ministry:

> The genius of Pietism lay in the adjectives it employed: *true*
> Christianity; *heartfelt, living* faith; a *living* knowledge of God;
> the *inward* Christ and the *inner* Word . . . Born-again laypeople
> became agents of their own spirituality, reading the Bible for
> themselves and teaching and encouraging one another in non-
> church settings.[21]

While one impulse behind the origin of Pietism included intentional
criticism of the ministry exercised by pastors—who were theologically
trained in the categories of Lutheran Orthodoxy and sometimes constrained as leaders by their use of its theological abstraction in their
preaching and ministry—many scholars today find the conventional

20. Spener, *Pia Desideria*.

21. Shantz, *Introduction to German Pietism*, 284.

opposition between Orthodoxy and Pietism to be overdrawn.[22] Theologians identified with Orthodoxy integrated obvious characteristics of deep Christian piety into their theological writings. For instance, John Gerhard (1582–1637) was greatly influenced by his friendship with Johann Arndt (1555–1621), the author of *True Christianity*, a classic and exceedingly popular text used in the Pietism movement.[23] "In *Sacred Meditations* (1606), Gerhard emphasized that Orthodox Lutheran theology, medieval mysticism, and the new piety were complementary and an indivisible unity."[24]

Loehe clearly followed this trajectory as a figure who integrated a commitment to Lutheran Confessional Orthodoxy and the renewal of a living Christian faith as exemplified in the practices of Pietism. Loehe was insistent about the necessity of preserving Lutheran confessional integrity against all attempts to impose a union of the Reformed and Lutheran traditions as had taken place in Prussia in the early 1800s. After Fredrick William, King of Prussia, required all Lutheran and Reformed churches to take up the common name of Evangelical, there was severe reaction by many church leaders, especially on the Lutheran side. This offense was further aggravated in 1830, the year observing the three-hundredth anniversary of the Augsburg Confession, when the directive came for the united church to celebrate the Lord's Supper using a common order of worship. Lutheran dissenters to this policy became known as the Old Lutherans.

Some affected by this imposed union began pursuing emigration as an alternative, among whom were those who left Germany in 1838 under the leadership of Pastor Martin Stephan, later to form the Lutheran Church—Missouri Synod (LCMS) in 1847. Loehe was a vocal opponent of unionism with the Reformed, a struggle that nearly led to his departure from the Bavarian *Landskirche* (territorial church).[25] He was particularly focused on Lutheran-specific church discipline in relation to admission to the Lord's Supper and advocated Lutheran altars only for Lutheran communicants. It was during this conflict that Loehe's orthodox Lutheran Confessionalism became most pronounced. For this reason, there was theological affinity between Loehe and German emigrants who led

---

22. Lindberg, *Pietist Theologians*, 6.
23. Shantz, *Introduction to German Pietism*, 28–30.
24. Shantz, *Introduction to German Pietism*, 39.
25. Geiger, *Wilhelm Loehe*, 116–27.

the LCMS, so that at the organization of the LCMS, Loehe became one of its major supporters in Germany and is counted as one of its founders, sending both theological candidates and material support in the synod's earliest years.

However, Loehe's commitment to Lutheran Orthodoxy always remained tempered by his concern for religious practices as expressed both at worship and in Pietism.

> Confessional Lutheranism was one of Loehe's great guiding principles. It meant to him staunch adherence to the doctrines of the Reformation, but not a rigid assumption that all doctrinal development had come to an end in the sixteenth century . . . United in the faith that is the basis of justification, Christians must struggle against godlessness and form a communion devoted to worship and service.[26]

"Because of this we should not speak of Loehe as returning to a Lutheran Orthodoxy interested only in correct doctrine for its own sake . . . Without corresponding practice, such a doctrinal position has no value."[27] This is as true about Loehe's grounding in Pietism as it was true of his liturgical commitments. The legacy of Wilhelm Loehe strikingly demonstrates the melding of Orthodoxy and Pietism in creative synthesis.

Evangelical Proclamation and Diaconal Servanthood

While Loehe was committed to the recovery and renewal of liturgy for the church in his time, he was also fully engaged in the practice of evangelical preaching and teaching. His service to the proclaimed Word, however, lived in creative relationship with active diaconal service to the needs of neighbors, especially those on society's margins, through the development of the deaconess community and institutions at Neuendettelsau. In Loehe's concept, evangelical proclamation and diaconal servanthood belong together.

As a theological candidate, Loehe was a keen student of the preached Word. "In his younger years Loehe studied published sermons closely, reading those of most eminent Lutheran preachers, with especial emphasis on Luther, and giving attention also to noted preachers of the

---

26. Ottersberg, "Wilhelm Loehe," 190.

27. Briese, "Wilhelm Loehe and the Sacrament of the Altar," 33.

old church."[28] During his brief period of study at Berlin, it was not the theological lectures of Schleiermacher that drew his attention but his preaching. Loehe would listen to as many as three or four sermons on a given Sunday, including those of Schleiermacher and Franz Theremin, the latter influencing him even more.[29] Loehe was devoted both to the renewal of the Christian liturgy based on ancient sources, and to the practice of evangelical and scriptural preaching.

Loehe's opportunities to preach were regular and frequent. Services with preaching took place three times a week: Sunday, Wednesday, and Friday. "On the great festival days there were two services and on the numerous communion Sundays additional confessional addresses. In addition, a total of about twenty lesser festivals, such as the days of the apostles, were observed with services, although some of these would coincide with regular service days. Loehe also practically always spoke when ministerial acts took place."[30] These included the performance of baptisms, weddings, and funerals. Ottersberg notes that the occasions for public speaking, including sermons and occasional addresses, numbered about two hundred times per year.

Loehe followed the lectionary for Sunday preaching, but would employ other texts on festival days or special occasions, selecting these with devotion and pastoral concern.[31] He also preached sermon series on particular books of the Bible, especially during the week. Over the years Loehe evolved from preaching with a prepared manuscript to preaching with outlines and notes. More than anything else, his sermons were attuned to the hearers, who often filled the village church, not only local parishioners but interested parties who chose to travel considerable distances to come and hear him, including students from Erlangen University.

> He used a wealth of illustrative material, but it was rarely narrative, usually descriptive, suited to the mentality of his audience, often drawn from nature or from the divine Word itself. He had a powerful voice; when he preached before large audiences in great city churches he was easily understood, but he adapted its volume to the village church where he preached regularly. The effectiveness of his delivery was achieved through the modulation

28. Ottersberg, "Wilhelm Loehe," 177.

29. Kressel, *Wilhelm Loehe als Prediger*, 24–32.

30. Ottersberg, "Wilhelm Loehe," 176.

31. Ottersberg, "Wilhelm Loehe," 176–77.

of the voice. He was capable of carrying away his hearers into rapt devotion, especially on festival days when adoration was the keynote of his preaching, and to touch the emotions, though he never appealed to shallow sentimentalism. Behind the delivery the hearer was always conscious of the personality, of the intense passionate sincerity of the preacher.[32]

Loehe was able to establish a personal connection with his hearers. Many volumes of his sermons have been collected and published over the years as a record of his full and committed engagement in evangelical proclamation.[33] However, as is often the case with the homiletical genre, the printed versions do not capture the spiritual power of the living Word as it affected the original hearers.

Loehe's concept for the ministry of deaconesses was to have their work closely connected to parish congregations. He imagined that the service of trained deaconesses would have its primary expression as an extension of the ministry of local congregations and under the oversight of local pastors. A church "which promotes God's Word among the nations without diakonia . . . is like a person with only one leg."[34] Liebenberg comments: "According to its substantive form he insisted that the practice of piety by the deaconesses corresponded both to the liturgical standards of the Lutheran church to which he ascribed and also to service character of the preaching office."[35] Evangelical proclamation and diaconal service are to be inseparable, even as today we would seek to hold together evangelizing and social ministry as core to holistic Christian mission.

Early in his pastoral ministry at Neuendettelsau, Loehe saw and organized opportunities for training women for diaconal service to others, initially as school teachers.[36] While Loehe was well informed about the deaconess movements started by Fliedner and Wichern, he focused on developing a deaconess order along the Lutheran confessional line. A society was formed in 1854 with efforts to organize local branches related to congregations. When this effort failed to take hold, Loehe consolidated the deaconess work by building a Mother House with facilities for a

---

32. Ottersberg, "Wilhelm Loehe," 177–78.

33. Three volumes of his collected works provide documentation of his activity as a preacher. See Loehe, *Gesammelte Werke*, 6.1, 6.2, and 6.3.

34. Loehe, "Das zehnte Jahr der Diakonnissenanstalt Neuendettelsau," 419.

35. Liebenberg, *Wilhelm Loehe*, 72.

36. Liebenberg, *Wilhelm Loehe*, 57.

hospital and a school for children with intellectual disabilities.[37] Young women began to train as deaconesses to serve in this work:

> Loehe himself took charge of the instruction as well as of general management, while the deaconesses, again for training purposes, took charge of the details of administration. A physician gave medical instruction. The deaconesses were organized into the order of the house of Stephen, adopted their distinctive garb, and soon began their own publication.[38]

Amalie Rehm became the first overseer of the deaconess order, serving from 1858 until her death in 1883. However, Loehe exercised strong leadership as the rector in the three-person Directorate, serving together with the overseer and the co-rector, Ernst Lotze, who was the first to hold this position from 1860 to 1866.[39]

The weekly chapter meeting of the deaconesses normally took place on Sunday evenings, at which they gathered for worship, devotional Bible reading, prayer, mutual admonition, and pastoral care. Concerns by members of the deaconess community were to be reported regularly to the Directorate. The motto of the deaconesses [Diakonissenspruch], first written by Loehe in the schoolbook of a fifteen-year-old deaconess student and adopted by the Society, reads:

> What do I want?
> I want to serve.
> Whom do I want to serve?
> The Lord among his suffering and poor ones.
> And what is my reward?
> I serve neither for reward nor thanks,
> But out of thanks and love;
> My reward is that I may do it!
> And if thereby I might die?
> If I die, so I die.
> Thus Esther spoke, who did not know Him
> And for whose sake I would die out of love
> And who would not let me die.
> And what if I thereby become old?
> So will my heart bud green like a palm tree,

37. For a detailed account of nursing education, see Honold, "Wilhelm Löhe and Nursing Education," and "Deaconesses in Nursing Care," in Kreutzer and Nolte, *Deaconesses in Nursing Care*, 65–77.

38. Ottersberg, "Wilhelm Loehe," 183.

39. Liebenberg, *Wilhelm Loehe*, 63–65.

And the Lord will fill me with grace and mercy.
I go in peace and lack for nothing.[40]

The deaconess work expanded in many directions and to many locations. The institutions founded and administered by the Neuendettelsau deaconesses included schools for the young, hospitals for men and women, homes for persons with intellectual disabilities, an industrial school, sheltered workshops, a home for abandoned girls, a home for single mothers, homebound nursing services, and a chapel. "Deaconesses were sent into service in various German states wherever demand for them arose; only gradually did sufficient demand develop in Bavaria to lead to the concentration of the work there."[41] The Neuendettelsau deaconess institutions became the foundation for the social services provided by the Lutheran Church in Bavaria in the following decades and to this day. Loehe maintained primary stewardship over this charitable work to the end of his life, and it remains a lasting part of his legacy. Evangelical proclamation and worship lead the church into diaconal service of neighbors in need, starting with the most vulnerable.

Theological Imagination and Pragmatic Skills in Administration and Financial Management

"Imagination is more important than knowledge" (Albert Einstein). Theological imagination is the capacity to envision the world that God in Christ by the power of the Holy Spirit is seen to be actively involved in human life and throughout all of creation. Jesus evoked theological imagination about the dynamic participation of God in all of life as often as he told parables of the kingdom and summoned people to receive God's gifts, trusting in the reality of God's mercy, healing, and transformation. In every generation, ministers of the Word are called by God to heighten human capacity to believe, trust, and hope in the Triune God's active presence and involvement in all that unfolds in life. The kingdom of God is near!

Wilhelm Loehe was one such minister of the Word, and his ministry invited the people of his generation to "fear, love and trust in God above all things" (Luther). Loehe exercised a theological imagination for shaping Christian identity and vocation for the life of the world in several facets:

40. Loehe, *Diakonissenspruch.*

41. Ottersberg, "Wilhelm Loehe," 183.

liturgical imagination, missional imagination, confessional imagination, pious imagination, evangelical imagination, diaconal imagination, and overall scriptural imagination. Now more than two hundred years after his birth, Loehe's legacy continues to fund a theological imagination for the church and mission in our time. Recent research on the life and contributions of Loehe demonstrate his lasting significance for shaping a matrix that is fruitful for reconstructing theological imagination today.[42]

Loehe's use of language, whether in service of the liturgy or in service of the Word, was performative. He understood the evocative character of theological language to create that to which it points. Loehe understood how the Lord's Supper not only was *communio* between the communicant and Christ, but also how the Christian assembly itself becomes a *communion* by participation in this meal. "This liturgical center should also hold for us in contemporary discussions surrounding the church as *communion* . . .

- the ground of communion in the triune God, who exists and relates to the world in the communion of trinitarian relationships

- the practice of communion in the Christian assembly gathered for worship in word and sacrament

- the nature of the church, its structures and ministry

- the social interest and engagement of the church

- the mission of the church to further God's mission of communion (the *missio Dei*)

On these topics, Loehe made significant contributions and helped to begin a critical and constructive practical-theological conversation that continues to this day."[43] Moreover . . . Loehe entertained reflection "about the success or failure" of the worship event . . . Wilhelm Loehe should have the last word: "All of that, as should be evident, is *not a requirement*, but only *advice to those*, who are capable of such things and have the will to do them."[44] Liturgy has an event character, in which God in Christ by

---

42. An International Loehe Society was founded in 2005 and holds meetings every third year. Examples of Loehe's theological imagination are drawn from Loehe research presented at the meetings in 2008 and 2011.

43. Schattauer, "Reclaiming the Christian Assembly as *Communio*," 65.

44. Seitz, "Gottesdienst und liturgische Sprache bei Wilhelm Loehe," 49.

the power of the Holy Spirit actually brings into existence things that were not.

Loehe's contributions as an educator and pastoral caregiver also deserve recognition as lasting accomplishments for the integration of pastoral work. "Loehe's ministry as a religious instructor is embedded in what he considered as a comprehensive catechumenate of the home, school, and church. Christian education comes to fulfillment in the church, therefore in Loehe's understanding religious instruction is on all levels a function of the church."[45] Such religious education takes place not only in the gathering of people in congregations but also as catechetical instruction when the church is scattered into their homes and through formal religious instruction in schools, observing confessional differences, as it exists today in Germany. This work of religious education was inseparable from the work of pastoral care. "For Loehe, pastoral theology is necessary for a genuine curacy of souls. The practice of pastoral care is embedded in the life of the church as the pastor is ordained to the office of preaching and sacraments. Thus the 'ordinary means' of pastoral care include preaching, catechization, and the Lord's Supper."[46]

Loehe brought a distinctive form of engagement to the social questions of his time, particularly through the organization of the deaconess institutions, joining the ministry of the church to the world's need for social service. "Loehe here followed the same line as Martin Luther, who asserted that a good tree can do no other than bring forth many good fruit, while many good fruit can themselves never turn a bad tree into a good one . . . Loehe knew that the people would not have wanted to set diaconal work at the end of the list. But he was convinced that inner mission from a diaconal perspective should never be placed over those things, which immediately have to do with the salvation of souls. Diaconal work can only issue forth from an understanding of the saving power of God's Word."[47] "Loehe took the role of ground breaker when he determined that the Reformation to be sure knew that deacons and deaconesses were based on Scripture, however he was not yet in the position to reestablish these offices and callings . . . Thereby the cornerstone was

45. Kothmann, "Wilhelm Loehe als Erzieher, Religionslehrer und Katechet," 253.

46. Pless, "Wilhelm Loehe als seelsorgerlicher Theologe," 276.

47. Schwarz, "Wilhelm Loehe zu sozialen Fragen seiner Zeit," 243–44.

laid for a diaconal church, in which again in the future the [ordained!] office and service of the deacon would regain its due place."[48]

One vital arena where the Loehe legacy continues to make a lasting impression is mission theology. "In Loehe's teaching of the church, mission plays a significant role in the characterization of the church as one holy catholic and apostolic body. Springing up from the manifestation of the Holy Spirit in Pentecost and the sacrificial death of Jesus Christ, the church, like a beautiful, lovely, and wonderful river flows through all ages until consummated into 'the famed sea of eternal blessedness.'"[49] One concretion of the ongoing significance of Loehe's missionary theology took place in the Congo:

> What use is a theology of mission in a situation that gives rise to pessimism? What was his central point in view of extreme social and ecclesial conditions and personal failure? Loehe was a realist—for that reason he took the small necessary steps and for that reason *diakonia* was dear to his heart. Loehe was a visionary—for that reason he lived in the rhythm of the liturgy and did not lose the larger perspective in the midst of the trifles. Loehe understood mission plainly as discipleship along the passion way of Jesus, which gave him energy to confront the ruling pessimism.[50]

Loehe's rich theological imagination continues to inspire theological reflection for the life of the church and its mission in our time. Theological imagination, however, went hand in hand for Loehe with his dedicated work as a highly competent administrator and financial manager. Given the many facets of the Loehe matrix explored in this chapter, it would be easy to overlook his astounding accomplishments as an organizer and administrator. Even though Loehe never earned more than $250-$300 per year during his thirty-five years of pastoral ministry in Neuendettelsau, he managed his family household and local congregation as well as a vast array of complex mission and diaconal enterprises.[51] Loehe was an entrepreneur for God's mission in the world!

Consider the scope of Loehe's involvements in developing infrastructure to initiate and sustain mission endeavors in Germany, the Baltic, and North America: publicizing and soliciting support for mission work

48. Strohm, "Wilhelm Loehes Verständnis der Diakonie," 274.

49. Chung, "Confession and Mission: Contextualizing Wilhelm Loehe," 64.

50. Weber, "Loehe in the Congo," 78–79.

51. Ottersberg, "Wilhelm Loehe," 170.

among German emigrants in North America, developing an emergency seminary for the education of teachers and pastors sent to serve these emigrants, planning mission work among the Chippewa in Michigan and the Crow in Wyoming, helping to direct the organization of two church bodies in North America, engaging in extensive correspondence with those for whom Neuendettelsau was the hub, initiating training programs for deaconesses, founding an order of deaconesses and the social service institutions where they served, constructing a Mother House and church building for the deaconess work, providing for the maintenance of these real estate assets, establishing the *Paramentik* for the manufacture of fine linens and paraments for church use, overseeing deaconess branches offering service at remote locations, and raising funds to undergird all of these ventures. This is only a partial list of the administrative and financial responsibilities assumed by Loehe over the course of his career. His attention to detail is well documented in his correspondence to the Iowa Synod in North America. Without Loehe's abilities and accomplishments in these areas, little else would have been possible. Administration is the skeleton upon which the church as the body of Christ in its institutional forms is constructed. Theological imagination without administrative ability is a mere idea. However, as Loehe demonstrates, when theological imagination and administration are held together, great things can and do emerge.

This chapter provides background on the origins of the Loehe legacy and maps the matrix of his significance for church and mission today. Loehe held in creative tension diverse gifts needed for a thriving ministry in service to others: liturgical worship and passion for mission, confessional orthodoxy and pietistic devotion, evangelical proclamation and diaconal servanthood, theological imagination and pragmatic skills in administration and financial management. Loehe was able to coordinate and sustain these varied contributions, which is one of his most notable accomplishments from which we can continue to learn. As next steps, the following three chapters explore the history and lasting impact of Loehe's work in North America. Chapter 2 explores Loehe's commitment to and support of the Iowa Synod.

2

Wilhelm Loehe's Influence
on the Iowa Synod

WILHELM LOEHE'S VISION FOR mission reached intensively within Germany and extensively to North America, encompassing what he called both inner and outer mission.[1] Chapter 1 gave an overview of that work, especially in Germany. This chapter looks at Loehe's pivotal influence upon the Iowa Synod. In the early 1840s Loehe already began missionary activity in partnership with a Lutheran seminary in Columbus, Ohio, followed later by material, financial, and personnel support of the Lutheran Church—Missouri Synod (LCMS). Loehe is counted as one of the founders of the LCMS, and its seminary in Fort Wayne, Indiana, and the four colonies organized in Michigan, the most well-known of these being Frankenmuth. From these colonies, German settlers and their pastors reached out to the Chippewa people almost immediately after their founding, a form of mission work of great importance to Loehe. This chapter gleans insights from the letters written between Loehe and two founders of the Iowa Synod, Johannes Deindoerfer and Georg Grossmann, about the next period of the Loehe legacy in North America. Four central characteristics of the Iowa Synod come to the fore in this correspondence: inner mission, outer mission, theological engagement, and "open questions." Each of these distinctive characteristics reflects the central theological and missiological concerns of Wilhelm Loehe himself.

---

1. Weber, *Missionstheologie bei Wilhelm Loehe.*

The Origins of the Iowa Synod in Relationship to Loehe

The story of Loehe as a central founder of the LCMS and the four Michigan colonies has been well preserved.[2] Lesser known are the events which transpired between Loehe and the leaders of the LCMS in the early 1850s, leading those who sought to remain loyal to Loehe to depart from Michigan in 1853 and form a new synod in Iowa in 1854. Controversial theological issues arise in every generation. In the late 1840s a fierce debate erupted over ordination and the pastoral office (*Amt*) between C.F.W. Walther, the leader of the LCMS, and Johannes Grabau, the founder of the Buffalo Synod. Grabau represented the view that ordination was based on divine authority imparted by God directly to the ordinand. In contrast, having experienced the tragic consequences of episcopal excess early in its history, the LCMS represented a view of ordination, sometimes characterized as the "transference theory," which was best articulated by Walther. According to this view, God grants the authority to ordain candidates to Word and Sacrament ministry to the congregation; the authority for that ministry is consequently transferred to the ordained pastor. Thus, the congregation retains primary authority in relationship to ordained pastors.

Loehe sought to navigate a path between Walther and Grabau on this divisive issue. However, pastors and theologians in the LCMS suspected him of favoring Grabau's "high view" of ordination, which was confirmed for them by Loehe's publication of *Aphorisms about the New Testament Offices and Their Relationship to the Congregation* in 1849.[3] The LCMS reaction was prolonged and sharply critical. Grossmann wrote to Loehe regarding this controversy with the leaders of the LCMS:

> Because I knew that, I offered the explanation at the very beginning that I would not again go into conversation about our mutual positions, until on behalf of the conference, perhaps through a commission which they appointed, the errors contained in your new *Aphorisms* are named.[4]

Although Loehe held that his position was grounded in Scripture (contrasting it with Walther's view, which he claimed was primarily based on

---

2. Maves, "How Firm a Foundation" and Zehnder, *Teach My People the Truth.*

3. Loehe, *Aphorisms on the New Testament Offices.*

4. Letter from Georg Grossmann to Wilhelm Loehe, June 1, 1853. Loehe Archive in Neuendettelsau. All translations of citations from the letters are the author's.

Luther), many in the LCMS accused Loehe of betraying the Lutheran Confessions.[5]

Attempting to salvage his relationship with the LCMS leaders, Loehe introduced the concept of "open questions," arguing that there are questions that are not definitively answered in Scripture or the Confessions that allow for differences of opinion among Lutherans without the need for them to become church dividing. Loehe wrote to Walther concerning the conflict with Grabau:

> so it remains certain, at least to me, that your mutual theological differences are resolvable or are not of the kind that they must upset the connection.[6]

Loehe elaborated in greater detail in a letter to Johannes Deindoerfer:

> To be sure there are points which divide; but the differences of insight and point of view about ordained ministry, which have existed for centuries, have not divided and should not divide, that is, upset church fellowship, especially where one is otherwise united.[7]

This position on open questions would later be adopted by the Iowa Synod; however, it was strictly rejected by the LCMS leadership.[8] This controversy over the pastoral office and ordination, which raged for decades, provides the immediate context for the events leading to the formation of the Iowa Synod.

Three figures played prominent roles in the drama unfolding at the emergence of the Iowa Synod: Johannes Deindoerfer, pastor of the Frankenhilf colony; Georg Amman, a key member of his congregation; and Georg Grossmann, the director of a teachers seminary in Saginaw, Michigan. During this controversy, Grossmann argued that the seminary in Saginaw was a donation from Loehe and therefore belonged to him, so he refused to surrender it to LCMS control. As the controversy intensified in Michigan, Grossmann and Deindoerfer, together with Amman,

---

5. Letter from Loehe to Grossmann, July 1, 1853. Concordia Historical Institute.

6. Letter from Loehe to C.F.W. Walther, December 6, 1852. Concordia Historical Institute.

7. Letter from Loehe to Johannes Deindoerfer, August 13, 1852. ELCA Region 5 Archives. Furthermore in a letter from Loehe to Grossmann, Weege, Deindoerfer, and Amman, March 31, 1853, Loehe wrote: "The Lutheran church has still more unfinished points, which on occasion can and will surface." ELCA Region 5 Archives.

8. Lohrmann, "A Monument to American Intolerance," 294–306.

became loyal defenders of Loehe and his theological views concerning ordination. Increasing pressure was placed upon Deindoerfer to join the LCMS and upon Grossmann to turn over the seminary to the LCMS. Grossmann wrote to Loehe that they had been accused of having "a schismatic institution."[9] Finally, both Deindoerfer and Grossmann were charged with heresy and threatened with excommunication if they persisted in support of Loehe and in defiance of the LCMS. The correspondence reveals heated polemic and sharp theological division between the two parties. Finally, the situation of the "Loeheaners" became intolerable.[10] Deindoerfer and Amman organized a scouting party to search for a new mission area in the west where there would be abundant German settlement, yet little organization by the LCMS.[11] That destination became Iowa.

In September 1853 a party of about twenty persons—including Deindoerfer, Amman, and Grossmann—set out for their new home. Loehe wrote:

> That is by far the best, that we go to a territory where the particular doctrine of the opponents (if they do not change) can leave us unharmed.[12]

Deindoerfer viewed Loehe's decision in this matter as "God's decision."[13] In spite of their great expectations, the trip (over 450 miles!) proved extremely difficult and the transport of goods very expensive. The party arrived in Dubuque "with completely empty pockets,"[14] reportedly spending their last coin fording the Mississippi River. Despite the hardship, Deindoerfer wrote ecstatically to Loehe:

> In Iowa it is beautiful, very beautiful, a thousand times more beautiful than in Michigan . . . It appears to us to be the most

9. Letter from Grossmann to Loehe, March 15, 1853. Loehe Archives in Neuendettelsau.

10. Letter from Grossmann to Loehe, March 15, 1853. Loehe Archives in Neuendettelsau.

11. Letter from Loehe to Grossmann and Deindoerfer, 1853. ELCA Region 5 Archives.

12. Letter from Loehe to Grossmann and Deindoerfer, 1853. ELCA Region 5 Archives.

13. Letter from Deindoerfer to Loehe, August 26, 1853. Loehe Archives in Neuendettelsau.

14 .Letter from Deindoerfer to Loehe, August 26, 1853. Loehe Archives in Neuendettelsau.

important place for the West. Daily immigrants arrive here, who travel westwards. Perhaps it would be the best place for the seminary.[15]

Thanks to the generous support of a local banker in Dubuque named Jesup, who loaned the new arrivals money based on a promissory note, the travelers were able to survive and began planning their future.

One of the frequently discussed decisions in the correspondence involved the choice of location for settlement. Among the locations under discussion were Dyersville, Garnavillo, Dubuque, and Strawberry Point, all in eastern Iowa. Jesup offered to donate lots for the building of a church in Dyersville; however, Deindoerfer, Amman, and a few others accepted the government terms for purchasing and settling land in Clayton County near Strawberry Point and moved there, giving the name "St. Sebald" to the settlement and new church.[16] We read from the correspondence that Deindoerfer and the members of the new settlement found themselves in dire financial straits, suffering harsh winters, illness, and strenuous labor to prepare the land for building and farming. Deindoerfer described in detail his personal hardship and poverty in letters to Loehe, seeking financial support for specific needs in the community. One of the most striking features of the correspondence is the detail given to accounting for various expenses and making pleas for support.[17] The correspondence with Grossmann also depicted the hardship suffered by the pioneers in Iowa. In a letter from September 1854, he communicated the death of his two young sons, Wilhelm and Karl, with Wilhelm dying on the anniversary of his wife's earlier death.[18]

While Loehe's commitment to the mission of the church in Iowa was unfailing, he faced complex decisions about how to steward his limited financial and material resources. His experience in Michigan made him question whether the correct approach should involve the founding of colonies following the pattern in Michigan. Deindoerfer and Grossmann shared Loehe's skepticism about whether colonization should be the approach taken in Iowa. At the same time as the beginning of mission activities in Iowa, Loehe was also deeply engaged in founding

15. Letter from Deindoerfer to Loehe, October 26, 1853. ELCA Region 5 Archives.

16. For the history of St. Sebald, see Hock, *The Pilgrim Colony*.

17. Letter from Deindoerfer to Loehe, April 29, 1854. Loehe Archives in Neuendettelsau.

18. Letter from Grossmann to Loehe, September 3, 1854. Loehe Archives in Neuendettelsau.

the deaconess institutions in Neuendettelsau. This new field of endeavor required much of Loehe's time, energy, and financial resources during the very same years as the organization and development of the Iowa Synod, which was founded on August 24, 1854.

Loehe's Commitment to Building Institutions

These different missionary commitments meant that Loehe had to become an even more frugal manager of his financial affairs, making careful decisions about where and why to distribute funds. He needed to deny many requests for ongoing support, not only in Michigan but also from Deindoerfer and the congregation at St. Sebald. Loehe's decision was firm: his primary support now would go to the establishment of institutions, like the seminary, and not to the support of new congregations which were expected to become self-supporting.[19] The correspondence makes clear Loehe's decision to distribute funds according to the priority of building institutions. Therefore, he turned over property to the Iowa Synod in April 1854[20] and, by the action of the Mission Society, turned over all other affairs in June 1855.[21] These acts were not taken out of disinterest about the development of the Iowa Synod. Instead, Loehe had learned a difficult lesson from his dealings with the Michigan colonies. There was much he simply could not manage at so great a distance from Germany.

Imagine the situation in which Loehe found himself in relationship to his missionary endeavors in the United States! He sought to respond both to the urgent needs of the German immigrants and to establish Christian outreach to American Indians. The requests for help from every side were overwhelming, not only the voluminous correspondence, but in the sheer number of requests for financial and material assistance, all of which required Loehe's response. Add to this the length of time it took for letters to arrive when dispatched by boat across the Atlantic. So many decisions required immediate action, it became unfeasible for Loehe to deliberate complicated matters that may have otherwise resolved themselves in the time it took for his written responses to arrive.

---

19. Deindoerfer objects to this decision in a letter to Loehe, May 21, 1854. ELCA Region 5 Archives.

20. Letter from Loehe to Deindoerfer, April 7, 1854. ELCA Region 5 Archives.

21. Letter from Loehe to Iowa Synod, June 20, 1855. ELCA Region 5 Archives.

It was impossible to communicate adequately by letter all the myriad details involved in even the least complex decisions.

Furthermore, there were dimensions of the North American situation that Loehe could scarcely comprehend. His defense of the German language and resistance to the "Americanization" of the German emigrants are just two acute instances of his separation from and limited knowledge about the United States context. Loehe could little appreciate the importance of the English language for missionary outreach on the North American frontier. Due in no small measure to Loehe's enormous influence, it would be decades before the Iowa Synod and its seminary would venture forth with instruction and ministry in English. Likewise, Loehe feared the Americanization of the Lutheran church among the German immigrants.[22] In his letters he often commented about his opposition to "Methodists" and other sects, lest the pure teaching of the Lutheran Confessions be tainted by other theologies and traditions. It is in these passages that the separation of Loehe from the North American context becomes most obvious. It was necessary for Loehe to learn to trust the reports from others in Iowa about matters far beyond his own experience and in a context complex beyond his comprehension.

It was primarily to the institution of the seminary that Loehe pledged his ongoing commitment and support. What began in Saginaw as a school to prepare teachers for primary and secondary instruction among the children of German immigrants became in Iowa a school with two distinct tracks. While the education of school teachers continued at the seminary as soon as it reconvened in Dubuque, it quickly became obvious that the need for a second track was even more urgent: the preparation of pastors for German-speaking Lutheran congregations. Wartburg College dates its founding to 1852 with the school that began in Saginaw, Michigan for teacher training. By contrast, Wartburg Theological Seminary dates its origin to 1854, when Inspector Grossmann introduced the theological curriculum and began to instruct men in study for pastoral ministry.[23]

The seminary remained in Dubuque for three years, before financial pressures guided the decision to move to Clayton County, near St. Sebald, where a two-story building was constructed, and the seminary

22. Letter from Loehe to Deindoerfer, August 13, 1852. Loehe Archives in Neuendettelsau.

23. For the report on the earliest curriculum in Iowa, see letter from Grossmann to Loehe, February 10, 1854. Loehe Archives in Neuendettelsau.

community could be sustained by farming the surrounding acreage. It was at this site that the name "Wartburg" was given to the school, in memory and honor of the great educational achievements of Luther at the original Wartburg in 1521. Moritz Braeuninger, who would later serve as missionary to the Native Americans, wrote to Loehe:

> You will be of the firm opinion that we want to do exactly as the inexhaustible worker at the Wartburg near Eisenach . . . we think very often about our dear devout man, Luther, at the Wartburg and follow his example.[24]

Wartburg College and Seminary remained at this site until 1874, when sustained growth in the number of students led to the relocation of the two schools for the first time to separate places: the college initially to Galena, Illinois and the seminary to Mendota, Illinois. Subsequent moves and institutional developments have continued to the present as Wartburg College is now located in Waverly, Iowa and Wartburg Theological Seminary in Dubuque since 1889.[25]

The early correspondence reveals how in Michigan, the relationship between Loehe and Deindoerfer could be described as filial, while Loehe's relationship with Grossmann was much more businesslike. In Iowa and with Loehe's decision to commit his major support to the seminary, there is a noticeable shift. Deindoerfer expressed a sense of distance from Loehe at times; for example, whenever he compared the support for his ministry in Iowa to the previous colonization efforts in Michigan. In the late 1860s this would change again, due to Deindoerfer's involvement in the founding of an orphanage institution in Toledo, Ohio.[26] At the same time, Loehe's contacts and relationship with Grossmann as director of the seminary became more extensive. In all correspondence, Loehe was keen to receive exact accounting and receipting for the expenditures in which he had invested. The shortage of money by the Iowa settlers was a constant refrain in the letters, with Loehe intent on maintaining accountability for how the money was being spent.

---

24. Letter from Moritz Braeuninger to Loehe, January 11, 1858. ELCA Region 5 Archives.

25. For the history of Wartburg College, see Matthias, *Still on the Move*. For the history of Wartburg Theological Seminary, see Weiblen, *Life Together*.

26. Letters 4, 14, 15, 19, 26, 29, 31, 36, 49, and 51 between Deindoerfer and Loehe/ Bauer, dated June 29, 1868 to August 21, 1871. Deaconess Archives in Neuendettelsau.

It is striking how Grossmann at first served as both administrator and professor of the fledgling college and seminary in Dubuque. Grossmann expressed great relief at the sending of the gifted teacher, Sigmund Fritschel, to serve as a second professor for the school in 1854.[27] Sigmund Fritschel took over most of the theological teaching until the arrival of his younger brother, Gottfried at age twenty, who joined the faculty in 1857. Gottfried contributed special talent in biblical languages and learned the art of printing. Through the publication of the *Kirchliche Zeitschrift* and the *Kirchenblatt*, news from Germany and the Iowa Synod was published and distributed to German-speaking churches and their leaders.

One of the most moving passages in the correspondence records Gottfried's humble request that Loehe send to Iowa one of the deaconesses, who might become his wife:

> If my heart now turns to the thought of selecting for myself a pious virgin for a wife, so I must thereby place great emphasis that this one possess a suitable level of education.[28]

Indeed, Deaconess Elise Köberle (together with another deaconess) was sent to North America in the summer of 1858 and married Gottfried later that same year.[29] The sending of the Fritschel brothers to Iowa from the training school in Neuendettelsau helped replenish the energies needed for the many educational and missionary tasks at the seminary. Together this *par nobile fratrum* ("pair of noble brothers") served Wartburg Seminary as its core faculty members for several decades until their deaths—Gottfried in 1889 and Sigmund in 1900.

Throughout the early years of the Iowa Synod and until his death in 1872, Loehe supported the Iowa Synod through the sending of pastors, students, books, and money. Loehe maintained interest in the development of the school and the organization of the mission to the Native Americans. The Iowa Synod honored Loehe over the course of his lifetime, for example, sending warm greetings and prayers on the twenty-fifth anniversary of his pastoral ministry in 1862.[30] Deindoerfer pledged to Loehe his loyalty as one who was "under the direction of my dear

27. Letter from Loehe to Deindoerfer, February 3, 1854. ELCA Region 5 Archives.

28. Letter from Gottfried Fritschel to Loehe, 1858. Loehe Archives in Neuendettelsau.

29. Liebenberg et al., *Diakonissen fuer Amerika*, 26, 31–32.

30. Letter from Iowa Synod to Loehe, August 7, 1862. ELCA Region 5 Archives.

father and brothers in Germany, whose faithfulness in the truth I know."[31] Upon departing from Michigan in September 1853, Grossmann wrote:

> Accompanied by your paternal blessing, we have moved into a new land and strengthened by your paternal blessing, we have begun to undertake the holy work which is commanded of us.[32]

Loehe's influence was clearly significant for the Iowa Synod. Based on the correspondence, Loehe also had an ongoing influence on the LCMS, including the institutions in Michigan and Fort Wayne, Indiana, which will be explored in detail in chapter 3. The missiological and theological influence of Loehe on the Iowa Synod can be documented in many areas. In this chapter, we will focus on four of these: inner mission, outer mission, theological engagement, and open questions.

Inner Mission

The first missionary endeavor of the Iowa Synod was in the area of "inner mission," which included outreach to the German immigrants, through the organization of preaching points that would be developed into congregations. While at its founding, the synod consisted of only two congregations at St. Sebald and Dubuque, one year later there were sixteen places where the Gospel was being preached. Friendly relations soon commenced with the Buffalo Synod, such that the Iowa Synod began to provide pastors for vacant Buffalo Synod congregations. In 1857 the Iowa Synod thereby extended its work to Michigan and Ohio.

Pastors who had finished at the seminary were sent out to form and serve congregations at places as distant as Des Moines, Jonesboro, Illinois, and Pocahontas, Missouri. Meanwhile, the mission field spread to the areas surrounding St. Sebald and Dubuque. By 1858 there were seventeen pastors, nineteen congregations, and twelve preaching points. In 1864 these numbers had increased to forty-one pastors and fifty congregations (in seven states!), and innumerable preaching points. Loehe continued to encourage and send candidates for ordained ministry to be prepared at Wartburg Seminary throughout this and subsequent period.

---

31. Letter from Deindoerfer to Loehe, September 28, 1853. ELCA Region 5 Archives.

32. Letter from Grossmann to Loehe, February 10, 1854. Loehe Archives in Neuendettelsau.

In the latter portion of the nineteenth century, the Iowa Synod continued its trajectory of steady growth in the number of pastors and congregations. In 1896 the synod roster listed 334 pastors, forty parochial school teachers, 534 congregations, and 149 preaching points. After its merger with the Texas Synod in 1896, the number of pastors swelled to 400 and congregations to 600, with a confirmed membership of nearly 65,000. Although its doctrine came under repeated challenge from representatives of the LCMS (involving issues as divergent as predestination and the eschatological events of the end times), the synod never wavered from its central purpose of spreading the ministry of the Gospel to the large number of German immigrants continuing to flow into the Midwest.

By 1930, when the Iowa Synod merged with the Ohio and Buffalo Synods to form the "old" American Lutheran Church, it had grown to nine geographical districts including 915 congregations, 638 pastors, and approximately 212,000 baptized members. Wartburg Seminary had been a key partner in this development, which began with the two congregations at Dubuque and St. Sebald in 1854. When the history of the Iowa Synod was written in 1929, just prior to the merger forming the American Lutheran Church, it was apropos that the author, Professor G. J. Zeilinger of Wartburg Seminary, selected the following title for the book: *A Missionary Synod with a Mission.*[33]

Outer Mission

From the beginning of Loehe's endeavor to send "emergency helpers" (*Nothelfer*) to North America, he never flagged in his zeal for outreach to the Native American people, an endeavor he counted as "outer mission."[34] This effort began with outreach to the Chippewa tribe in the four colonies of Michigan, starting with Frankenmuth, which were established in the 1840s and continued through new labors by his Iowa Synod partners. By 1856 efforts were already underway in the Iowa Synod to organize missionary work among Indians in Canada through the leadership of Pastor John Jakob Schmidt. While these initiatives met insurmountable obstacles, Schmidt learned of another possibility from a government

33. Membership statistics are primarily from Zeilinger, *A Missionary Synod With a Mission.*

34. Letter from Loehe to Deindoerfer, February 3, 1854. ELCA Region 5 Archives.

agent named Redfield to work among the Upsaroka tribe in Montana. Loehe committed financial and personnel support to organize mission among the Upsaroka people, making application for assistance to the Bavarian Mission Society.[35] Redfield led Schmidt to Montana in the spring of 1858, accompanied by Moritz Braeuninger from Wartburg Seminary. The two missionaries, Schmidt and Braeuninger, lived for several months among the Upsaroka, building relationships and learning the language. As the missionaries traveled with the tribe for several weeks, they became trusted friends, so much so that tribal leaders pleaded with them to continue the journey through the winter.[36] In spite of this request, they decided to return to Iowa for supplies and replenishment, departing from the Upsaroka until the next year.

The encouraging report given to the Iowa Synod that winter generated contributions from supporters not only in the Iowa and Buffalo Synods but especially from mission societies in Germany. In July 1859 Schmidt, Braeuninger, two additional missionaries, and two colonists returned to Montana. After a difficult winter during which there was no contact with the Upsaroka, they followed the previously established pattern of constructing a mission station, rather than seeking to accompany the people in their nomadic way of life. When Schmidt returned with one of the other missionaries to Iowa for additional provisions, Braeuninger and the others erected a mission station on the banks of the Powder River. Here tragedy struck. Thinking they had built their log house in Upsaroka territory, they were in the border area between two tribes instead. According to the most probable reconstruction of events, Braeuninger was killed by representatives of a neighboring tribe that was resisting the settlement of whites in the region. His death was a deep blow to the Iowa Synod's missionary efforts among the Native Americans.

Nevertheless, additional missionary work followed among the Cheyenne at a mission station constructed at Deer Creek, Wyoming. Between 1861 and 1863 various missionary ventures were explored, including preaching services for Native Americans near the Deer Creek station. Three orphaned Cheyenne boys were entrusted to the missionaries in 1863 and baptized shortly thereafter. Whatever encouragement this might have generated soon dissipated through the eruption of new waves

35. Application from Loehe to the Royal Bavarian Mission Society, May 29, 1858. ELCA Region 5 Archives.

36. Letter from Johann Jakob Schmidt to Loehe, December 8, 1858. Loehe Archives in Neuendettelsau.

of violence between the Indians and their colonizers. By January 1865 the entire missionary team had withdrawn. One later attempt to resume the Native American mission work was undertaken in 1866 but this was short-lived. There are many reasons for the failure of the Iowa Synod's mission to the Native American people. Schmutterer and Lutz named the following:

> the involved chain of command from Bavaria via Iowa to the frontier; the haphazard planning, lack of funds, and inexperience of the synod's mission board; the faulty logistics and exhausting travel routes to the frontier; the intertribal conflicts among the Indians; the dishonesty of many whites with whom the Indians dealt; the routine violation of treaties by whites in general; the untimely outbreak of the Civil War and the concomitant withdrawals of military forces in the West; and finally the inexperience, isolation, and naiveté of the German-speaking missionaries operating in a twice-foreign environment.[37]

A memorial to Braeuninger was erected in the church cemetery at St. Sebald, together with the graves of two of the young Cheyenne converts, the only tangible evidence remaining from the Iowa Synod's missionary outreach to Native Americans.

The most promising moment in this entire enterprise occurred in the summer of 1858 when the two missionaries, Schmidt and Braeuninger, asked the Upsaroka chief if they could travel along with the tribe and live as they lived.[38] The next six weeks were spent traveling among the tribe in the Powder River valley, learning the language, becoming familiar with Upsaroka culture, and engaging in theological conversation with Indian leaders. As a result of this period of "accompaniment," the Upsaroka were reluctant to let them depart and, as Schmidt reported: "A thousand times they asked us if we would really return when the winter had passed."[39] How might the history of American Indian missionary endeavor by the Iowa Synod been different had the missionaries chosen to persist in this approach, rather than returning the next year to build the ill-fated mission station?

---

37. Schmutterer and Lutz, "Mission Martyr on the Western Frontier," 140.
38. Schmutterer and Lutz, "Mission Martyr on the Western Frontier," 132–33.
39. Schmutterer and Lutz, "Mission Martyr on the Western Frontier," 133.

The prevailing model of mission engagement in the Evangelical Lutheran Church in America (ELCA) today is described as "accompaniment." ELCA Global Mission explains the meaning of accompaniment:

> We understand *accompaniment* as walking together in a solidarity that practices interdependence and mutuality. The basis for this *accompaniment*, or what the New Testament calls *koinonia*, is found in the God-human relationship in which God accompanies us in Jesus Christ through the Holy Spirit.[40]

In this nineteenth-century case, the missionaries engaged in an accompaniment model, which might have succeeded in developing lasting and trustworthy relationships with the Native American people, whereas the institutional model of building a mission station failed. How different this history might have been, if the missionaries had persisted in the method that has come to be called accompaniment![41]

In 1885 the Iowa Synod transferred all remaining funds from Native American missions to the Neuendettelsau Mission Society for its work in Papua New Guinea. The missionary work in Papua New Guinea became a major focus for the Iowa Synod during World War I, when the involvement of German missionaries was severely curtailed. An Iowa Synod committee for foreign missions was established in 1917. This became a vehicle for supporting the work of the Neuendettelsau mission in New Guinea, as well as other mission work in east Africa. By 1930 the Iowa Synod had sent twenty-three missionaries to Papua New Guinea, seven of whom were ordained ministers prepared at Wartburg Seminary. In addition, five other ordained pastors had spent at least a portion of their studies at Wartburg prior to setting out as missionaries to Papua New Guinea. This significant missionary connection continued in subsequent years through Wartburg Seminary's theological preparation of students from Papua New Guinea.

Theological Engagement

Wartburg Seminary was instrumental in serving the needs of the Iowa Synod for educating pastors and teachers. The seminary was compelled to move twice due to outgrowing its facilities: in 1874 to Mendota,

---

40. *Global Mission in the Twenty-first Century*, 5.

41. Nessan, "Lernendes Begleiten," 36–38, and Rössler, "Neuendettelsauer Missionare bei den Chippewas," 227–34.

Illinois and in 1889 back to Dubuque. Whatever the seminary's location, it continued to initiate mission work in the surrounding area and
to prepare graduates as candidates for ordained ministry in the Iowa
Synod's congregations. During the years of service by Sigmund Fritschel
(1854–1900) and Gottfried Fritschel (1857–1889) as the faculty of Wartburg Seminary, hundreds of students were prepared for pastoral ministry,
which included nearly all the pastors of the Iowa Synod. Their influence
as theological teachers of the church expanded through their publications, including two books and the editing of the *Kirchenblatt* from 1858
to 1871 by Gottfried and their many articles in various periodicals, especially the *Kirchliche Zeitschrift*. Besides their endeavors as educators, the
brothers served the mission of the church as synod leaders, preachers,
and "ecumenical" representatives to the General Council in the pursuit
of confessional faithfulness and unity among Lutherans.

One central concern by the teachers of the Iowa Synod was the interpretation of the Lutheran Symbols and the meaning of confessional
subscription. Sigmund Fritschel described the distinctive position of the
Iowa Synod this way:

> Accordingly, there is a distinction to be made between the *dog-
> mas, properly speaking, and other parts of the Symbols;* as e.g.
> the frequent exegetical, historical and other deductions, illus-
> trations and demonstrations. Only the former, i.e. the dogmas,
> constitute the Confession, whilst the latter partake of this dig-
> nity only indirectly, inasmuch as they define the dogmas more
> clearly. What the Symbols state and intend *as a confession*, the
> articles and doctrines of faith, this it is, to which the Synod is
> bound, not because they are the Church's decisions in contro-
> versies that have come up, but because they present the saving
> truth and doctrine of the Scripture. The Church is bound to ac-
> cept these doctrines which constitute the Confession in their
> totality, *without exception*, whilst the demand of doctrinal con-
> formity by no means includes *all unessential* opinions which *are
> only occasionally* mentioned in the Symbols.[42]

The Iowa Synod operated according to a hermeneutic that interpreted the
Lutheran Confessions by both reading them in their historical context
and distinguishing in them what was essential (articles of faith) from
what was "unessential." This distinction was the basis for the consistent

42. Fritschel, "The German Iowa Synod," 66. On page 62, he describes the viewpoint of the Iowa Synod as "a strictly confessional as well as ecumenical Lutheranism."

assertion by the Fritschel brothers and the Iowa Synod that there were matters that remain "open questions" and that full agreement on such questions was not necessary for church fellowship.

Open Questions

Throughout the nineteenth century, the Iowa Synod was embroiled in theological controversy. The departure from Michigan and the conclusion of the common work with the LCMS was the consequence of doctrinal controversy about the theological understanding of the pastoral office.[43] Moreover, in the latter half of the nineteenth century, the theologians of the Iowa Synod engaged in debate concerning many other theological controversies, including chiliasm, the anti-Christ, Sunday worship, usury, and especially predestination. The circulation of periodical articles, tracts, and books contributed to a fierce discussion of these issues.[44] Each of these issues was highly contested; even more, the theological stance of the Iowa Synod was attacked. Crucial to these debates, the theological stance of the Iowa Synod included support for the possibility of "open questions." In the controversy over the office of ministry in Michigan, Loehe argued that holding different views about ordination should not be understood as church dividing. Because neither Scripture nor the Lutheran Confessions take a definitive stance, this allowed for a legitimate range of theological viewpoints and differences. Loehe's defense of open questions became itself another basis for theological controversy.

From its origin, the Iowa Synod adopted Loehe's approach to open questions.[45] In 1858 the theological position of the Iowa Synod was firmly established. Referring to the letters of Paul and to the writings of Luther, the theologians of the Iowa Synod defended open questions:

> About this there is no question, that Luther in the great and pointed questions which concern *the salvation of souls and the way of blessedness* tolerated *no* differences in doctrine . . . That does not contradict that in the subordinate questions he allowed for differences.[46]

43. Schaaf, "The Controversy about *Kirche* and *Amt*," 121–62.

44. Fritschel and Fritschel, *Iowa und Missouri.*

45. Lohrmann, "A Monument to American Intolerance."

46. Fritschel, *Quellen und Dokumente*, 312.

Granted, one must proceed conscientiously in determining whether a given teaching is—or is not—a matter of essential doctrine or an open question.[47] Yet in contrast to many other North American religious groups, "the Iowa Synod admitted that they knew too little."[48] Whether the controversy was over millennialism, the anti-Christ, or Sabbath observance, the Iowa Synod sought to take a less fixed stance and more mediating position by appealing to the possibility of open questions. Although the Iowa Synod eventually did take a stand against the LCMS on the issue of predestination, it did not constitute the abandonment of open questions in principle.[49]

The degree to which the Iowa Synod was forced to defend itself from attack regarding the controversies of the time is well documented by the 111 pages devoted to open questions in the book, *Iowa und Missouri*, written by Sigmund and Gottfried Fritschel. In painstaking detail, the Fritschel brothers explain the importance of open questions and articulate the fundamental distinction between essential and non-essential doctrines:

> regarding why both views are able to stand next to each other in the church . . . this sentence resonates overall: "Because the question is not decisive in the Symbols [Confessions], so there can be also different opinions about it."[50]

Although it might be tempting to view the controversy over open questions as an antiquated quarrel from the nineteenth century, in many respects, it still reflects one of the major differences between those churches open to ecumenical rapprochement and those insisting on an all-encompassing and thereby exclusive understanding of truth.

One of the defining characteristics of the Iowa Synod was its conciliatory posture toward other churches, deeply grounded in its commitment to open questions. This allowed the leaders of the Iowa Synod, even when pushed to the limit by their critics, to state:

> We want to bear patiently by Jesus' power what you have done to us unjustly and continue to acknowledge you as our closest neighbors in the faith and brothers, and to pray for you. We also want to hold ourselves at all times to peace and brotherly

47. Fritschel, *Quellen und Dokumente*, 317.

48. Lohrmann, "A Monument to American Intolerance," 301.

49. Lohrmann, "A Monument to American Intolerance," 304–5.

50. Fritschel and Fritschel, *Iowa und Missouri*, 187.

understanding with you, and not become too weary thereby to sigh and to implore. However, we would rather die, than that we would abandon and betray the truth, which [God] has granted us to preserve and which we have represented against you.[51]

The heritage of Wilhelm Loehe in the Iowa Synod was embedded deeply into its very fiber. This legacy is reflected in the deep and lasting commitments to inner mission, outer mission, theological engagement, and open questions, which were inherited from him. In the next chapter, we trace and compare the two distinctive trajectories of the Loehe legacy in the Iowa Synod and Lutheran Church—Missouri Synod.

---

51. Fritschel and Fritschel, *Iowa und Missouri*, 280.

3

Two Historical Trajectories
in the Missouri and Iowa Synods

IN *THREE BOOKS ABOUT the Church*, Loehe vividly described the place of the church in history: "Springing up on Pentecost and Calvary, the church flows through the ages like a river, and that same river and no other will flow unchangingly on through the ages until that great day when it will empty completely into the famed sea of eternal blessedness."[1] Loehe entertained a vision of the one holy catholic and apostolic church through the ages and dared to claim that the Lutheran church, with its confessional clarity, was the fullest expression of that church. As the river named "church" has continued to flow from the nineteenth century to the present, what has been the influence of Loehe on the historical development of specific churches in the United States? Are there any notable trajectories that demonstrate that influence?

Whereas chapter 2 examined Loehe's influence on the Iowa Synod through several themes in his direct correspondence with its leaders, this chapter compares the reception of Loehe as it has unfolded in two distinct North American Lutheran church bodies. After providing some historical background, we examine how the Loehe legacy has informed the Lutheran Church—Missouri Synod (LCMS) and the Iowa Synod, one of several church bodies that eventually flowed into the Evangelical Lutheran Church in America (ELCA).

1. Loehe, *Three Books about the Church*, 55.

Tracing Loehe's Influence on Lutheranism in the United States

To map the influence of any figure, especially one from the nineteenth century, on contemporary Lutheranism is a difficult undertaking. The factors that contribute to the historical development of a church body are manifold, complicated, elusive, and mysterious. Moreover, it is exceedingly complicated to document specific influences on something as fluid as a living tradition. At the same time, however, it is possible to note certain tendencies and analogies between what a given historical figure represented and the distinctive characteristics of a contemporary church body. Granted, the chain of cause and effect for any contemporary expression of a distinctive characteristic is complex; nevertheless, some generalizations may be ventured.

The five dimensions of the Loehe legacy outlined in chapter 1 serve as an interpretive lens for reflecting on Loehe's influence within two particular church bodies: the LCMS and the Iowa Synod. Following a brief description of the historical connections between Loehe and each church body, arguments will be offered about how these five dimensions have—or have not—been influential for the historical development of that church body. This will sketch the shape of Loehe's influence on that church body, which is notably different in the two trajectories.

One of the striking features of the Loehe legacy is the unique configuration of elements that characterized his ministry. As we have seen in chapter 1, characteristics that would normally be considered antithetical are brought together in distinctive combinations, for example, nineteenth century Pietism and Lutheran Confessionalism. The five-dimensional matrix sketched in the Introduction—consisting of pietism, confessionalism, liturgical renewal, *diakonia*, and mission—offers a framework for interpreting the patterns of influence which Loehe exerted upon these contrasting church traditions. Although the reception of the Loehe heritage has taken a quite different shape in the LCMS than in the Iowa Synod, both church traditions still look to Loehe as their theological and ecclesial ancestor.

Loehe in the Lutheran Church—Missouri Synod

The impetus for Loehe's material response to the needs of German immigrants in North America was F. C. D. Wyneken's appeal for help, published in 1840. In direct response to this plea, Loehe wrote "Die lutherischen Auswanderer in Nordamerika: Eine Ansprache an die Leser des Sonntagsblattes" [The Lutheran Emigrants in North America: An Address to the Readers of the *Sonntagsblatt*].[2] Loehe and Pastor Johann Friedrich Wucherer, his colleague and the editor of the paper, were soon overwhelmed by donations to this cause. As another response, Loehe began a training program in Neuendettelsau for those who volunteered or were recruited to serve the German immigrant communities in North America. Adam Ernst, the first to respond, and Georg Burger were instructed to become schoolteachers and sent as missionaries to North America in 1842.

Upon their arrival in New York, Ernst and Burger were received by Friedrich Winkler, who was newly called professor to the Evangelical Lutheran Theological Seminary at Columbus, Ohio. Because of the urgent need for pastors, Ernst and Burger soon found themselves in Columbus studying for the ministry. Thereby, the earliest relationships of Loehe's *Sendlinge* (missioners) in North America were with a seminary that eventually became part of the ELCA. After examining the faith commitments of the seminary according to its confessional loyalty, Loehe began sending students, books, and other material support. However, a breach developed between Loehe and the Columbus seminary in 1845 over the issue of confessional subscription. Loehe perceived the Columbus seminary to be overly influenced by Samuel S. Schmucker's project to forge an "American Lutheranism."[3] To Loehe this appeared to be unionism in a new guise—something he emphatically rejected—turning instead to the founders of the LCMS as partners more aligned with his own confessional commitments.

Through the mediation of Ernst and others sent from Neuendettelsau, Loehe soon entered into planning for the founding of the LCMS in April 1847. Over half of the founding pastors were those trained by Loehe. Pless writes:

> Loehe had reservations about the constitutional foundation of the Synod from the beginning. He was especially uneasy regarding the notion of equal representation of clergy and laity in church governance. This seemed to him to reflect a democratic form of church life more reflective of American principles than the ecclesiology of the New Testament. Such a democratic

2. Ratke, *Confession and Mission, Word and Sacrament*, 24.
3. Pless, "Wilhelm Loehe and the Missouri Synod," 126–27.

approach, Loehe feared, would subordinate the pastor to the will
of the congregation. But at this early stage, Loehe was unwilling
to protest too strongly, believing that over time the weaknesses
of this approach would be realized and appropriate adjustments
made in the constitution.[4]

Loehe continued to communicate these theological concerns through his
regular correspondence, even as he invested energy and financial support
toward the development of the seminary founded in 1846 at Fort Wayne,
Indiana and the organization of the four colonies established in Michigan, which included the most well-known settlement at Frankenmuth.

Loehe is considered a founder of the LCMS seminary at Fort Wayne,
with Wilhelm Sihler, a Loehe missioner, as its first president.[5] By 1853,
when Loehe's formal connection with the LCMS ended, eighty-two additional "Loehe men" had been sent to the LCMS via the Fort Wayne
seminary. At the organizing convention of the Missouri Synod, Loehe
agreed both to transfer the seminary to the synod and to continue supporting it through donations of money and books. The establishment of
the seminary at Fort Wayne belongs to the enduring legacy of Loehe in
the LCMS.

Meanwhile, Loehe took great interest in the formation and development of the four colonies founded in Michigan southeast of Saginaw. He
was involved in ordering the life of the colonies and sending both settlers
and pastors to lead them. Moreover, Loehe had keen interest in outreach
to the Chippewa people. In 1852 Loehe founded a "seminary" in Saginaw,
originally a teachers' college, which would eventually become Wartburg
College. This school, however, was not handed over to the LCMS. Its
director, Georg Grossmann was, together with Pastor Johannes Deindoerfer of the Frankenhilf colony, a key figure in representing the views of
Loehe in the controversy which erupted over the doctrine of ministry.
Loehe maintained the divine origin of the pastoral office in contrast to
the views of Walther, who held that the pastoral office was bestowed
upon the congregation which then transferred its authority to the pastor.
Loehe feared that North American individualism and congregationalism
were exerting undue influence on church doctrine.[6] This controversy

4. Pless, "Wilhelm Loehe and the Missouri Synod," 129.

5. Heintzen, *Prairie School of the Prophets*, 30–41.

6. For a detailed account of several aspects of this controversy, see Pless, "Wilhelm Loehe and the Missouri Synod," 129–35 and Schaaf, *Wilhelm Loehe's Relation to
the American Church*, 121–61.

culminated in the departure of Grossmann and Deindoerfer, who led the band of twenty-two persons journeying to Iowa in 1853, where the Evangelical-Lutheran Synod of Iowa was founded in 1854.

For nearly a century, the influence of Loehe on the LCMS continued, especially in worship practices. In the late 1940s explicit interest in the Loehe heritage began to revive through the influential teaching, research, and writings of Hermann Sasse, Walter Baepler, Erich Heintzen, John Tietjen, Walter Bouman, and Kenneth Korby.[7] At the 200th anniversary of Loehe's birth in 2008, he was reclaimed as an important ancestor in the history and life of the LCMS. What is the shape of the Loehe legacy in the Missouri Synod according to the five dimensions of Loehe's ecclesial theology?

Pietism

In his own time and context, Loehe's pietism was a reaction to the failure of the state church to instill a vital spirituality into the life of the congregation. The pietistic impulse drove much of Loehe's interest for a church in mission. While pietism shaped those figures directly trained by Loehe in Neuendettelsau, the impact of pietism is not well documented in the materials pertaining to the influence of Loehe on the LCMS. Although more influenced by North American evangelicalism, the renewal of interest in evangelical outreach in recent LCMS initiatives bears some resemblance to Loehe's concern; however, there is no direct evidence that Loehe's pietism has fueled this development.

Confessionalism

One of the most prominent influences of Loehe on the theology of the Missouri Synod relates to his confessionalism. In origin, Loehe's strong confessional commitments were impelled by the threat of "unionism" in the Bavarian Lutheran church of his time. This concern matched that of the Saxon Lutherans who emigrated from Germany in 1838 due to the forced union of the Lutheran with the Reformed churches and who settled in Perry County and St. Louis, Missouri, founding the LCMS in

7. For bibliographical references and elaboration, see Pless, "Wilhelm Loehe and the Missouri Synod," 135–36.

1846.[8] When Loehe shifted his support from the seminary in Columbus to the new seminary in Fort Wayne, it was chiefly a consequence of his suspicion of unionist tendencies with Schmucker's "American Lutheranism."[9] In the LCMS Loehe found a rigorous theological confessionalism more in accordance with his own views. Fully half of the founders of the LCMS were missioners sent from Germany by Loehe.[10] It is therefore somewhat ironic that it was a controversy over the confessional understanding of the doctrine of ministry that led to the parting of ways between Loehe and Walther.[11] Nonetheless, Loehe's strict adherence to the standards of the Lutheran Confessions has been highly valued and affirmed in the LCMS from the nineteenth century to the present.[12]

Liturgical Renewal

The influence of Loehe on the liturgical practices of German-speaking Lutherans in North America was enormous. Starting with the missioners who became founders of the LCMS, their training by Loehe "included drilling in the hymns and liturgical forms that he was trying to restore. In 1844 Loehe published an *Agende* with his 'brethren in North America' in mind, and dedicated it to Pastor Friedrich Wyneken of Fort Wayne."[13] Loehe also commended various forms of liturgical renewal that had already been introduced within the life of his own congregation. For example, the "practice of every Sunday communion preceded by private confession in Frankenmuth and the surrounding area would continue for several decades."[14]

While Loehe's liturgical material had an early and lasting influence on the LCMS, another primary influence was the *Saxon Agenda*. "In 1856 a revision of the Saxon Agenda was approved and published by the Missouri Synod."[15] The *Saxon Agenda*, Friedrich Lochner's publication of

8. Forster, *Zion on the Mississippi*.

9. Schaaf, *Wilhelm Loehe's Relation to the American Church*, 50–65.

10. Baepler, *Century of Grace*, 69–70. The *Sendlinge* of Loehe to America were required to make "a pledge of allegiance to the Confessional Writings of the Lutheran Church."

11. Sasse, "Walther and Loehe: On the Church," 176–82.

12. Schaaf, "Wilhelm Loehe and the Missouri Synod," 54–59.

13. Schalk, "Sketches of Lutheran Worship," 86.

14. Pless, "Wilhelm Loehe and the Missouri Synod," 137.

15. Reed, *The Lutheran Liturgy*, 176.

Der Hauptgottesdienst in 1895, and the adoption of the Common Service by the English District of the LCMS in 1899 were the main influences upon the worship book, *Liturgy and Agenda,* published in 1917.[16] Regarding the influence of Lochner's *Der Hauptgottesdienst,* Pless writes: "What Lochner learned from Loehe in the way of liturgics he transmitted to his students at Springfield and published in his book" which "shows signs of Loehe's historical and confessional appreciation of the liturgy. It remained in print until 1935 and was used as a text in liturgics at both LCMS seminaries into the twentieth century."[17] It was through the use of these liturgical materials, including the use of the Common Service, that the influence of Loehe's liturgical renewal (as embodied in his *Agende*) was transmitted.[18]

With the publication of the *Lutheran Service Book* and its companion volume, *Agenda,* in 2006, the explicit influence of Loehe on the Missouri Synod's worship practices is evident. For example, January 2, the day of Loehe's death, is noted in the calendar of commemorations, and the hymn, "Wide Open Stands the Gates Adorned with Pearl," which was written shortly before Loehe's death, appeared in a North American Lutheran hymnal for the first time.[19] The worship book also included suggestions for daily prayer from Loehe's *Seed-Grains.* "Loehe's influence is especially apparent in the *Agenda* as the introduction lays out an approach to pastoral care that is centered in confession/absolution and framed by the liturgy. Loehe's liturgical formula for anointing the sick, which provoked both Bavarian and Missourian reaction in the nineteenth century, has found its way into the new LCMS Agenda."[20]

Diakonia

Loehe's original intent was to prepare deaconesses for service in congregations. This was his vision at the founding of the *Lutherische Verein fuer weibliche Diakonia* in 1853. However, the plan soon gave way to the establishment of a Mother House in Neuendettelsau in 1854. Loehe

16. Reed, *The Lutheran Liturgy,* 176–77.

17. Pless, "Wilhelm Loehe and the Missouri Synod," 137.

18. Reed, *The Lutheran Liturgy,* 153.

19. "Wide Open Stands the Gates Adorned with Pearl," *Lutheran Service Book,* #639.

20. Pless, "Wilhelm Loehe and the Missouri Synod," 137.

encouraged regular participation by the deaconesses in community worship, daily private prayer, and private oral confession/absolution. "During
Loehe's life, there were 163 deaconesses consecrated. Forty-five percent
of them resigned, many to marry."[21] Two early attempts were made to establish deaconess activity in the United States. The first, in 1858, involved
sisters teaching at a school for girls in Ohio and the second involved
service as nurses, but both of these attempts were short-lived.[22] Interest in Loehe's diaconate revived in the late twentieth century, especially
through the work of Kenneth F. Korby, a student of Arthur Carl Piepkorn.
Korby wrote his doctoral dissertation on the theology of pastoral care in
Loehe, taught at Valparaiso University, and served as an adjunct professor at Concordia Theological Seminary in Fort Wayne in retirement.[23]
Korby's "instruction of future deaconesses at Valparaiso connected them
with the diaconal tradition of Neuendettelsau."[24] The heritage of Loehe
continues to influence the training of Valparaiso deaconesses, as does the
recently instituted deaconess program at Concordia Theological Seminary. In 2007, the Board for World Relief and Human Care of the LCMS
translated and published a portion of Loehe's "Von der Barmherzigkeit"
under the title, *Loehe on Mercy.*[25]

Mission

The early history of the LCMS reveals Loehe's involvement in its first missionary efforts. Loehe was instrumental in the founding of the LCMS,
the establishment of the Fort Wayne seminary, and the four colonies
in Michigan, including the efforts to establish outreach to the Native
Americans in the vicinity surrounding Frankenmuth.[26] In Michigan and
at Concordia Theological Seminary, the Loehe heritage has been intentionally cultivated. Missioners trained by Loehe constituted most of the
founders of the LCMS. Through the ministry of these pastors and teachers, the influence of Loehe on congregational ministry and theological

21. Olson, *Deacons and Deaconesses,* 222–23.

22. Jenner, *Von Neuendettelsau in alle Welt,* 257–58.

23. Korby, *Theology of Pastoral Care.*

24. Pless, "Wilhelm Loehe and the Missouri Synod," 136.

25. Loehe, *Loehe on Mercy.* This is a translation of chapters 6 and 7 of Loehe's
"Von der Barmherzigkeit."

26. Schoenfuhs, "The German Lutheran Chippewa Indian Mission."

education was significant. The influence of Loehe on worship practices in the LCMS also has been substantial. Moreover, insofar as worship undergirds mission, Loehe has also exerted considerable influence in this arena. Through the histories of the Michigan colonies and Concordia Theological Seminary, and through cooperation in international mission in places that have a historical relation to Loehe (such as Australia), the LCMS connection to Loehe was maintained, though subdued, after the schism with Loehe in 1853. This changed with renewed interest in the heritage of Loehe at the end of the twentieth century, marked by dissertations on Loehe by doctoral students of the LCMS[27] and the publication of David Ratke's *Confession and Mission, Word and Sacrament: The Ecclesial Theology of Wilhelm Loehe* by Concordia Publishing House in 2001. The involvement of John Pless and others from the LCMS in the founding of the International Loehe Society in 2005 extended the focus on the Loehe legacy into the twenty-first century.

Loehe in the Iowa Synod

Johannes Deindoerfer was sent as pastor to the Michigan colony at Frankenhilf in 1851, and Georg Grossmann became director of the teachers seminary at Saginaw in 1852. As conflict emerged over the doctrine of ordained ministry between the Missouri Synod and Johannes Grabau, founder of the Buffalo Synod, the defenders of Loehe's mediating position, led by Deindoerfer and Grossmann, found themselves in an irreconcilable controversy with the leaders of the LCMS. This conflict prompted those loyal to Loehe to leave the work begun in Michigan and seek out a territory not yet under development by the LCMS. That destination was Iowa.

While Deindoerfer and the lay leader, G. Amman, went to Clayton County near Strawberry Point, Iowa to break ground for a settlement, Grossmann immediately went to work in Dubuque to reestablish the teachers seminary. The initial missionary vision was to establish schools in cities and towns that had significant populations of German immigrants. This soon led to the second missionary goal of forming Lutheran congregations in these localities. Events rapidly unfolded, and almost immediately, the teachers seminary also became a theological seminary.

27. Korby, *Theology of Pastoral Care*; Tietjen, *The Ecclesiology of Wilhelm Loehe*; and Bouman, "The Unity of the Church."

Wartburg Theological Seminary, which formally received its name in 1857, traces its origin to the expansion of the original teachers seminary when it incorporated theological studies for the preparation of pastors in 1854. This was the same year that Sigmund Fritschel arrived to assist Director Grossmann as a professor at the seminary.

The Evangelical-Lutheran Synod of Iowa was founded at St. Sebald in Clayton County on August 24, 1854 with four charter members: Deindoerfer, Grossmann, S. Fritschel, and M. Schueller, a theological candidate. The synod's first missionary endeavor involved "inner" mission, through the organization of preaching points that could be developed into congregations. While the synod originally consisted of only two congregations at St. Sebald and Dubuque, outreach generated through mission activities by the faculty and students of the seminary led to the rapid founding of many additional member congregations for the Iowa Synod. Pastors who finished at the seminary went out to form and serve congregations. Loehe continued to encourage and send candidates for ordained ministry to be prepared at Wartburg Seminary throughout the early and subsequent periods. While the greatest gains from the Iowa Synod's early missionary efforts were among the stream of immigrants from Germany, the vision for "outer" mission as outreach to American Indian people continued to inspire its founders.[28] The Iowa Synod continued its steady growth in the number of pastors and congregations through the end of the nineteenth century. Although its doctrine came under repeated challenge from representatives of the LCMS, the synod held to its central purpose of extending the ministry of the gospel to the large number of German immigrants flowing into the Midwest.

Wartburg Seminary was instrumental in serving the needs of the synod for pastors and teachers during this period. During their years of service on the faculty of Wartburg Seminary, Sigmund Fritschel (1854–1900) and Gottfried Fritschel (1857–1889) prepared hundreds of students for pastoral ministry, nearly all of the pastors belonging to the Iowa Synod. Beyond their endeavors as educators, both brothers served as synod leaders, preachers, and "ecumenical" representatives, for example, to the General Council in advocating for confessional faithfulness and unity among Lutherans.

The influence of Loehe on the Iowa Synod continued in the teaching of J. Michael Reu and other second-generation leaders, such as Max

28. Schmutterer and Lutz, "Mission Martyr on the Western Frontier," 117–42.

Fritschel and George Fritschel, and was renewed at Wartburg Theological Seminary through the leadership of William Weiblen as seminary president beginning in the 1970s. Weiblen authored a history of the seminary, *Life Together at Wartburg Seminary*, which drew directly on the Loehe legacy in underscoring the liturgical and missional commitments of the school.[29] Thomas Schattauer, professor of liturgics, has drawn upon the Loehe tradition for the worship practices of the seminary.[30] Paul Chung, professor of Lutheran Confessions and World Christianity, gave attention to Loehe's contribution to the renewal of *diakonia*.[31] Given these historical connections, what was the shape of the Loehe legacy in the Iowa Synod according to the five dimensions of Loehe's ecclesial theology and how has this legacy become manifest in the ELCA?

Pietism

Loehe's pietism was palpable in the Iowa Synod of the nineteenth century through a vital perception of the activity of the living God in the church, especially through the publication and distribution of devotional writings and materials authored by Loehe that were translated into English. For example, *Seed-Grains of Prayer: A Manual for Evangelical Christians* was translated and published in 1912.[32] Designed by Loehe to order private and family devotions, this work was still valued and used in the Iowa Synod in the early twentieth century. Moreover, the entire impulse toward mission in the Iowa Synod was coherent with Loehe's pietistic commitments.[33] In the twentieth century, the fostering of a "communitarian" ethos at Wartburg Theological Seminary has appealed both to Loehe and Bonhoeffer as sources.

Confessionalism

The theologians and pastors of the Iowa Synod understood themselves as fully loyal to the Lutheran Confessions. Compared to some expressions

---

29. Weiblen, *Life Together.*

30. Schattauer, "Sung, Spoken, Lived," 113–21.

31. Chung, *Christian Mission and a Diakonia of Reconciliation*, 100–16.

32. Loehe, *Seed-Grains of Prayer.*

33. Zeilinger, *A Missionary Synod with a Mission* describes the origin of the Iowa Synod as "the response of sympathetic hearts," 12.

of Lutheranism, such as the stance of the General Council for example, the Iowa Synod's position on pulpit and altar fellowship was strict.[34] In comparison to the confessional hermeneutic of the LCMS, however, the Iowa Synod was judged as moderate. For this reason, a series of controversial issues erupted in the nineteenth century that distinguished Iowa from Missouri: open questions, chiliasm, the anti-Christ, Sunday worship, usury, and especially predestination.[35] At the heart of the divide was the Iowa Synod's position on "open questions."[36] By "open questions" the Iowa Synod held that while agreement on the essentials of the Lutheran Confessions, centered on the doctrine of justification, was necessary for remaining in church fellowship, there were other non-essential issues about which Lutheran Christians were free to disagree without these differences becoming church dividing. Sigmund Fritschel described the confessional hermeneutic of the Iowa Synod:

> What the Symbols state and intend *as a confession*, the articles and doctrines of faith, this it is, to which the Synod is bound, not because they are the Church's decisions in controversies that have come up, but because they present the saving truth and doctrine of the Scripture. The Church is bound to accept these doctrines which constitute the Confession in their totality, *without exception*, whilst the demand of doctrinal conformity by no means includes *all unessential* opinions which *are only occasionally* mentioned in the Symbols.[37]

This confessional hermeneutic and the tradition about open questions have been two important contributions of the Iowa Synod to the American Lutheran Church and eventually the ELCA.

Liturgical Renewal

Loehe's *Agende*, published in 1844, became the primary worship book at the Iowa Synod's founding. Published in four German language editions (with the first three printings in Germany), the last edition was printed in the United States by the Iowa Synod in 1919, making Loehe's liturgical

---

34. Buehring, *The Spirit of the American Lutheran Church*, 45–46.

35. Fritchel and Fritschel, *Iowa und Missouri*.

36. Lohrmann, "A Monument to American Intolerance.

37. Fritschel, "The German Iowa Synod," 66. On page 62, Fritschel describes the Iowa Synod as "a strictly confessional as well as ecumenical Lutheranism."

materials available for use in the Iowa Synod's many German-speaking congregations into the twentieth century.[38] The influence of Loehe also exerted itself on English language worship materials, for example, through the publication in 1860 of an English version of the German liturgy of 1855.[39] Loehe's contributions were valued for helping to recover Lutheran materials, based on historic, catholic liturgical practice.[40] Through the participation of Sigmund Fritschel on a committee of the General Council, Loehe's liturgical materials also became a major influence on the publication of the *Kirchenbuch* in 1877.

> If [Beale] Schmucker could be called the father of the Common Service of 1888, then surely Fritschel is its grandfather, and Loehe its great-grandfather. Because of the success in reaching the German immigrants, work in English was slow to begin. The use of the Loehe *Agende* or the General Council's *Kirchenbuch* made the transition to the Common Service for English worship quite natural.[41]

Loehe's *Agende* was translated and employed in North American Lutheranism in the eastern states already in 1902.[42] It was one of the most formative influences on the widely used Common Service and thereby on the *Service Book and Hymnal* (1958) and *The Lutheran Book of Worship* (1978).[43] The most recent worship book of the ELCA, *Evangelical Lutheran Worship* (2006), designates January 2 for commemoration of Wilhelm Konrad Loehe as a "Renewer of the Church" and has incorporated Loehe's prayer for church unity.

Diakonia

The founding of the deaconess order by Loehe in Neuendettelsau also led to their being sent into service in other places. "In 1857 and 1858,

---

38. The Evangelical-Lutheran Synod of Iowa, ed. *Agende von Wilhelm Loehe.*

39. Brand, "The Lord's Supper," 362.

40. For the influence of Loehe on Lutheranism in the Northeastern U.S., see Lohrmann, "Loehe and the Ministerium of Pennsylvania," 72–79.

41. Muenich, "The Victory of Restorationism," 32. This includes material prepared by Muenich for a chapter of a worship textbook used at Luther-Northwestern Seminary, 1984/1985.

42. Loehe, *Liturgy for Christian Congregations.*

43. Brand, "The Lord's Supper," 355–56.

Wilhelm Loehe sent several deaconesses to the Iowa Synod. Of these deaconesses, two in succession became housemother at Wartburg Theological Seminary . . . In 1859 there were five deaconesses from Neuendettelsau in the United States. A report from Neuendettelsau about 1860 indicated they had all married."[44] In the 1860s, two further initiatives were undertaken by the Iowa Synod related to the Neuendettelsau deaconesses. First, Loehe was encouraged to give his support to establish an Association for Works of Mercy in conjunction with the founding of an orphanage at Toledo, Ohio in 1862.[45] While Loehe, through extensive correspondence, came to be in favor of the undertaking, his expectation that the institution have widespread financial support eventually limited his involvement, and the plans to establish a Mother House in Toledo connected to Neuendettelsau failed to materialize.[46] The second initiative also involved the founding of an orphanage in the state of New York. "In 1869 Sister Luise Adelberg of Neuendettelsau became housemother of St. John's orphanage near Buffalo, New York, though she eventually returned to Neuendettelsau."[47] Regarding the impact of Loehe deaconesses, Olson writes:

> Neuendettelsau influenced other deaconess establishments in North America, providing personnel, worship practices, and training. The first full-time training sister recruited for the deaconess training school that opened in Philadelphia in 1889 was Magdalene Steinmann, a deaconess from Neuendettelsau. The liturgy at Neuendettelsau became a model for this Philadelphia motherhouse. Catherine Dentzer, an American who became the second training sister at the Milwaukee motherhouse in 1900, had taken a special course at Neuendettelsau. Just as some U.S.

44. Olson, *Deacons and Deaconesses*, 265. Regarding the Neuendettelsau deaconesses coming to the U.S.: Sophie List served as a teacher in Des Moines, Iowa from 1858 to 1869; Luise Adelberg served the orphans' home in Buffalo, New York from 1869 to 1879; Anna Lutz served the orphans' home in Toledo, Ohio in 1874; and, Magdalene Steinmann served as part of the Philadelphia Mother House at the Lankenau Hospital in Ardmore, Pennsylvania from 1890 to 1908, spending October 1896 to June 1899 as a Training Sister at the Milwaukee Mother House. Regina Scheid, Katherine Scheid, and Rosette Wibel came to serve in the Iowa Synod, each resigning in 1860, presumably in order to marry.

45. Gebhardt and Honold, "Internationale Beziehungen der Diakonie Neuendettelsau," 52.

46. Jenner, *Von Neuendettelsau in alle Welt*, 258.

47. Olson, *Deacons and Deaconesses*, 265.

deaconesses went to Kaiserwerth for training, they also went to Neuendettelsau.[48]

Loehe was a key historical figure in the Neuendettelsau deaconess movement, which provides one historical precedent for establishing the roster of diaconal ministers in the ELCA in 1993.

Mission

The chief dimension of the Loehe heritage that was championed in the Iowa Synod was his commitment to the church in mission. The early history of the Iowa Synod documents its widespread involvement in founding congregations and preparing pastors for congregational ministry. The Iowa Synod also shared and participated in Loehe's commitment to outer mission, through outreach to Native Americans in the 1860s and in Papua New Guinea beginning with the First World War.[49] At Wartburg Theological Seminary, international partnerships have been nurtured with churches in Germany, Norway, Papua New Guinea, Tanzania, Namibia, Guyana, Brazil, and other countries. Wartburg Seminary also operates a Center for Global Theologies and has had a long tradition of educating students on behalf of global partner churches, underscoring this commitment to global mission. We can recall how both F. Braun and G. J. Zeilinger heralded mission as the defining characteristic of the Iowa Synod.[50] Although the Iowa Synod was only one stream that eventually flowed into the formation of the ELCA, Loehe's focus on mission continues to inform the life of that church body through the commitments of pastors, congregations, and institutions that originated in partnership with Loehe in the nineteenth century.

Comparing Influences

Employing the five dimensions of Loehe's ecclesial theology to interpret the influence of Loehe on the LCMS and Iowa Synod reveals two distinctive patterns. In the LCMS, the most prominent aspects of the Loehe heritage are his influence on confessionalism and on worship, with some

48. Olson, *Deacons and Deaconesses*, 265.

49. Nessan, "Loehe and the Iowa Synod," 140–144.

50. Braun, *Zum diamentenen Jubilaeum*, 43–58. Also, Zeilinger, *A Missionary Synod with a Mission*.

attention also to mission. The affinity in confessional outlook was generated by a shared resistance to the forces of unionism. Loehe's influence on *diakonia* has been either confined to the nineteenth century or is more theoretical in nature, as general appeals to his legacy which inform the present life of the church. The element of pietism is muted.

In the Iowa Synod, the two most distinctive aspects of the Loehe heritage were mission and worship. While the Iowa Synod also claimed solidarity with Loehe's confessionalism, it did so through a differentiated hermeneutic for interpreting the Confessions and its distinctive emphasis on "open questions." As in the LCMS, Loehe's influence on *diakonia* has been either limited to the nineteenth century or remains more theoretical for the recent renewal of the diaconate in the North American church. In addition to its contribution to the church's emphasis on mission, the influence of Loehe's pietism on the Iowa Synod was primarily through the publication and translation of Loehe's devotional writings.

Although Wilhelm Loehe never traveled to North America, his influence on Lutheranism there continues to this day, albeit in two distinctive trajectories. In the LCMS, Loehe is being reclaimed as a church father who contributed to a strong emphasis on Lutheran Confessionalism, renewed worship through liturgical materials that continue to be used, and furthered the church's mission. In the Iowa Synod, Loehe was acknowledged as the inspiration for its missionary endeavors, the primary source for its liturgical practices, and a confessional theologian who authorized the possibility of open questions. In both trajectories, Loehe's contributions to the diaconate have been revived since the end of the twentieth century, while his emphasis on pietism remains mostly latent.

In the LCMS, the influence of Loehe is strongest in those congregations and institutions founded by his missioners; however, his heritage appears in the process of being retrieved by the denomination itself. In contrast, given the Iowa Synod's incorporation into the ELCA through a series of mergers, the significance of Loehe on the entire denomination is less noticeable. It does remain prominent, however, in those parts of the church that were, at one time, directly related to Neuendettelsau and in those institutions founded by Loehe and his missioners. Because the effects of these mergers would nuance the transmission of the Loehe legacy, chapter 4 provides a snapshot of how one major historian of the Iowa Synod, Johannes Deindoerfer, depicted the influence of Loehe upon the Iowa Synod as it approached its own fiftieth anniversary and the beginning of the twentieth century.

4

Wilhelm Loehe in Deindoerfer's History
of the Iowa Synod

EVERY COMMUNITY IS SHAPED by its origin story. For a church body, the
story of origin communicates foundational information about its identity and mission. For the Iowa Synod, classic expression was given to its
origin story in the historical account of Pastor Johannes Deindoerfer
(1828–1907), one of the four founders of the Iowa Synod and author of
*Geschichte der Evangelisch-Lutherischen Synode von Iowa und anderen
Staaten*, published at Chicago by the Wartburg Publishing House in 1897.
This chapter gives a snapshot of how the influence of Wilhelm Loehe
had been received and was valued by the Iowa Synod at the end of the
nineteenth century according to Deindoerfer's history.

Deindoerfer serves as a primary source for the history of the Iowa
Synod in its relationship to the Loehe for the first fifty years of its existence. Moreover, Deindoerfer's involvement predates the founding of
the Iowa Synod through his service as a congregational pastor in one
of the original colonies founded by Loehe in Michigan in the 1840s. As
we examine Deindoerfer's historical account, we will discover the three
most important sources of authority for the Iowa Synod: Holy Scripture,
the Lutheran Confessions, and the Loehe legacy. This chapter documents
Deindoerfer's interpretation of the influence of Loehe on the Iowa Synod's identity and mission.

Johannes A. Deindoerfer was born at Rosstal, near Nuremberg, on
July 28, 1828, and was educated at Nuremberg and Neuendettelsau, where
he studied under Loehe. He was ordained at Hamburg in 1851, sent as an
emissary (*Sendling*) by Loehe to the colonies in Michigan, and became
pastor of the congregation at Frankenhilf in 1851. Deindoerfer joined the

Lutheran Church—Missouri Synod (LCMS) in 1852. As we have seen, theological controversy led to his departure from both Michigan and the Missouri Synod to Iowa in 1853, together with Georg Grossmann and eighteen others. Deindoerfer subsequently served as a pastor in the Iowa Synod at St. Sebald, Iowa; Madison, Wisconsin; and Toledo, Ohio. He was elected president of the Eastern District and then president of the entire Iowa Synod, in which office he served from 1893–1904. Deindoerfer's *Geschichte* encompasses the founding and almost five decades of Iowa Synod history. Significant for his credentials as synod historian, he served as editor of the synodical publication, the *Kirchenblatt*, from 1878–1904. Deindoerfer died on May 14, 1907.

Origins

The countenance of Wilhelm Loehe graces the opening pages of Deindoerfer's history.[1] Loehe is depicted as the "father" and guiding light for the Iowa Synod from its beginning. Loehe's influence informs the forty-six pages of material devoted to Deindoerfer's depiction of the synod's "*Vorgeschichte*" (pre-history). From the outset, Loehe was deeply concerned for both the spiritual care of German immigrants to North America and the mission to Native Americans. Regarding "inner mission" to German immigrants, Loehe was concerned about three main challenges: doctrinal indifference among existing Lutheran bodies, "Methodist" (that is, "free church") influences on church praxis, and insufficient numbers of teachers and pastors. In response to the plea for help by Pastor Friedrich Wyneken (1810–1876) in 1840, Loehe issued his "Address to the Reader" in January 1841. Through this appeal donations, both of money and volunteers, began to arrive. Loehe took it upon himself to train the first two volunteers, Adam Ernst and Georg Burger. This was the beginning of the *Neuendettelsauer Missionsanstalt*, which would continue to prepare and send candidates as teachers and pastors to North America throughout the nineteenth century.

Beginning in 1843, Loehe composed regular messages about the work in North America that were published as *Kirchliche Mitteilungen aus und über Nordamerika* ("Church News from and about North America"), which Deindoerfer reports gained a circulation of eight thousand

---

1. In its review of historical developments, this article closely follows Deindoerfer's account in Deindörfer, *Geschichte*.

copies. This communication generated even more financial donations and volunteers for service. In 1845 Loehe wrote and published his "Call from the Homeland to the German-Lutheran Church in North America." Loehe built a strong constituency of supporters in Germany for North American outreach. His initial efforts at cooperation with the Lutheran seminary at Columbus, Ohio (supplying books and supporting the continued training of Ernst and Burger for the pastoral ministry) ended in a parting of the ways over matters of confessional interpretation and use of the English language.[2]

Loehe next turned his attention to Lutheran mission efforts in Michigan, including support for the German immigrant congregations and their Indian mission in Frankenmuth and the related colonies.[3] In cooperation with Loehe, Pastor Wilhelm Sihler (1801–1885) organized a Lutheran seminary at Fort Wayne, Indiana, in 1846. Loehe also engaged in preparatory work with C. F. W. Walther (1811–1887) toward the founding of a new synod, the Missouri Synod.[4] At an organizational meeting at Fort Wayne in July 1846, no fewer than twenty-four participants had been sent by Loehe to North America. Deindoerfer commented that this development was surprising considering the unresolved differences over the office of ministry.[5] According to Deindoerfer, although Loehe had reservations about its constitution, he approved and released his *Sendlinge* (emissaries) to the work of the Missouri Synod. Loehe and Wucherer agreed also to hand over the Fort Wayne seminary to the Missouri Synod upon receiving a pledge that German would remain the language of instruction. At the same time, Loehe was asked to continue providing support.

A bitter controversy broke out between Walther and Johannes Grabau (1804–1879), founder of the Buffalo Synod, over the nature of the church and the office of ministry. While Loehe pleaded for reconciliation and sought to mediate their differences, he was drawn inexorably into the controversy, insofar as his position was perceived to be closer to Grabau than to Walther. Loehe's publication of *Aphorisms about the New Testament Offices and Their Relationship to the Congregation* in 1849 further exacerbated his differences with the Missouri Synod. Deindoerfer

2. Deindörfer, *Geschichte*, 10–12.

3. For the following, see Deindörfer, *Geschichte*, 13–28.

4. The Lutheran Church—Missouri Synod will be referred to as "the Missouri Synod" in this chapter, following Deindoerfer's usage.

5. Deindörfer, *Geschichte*, 17.

commented that in 1850 it had already become clear that cooperation between Loehe and the Missouri Synod would need to come to an end.[6] Seeking to reestablish positive relations, Walther and Wyneken visited Loehe in Neuendettelsau in fall 1851 but hope for reconciliation soon collapsed.

Even so, the Missouri Synod made an appeal for Loehe to support a seminary for the preparation of teachers.[7] Loehe offered to support a *Pilgerhaus* (pilgrim house) in Saginaw, Michigan, to serve as the first refuge for German immigrants arriving there. He also pledged continued support to the four colonies in Michigan (including Frankenmuth and Frankenlust), with the aim of preserving German church, language, and culture in North America. These colonies would also become the base for "outer mission" to Native Americans. The teachers seminary would initially be housed in the *Pilgerhaus*. While a frame building was being constructed in Saginaw, five students began their studies with Pastor Georg Grossmann (1823–1897) as Director in a rented storefront in summer 1852. This was the first German-Lutheran teachers seminary in North America and the beginning of what would become Wartburg College. This work was complicated when Pastor Cloeter, the local pastor in Saginaw, charged Grossmann of being a "Loeheaner" and of teaching false doctrine about the office of ministry, threatening him with church discipline. As the conflict intensified, Grossmann was pressured to leave the congregation.

Pastor Deindoerfer of the Frankenhilf colony, sent by the *Gesellschaft für innere Mission* in 1851, had developed a strong collegial bond with Grossmann. Together they understood themselves as loyal to Loehe and representatives of his theological commitments. This included the matters regarding the office of ministry currently in dispute. Like Loehe, they held that these were not essential doctrines but subordinate teachings that should not to be considered church dividing. This was the origin of the Iowa Synod's position regarding "open questions" (that is, differences that ought not to be church dividing). Despite the interventions of Wyneken, a local pastors' conference demanded that the teachers seminary should either be handed over to the Missouri Synod or dissolved. As an alternative, Grossmann and Deindoerfer submitted to Loehe that his ongoing mission work in North America needed to separate from the

6. Deindörfer, *Geschichte*, 23.

7. Deindörfer, *Geschichte*, 28–33.

Missouri Synod and be transplanted to a location, perhaps Iowa, where it would be unhindered by such conflict. Under the charge that the teachers seminary was a "schismatic institution," Loehe was convinced that continued cooperation with the Missouri Synod was not possible and he wrote a passionate letter of farewell dated August 4, 1853.

Supported by a lay founder of the Frankenhilf colony, Gottlob Amman (1812–1877), an exploratory journey to Iowa was undertaken by Amman and Deindoerfer.[8] The conditions appeared advantageous to them for relocation to Iowa for the purposes of colonization and mission. Dubuque seemed a strategic site and land for homesteading was available for a reasonable price in Clayton County. At the end of September 1853, twenty persons departed for a new beginning in Iowa. Although their finances barely held out, by God's providence and the assistance of Mr. Jesup, a banker in Dubuque, the party arrived in Iowa to reestablish the teachers seminary at Dubuque and to found a colony in Clayton County, named "St. Sebald" (after the beloved parish in Nuremberg). Grossmann reopened the teachers seminary in a rented house in Dubuque on November 10, 1853. Worship services were held in the local community and the congregation of St. John Lutheran Church was organized. It soon was apparent that the need for the preparation of pastors to serve congregations was even more urgent than the need for teachers in parochial schools. Therefore, plans were made to expand the seminary into a *Predigerseminar* (preacher seminary) to supply pastors for the new congregations that began to emerge through their mission efforts. While financial gifts from Germany became less plentiful, due to Loehe's discouragement at the controversy in Michigan, he continued to send candidates for ministry to Iowa. Among them was Sigmund Fritschel (1833–1900), a gifted young man, who arrived in 1854 and immediately took up his calling as seminary teacher.

Identity and Mission

The Iowa Synod was founded on August 4, 1854, at St. Sebald, Clayton County, Iowa with four founding members: Georg Grossmann, Johannes Deindoerfer, Sigmund Fritschel, and Michael Schueller, who was ordained at this meeting.[9] The synod subscribed to the Lutheran

8. Deindörfer, *Geschichte*, 31–36.

9. For the following, see Deindörfer, *Geschichte*, 40–55.

Confessions, interpreted according to the Word of God for the fulfillment of the Lutheran church, and was dedicated to the preservation of the ancient catechumenate, the apostolic life, and the exercise of church discipline. The founders of the Iowa Synod aimed to establish a confessional hermeneutic that distinguished between doctrinal essentials and secondary matters about which full agreement would not be necessary for maintaining church unity ("open questions"). The Iowa Synod articulated its distinctive confessional direction that was open to God's unfolding work in history. This confessional position set the Iowa Synod apart from other Lutheran bodies in the many doctrinal controversies which ensued in the late nineteenth century. The emphases on the catechumenate, apostolic life, and church discipline translated these aspects of Loehe's program of renewal into congregational life. Deindoerfer pays attention to how these characteristics were expressed in church life over the early decades of the Iowa Synod.

The primary focus of the Iowa Synod was on inner mission—establishing and building up German-Lutheran congregations. Seminary faculty and students went out as missionaries to preaching points to proclaim the Gospel and form new congregations. Providing pastors for the Buffalo Synod extended the geographical reach of the Iowa Synod and was enabled by the steady flow of theological candidates sent by Loehe and colleagues from Germany.

The Iowa Synod also preserved Loehe's vision for outer mission, particularly through outreach to Native American people.[10] Outer mission was a high priority for Loehe and his *Sendlinge* (emissaries), beginning with his support for outreach to Indians in the Michigan colonies. Deindoerfer recounts the narrative of the Iowa Synod's outreach to the Crow (Upsaroka) in Montana through the leadership of J. J. Schmidt and Moritz Braeuninger.[11] In addition to his account of the martyrdom of Braeuninger on July 22, 1860, Deindoerfer explains how missionary work nevertheless continued among the Cheyenne at a mission station constructed at Deer Creek, Wyoming. Between 1861 and 1863 various missionary ventures were explored, including preaching services for Native Americans near the Deer Creek station. For a short time, the missionaries again experimented with traveling in accompaniment with

---

10. For the following, see Deindörfer, *Geschichte*, 55ff.

11. Schmutterer and Lutz, "Mission Martyr on the Western Frontier," 117–42.

the Cheyenne and the Arapaho.[12] Three orphaned Cheyenne boys were entrusted to the missionaries for instruction in 1863, and each was baptized. This effort soon dissipated through the eruption of a new wave of Indian insurrections. By January 1865 the entire missionary team had withdrawn. An attempt was made to resume Native American mission work in 1866 but was short-lived. In 1885 the Iowa Synod transferred remaining funds from Native American missions to the Neuendettelsau Mission Society for its work in Papua New Guinea (an initiative closely aligned to the commitments of Loehe). In its understanding of inner and outer mission, the Iowa Synod looked to Loehe as its founder, supporter, source of authority, and inspiration.

Seminary, Worship, Confessional Direction

From the founding of the teachers seminary in Saginaw to the development of Wartburg Seminary and Wartburg College in Iowa, Loehe displayed unflagging interest and support. This was evident in his continuing to send candidates for pastoral ministry from Germany for training at Wartburg Seminary.[13] While requests for financial support from the Iowa Synod (among others) overwhelmed the capacity of Loehe to fulfill them, he remained committed to providing leaders for the fledgling synod. Sigmund Fritschel, who arrived in 1854 to assume duties as professor at the seminary, also served as congregational pastor and missionary in a career in the Iowa Synod that spanned forty-six years. Sigmund's brother, Gottfried, was sent from Neuendettelsau in 1857 to serve as a second professor at the seminary. Gottfried Fritschel (1836–1889) was a gifted linguist. He learned the art of printing to prepare synod publications and was a major theological spokesman for the Iowa Synod until his death. Together the brothers served as primary faculty for nearly all the pastors prepared by the Iowa Synod in the nineteenth century.

Financial challenges plagued the seminary from its earliest years. Although the *Gesellschaft* wished to provide resources, at Loehe's direction the Iowa Synod was told that in the future it would be necessary

---

12. Deindörfer, *Geschichte*, 61–62.

13. For a comprehensive listing of the names of those sent to North America, including those specifically sent to the Iowa Synod in the nineteenth century, see Koller, *Die Missionsanstalt in Neuendettelsau*, 36–57.

to entrust the seminary "into God's hands."[14] As a result, the seminary was given to the Iowa Synod as a donation by the *Gesellschaft* that was gratefully accepted at the synod's 1855 assembly. Financial pressures also contributed to the relocation of the seminary to Clayton County in 1857, where a two-story wood frame building was constructed on 160 acres of land. The seminary was supported by farming, with seminarians working the farm and nourished by its produce. Here the school received its name, Wartburg, "a mighty fortress" and sign of God's faithfulness. In 1860 Sigmund Fritschel was sent on a fundraising mission for the seminary to Germany, where he was well received by Loehe. Loehe mediated many contacts in Germany, Holland, and Eastern Europe. Sigmund Fritschel traveled as far as St. Petersburg, where he met generous supporters, some who would remain so for life. At St. Petersburg he welcomed Auguste von Schwartz, who volunteered to come to Iowa to serve as housemother for the seminary, a service that continued to the end of her life.[15] Loehe facilitated these relationships on behalf of the seminary to address its financial crisis.

The worship life and congregational practices of Iowa Synod congregations were decisively shaped by Loehe's vision for the renewal of the church. Loehe's *Agende* served as the standard for liturgical worship. Through connections with parish life in Neuendettelsau, the synod's pastors gained an appreciation for the beauty and order of worship.[16] Loehe included the worship of North American congregations as part of his intent when composing his *Agende*, which contributed to a glorious liturgical life for the synod in place of less desirable alternatives. Deindoerfer lamented the relative infrequency of participation in Holy Communion in many congregations, noting how this had also become the norm in many quarters of the church in Germany.[17] A revised edition of Loehe's *Agende* was edited by Pastor Johannes Deinzer, Loehe's successor in Neuendettelsau, for a new printing that appeared in 1884.[18] This helped to counter the use of other worship books in the Iowa Synod, including some in the English language.

14. Deindörfer, *Geschichte*, 93–94.
15. Lohrmann, "Prairie Royalty."
16. Deindörfer, *Geschichte*, 104.
17. Deindörfer, *Geschichte*, 182–83.
18. Deindörfer, *Geschichte*, 307.

Based on the pastoral practice of Loehe, the Iowa Synod fostered the use of private confession.[19] This was a key component in the Iowa Synod's commitment to the preservation of the apostolic life and exercise of church discipline. Private confession highlighted the importance of absolution for the Christian life. Unfortunately, the implementation of private confession frequently met resistance from church members as being a Roman Catholic practice. Deindoerfer also emphasized the importance of the church year and liturgical calendar in the congregations of the Iowa Synod, following the model of Loehe. In the late 1880s, a new edition of Loehe's *Question and Answer Booklet for Luther's Small Catechism* was produced by the seminary faculty for congregational use.[20]

The commitments of the Iowa Synod to the Lutheran confessional tradition were decisively shaped by Loehe in the theological controversies of the nineteenth century. Especially influential was his interpretive approach that distinguished between core articles of faith and open questions. The Iowa Synod insisted on full agreement in all matters of core Lutheran doctrine as the basis for pulpit and altar fellowship with other Lutheran church bodies. This was palpable in the Iowa Synod's reservations to joining the General Council in the years after 1867. The Iowa Synod subscribed to what was articulated in the Galesburg Rule in 1875: "Lutheran pulpits are for Lutheran ministers only, and Lutheran altars are for Lutheran communicants only." Furthermore, the Iowa Synod's clarity about full agreement on matters of core Lutheran doctrine was evident in its opposition to secret societies and lodge membership by church members, matters to which Deindoerfer refers several times.

The Iowa Synod understood itself to be faithful to Loehe in "open questions" regarding non-essential church teachings. These included issues that were not definitively settled either by Scripture or the Confessions, where holding different views should not be viewed as church dividing. This method of interpreting the Confessions both allowed consideration of historical circumstances that conditioned a specific theological claim and affirmed the ongoing development of Christian teaching. One finds reference in Deindoerfer to the argument that Luther himself allowed for open questions in matters of subordinate importance.[21]

---

19. Deindörfer, *Geschichte*, 106–7.

20. Deindörfer, *Geschichte*, 268–69.

21. Deindörfer, *Geschichte*, 125–26.

In response to theological attacks (for example, the claim that the pope is the anti-Christ, or particular views regarding chiliasm or predestination), the Iowa Synod appealed to open questions as a defense against dogmatism on unessential matters. Thereby the Iowa Synod defended church unity against unnecessary forces of schism within the church. In one passage Deindoerfer referred to a proposed action within the synod that would have abandoned the term "open questions," as long as substance would be maintained regarding matters that need not be church dividing. If that view had prevailed, the use of the term "open questions" might itself have been understood as an open question![22]

Lasting Influence

The devotion of the Iowa Synod to the commitments of Loehe persisted until its merger into the American Lutheran Church in 1930, and beyond! Loehe died in 1872, having offered encouragement and support to the Iowa Synod for the last eighteen years of his life. Although Loehe could not be present for the twenty-fifth anniversary of the Iowa Synod in 1879, his successor, Johannes Deinzer (1842–1897), crossed the Atlantic to participate in the festivities and represent the Loehe tradition for the ongoing life of the synod. In one of his speeches Deinzer movingly said:

> I am now fifteen years into the service of our common work and have been able to work for the greater part of this time at the side of our fathers who now rest in God, the honorable Pastor Loehe and honorable Mission Director Bauer. Also, in the name of these our blessed fathers I want here to rejoice; for while they celebrate in heaven, I may see it here and grasp it with my hands, how their seeds have grown up and their work in the Lord has not been in vain.[23]

In response to the blessings received from Loehe, the *Missionsanstalt*, and the *Gesellschaft für innere Mission*, the Iowa Synod issued a formal Thanksgiving Declaration (*Dankschrift*) to express its profound gratitude for all God had provided through these partners. The solemn resolution (*Denkschrift*) of the synod assembly underscored the treasures bequeathed to them through Loehe's theological commitments: the work

---

22. Deindörfer, *Geschichte*, 143.

23. Deindörfer, *Geschichte*, 213 (author's translation).

of the seminary, commitment to mission among Native Americans, the liturgical order, and the nurturing of Christian life in its congregations.[24]

The next two chapters examine the specific contributions of Friedrich Bauer, Loehe's colleague in Neuendettelsau, for his work in theological education and the development of the theological curriculum. Although Bauer's work has been too long overlooked, it was his major accomplishment to serve as the primary guide in Neuendettelsau for the theological preparation of candidates sent to North America from the 1850s to the end of his life in 1874.

24. Deindörfer, *Geschichte*, 216–21.

5

Friedrich Bauer (1812–1874)

Hidden behind the Giant of Neuendettelsau

IF YOU VISIT THE beautiful cemetery in the Franconian village of Neuendettelsau, you will note the prominence and symbols of veneration at the grave of Wilhelm Loehe (1808–1872). Loehe, as we have seen, is one of the ecclesial giants of nineteenth century Lutheran confessionalism and pietism in Germany, as renewer of the liturgy, organizer of mission to North America, and founder of deaconess institutions that carry forward social service among people in need to this very day. The name and stature of Loehe have grown to immense proportions in subsequent generations. However, when one lines up one's vision looking straight at Loehe's grave, the observant visitor will notice the exact placement of another grave directly behind it. Clearly, not by accident! This grave belongs to Friedrich Bauer. Bauer is the figure hidden in the shadows, backing up the giant stature of Loehe, in death even as he did in life.

Bauer's Contribution to Theological Education in Partnership with Loehe

Friedrich Bauer (1812–1874) served as founder and director of the *Missionsanstalt* Neuendettelsau, which was first located at Nuremberg in 1846 and relocated to Neuendettelsau in 1853. Bauer worked in close partnership with Loehe as a colleague and friend for more than twenty-five years. While Loehe's legacy is remembered and cherished in the history of Lutheranism in North America, Bauer's contributions have been almost entirely neglected and forgotten over the decades. In the course of history, succeeding generations often remember individual figures who function as heroes of the faith. But the memory of the team of colleagues, who lived and worked with the "giant" in their own lifetimes, is often lost to history. The 200th anniversary of Bauer's birth on June 14, 2012 gave occasion for recollecting that the mission work generated from Neuendettelsau was not solely the consequence of the heroic figure of Loehe but was the result of genuine collaboration among many dedicated co-workers, not least of whom was Friedrich Bauer.

Between the founding of the *Missionsanstalt* Neuendettelsau by Friedrich Bauer in 1846 and his death in 1874, 190 students were educated and sent for the mission work in North America.[1] The 1904 *Wartburg Kalendar der Evangelisch-Lutherische Synode von Iowa und anderen Staaten* reported that "about 100" of these students had been sent to the Iowa Synod alone.[2] Bauer increasingly became the pivotal figure in the relationship between Neuendettelsau and the Iowa Synod, to some degree as much or more than Loehe himself. Within Bauer's lifetime, a steady stream of correspondence flowed to the Iowa Synod not only from Loehe but also—and often more significantly—from Bauer.

This chapter focuses on the collection of approximately twenty-six letters (and letter fragments) in the Region 5 Archives of the Evangelical Lutheran Church in America, housed at Wartburg Theological Seminary in Dubuque, Iowa. There is no evidence that this correspondence has ever been previously examined for its historical significance. The documentation reveals a lively communication and collaboration between Bauer and the first-generation founders of the Iowa Synod and Wartburg Theological Seminary, a relationship that today has been nearly forgotten.

Bauer played a lively, vital, and engaged role in the preparation of pastors for the Iowa Synod in the first generation of Wartburg College and Seminary, particularly in relationship to those leaders whom he knew first hand: Georg Grossmann, Johannes Deindoerfer, Sigmund Fritschel, and Gottfried Fritschel. The collected letters from Bauer to the leaders of the Iowa Synod are addressed exclusively to these four persons or collectively to the "dear brothers," who were presumably these same persons. The dates of the letters range from March 21, 1851 to July 26, 1869. The holdings in the United States' archives ends with Bauer's summary of a

1. Rössler, "Friedrich Bauer," 1.

2. *Wartburg Kalendar der Evangelisch-Lutherische Synode von Iowa*, 44. Schaaf, "Wilhelm Loehe's Relation to the American Church," 192–97, provides a corrected list of those sent to North America from 1842–1925 based on Koller, *Die Missionanstalt in Neuendettelsau*.

Denkschrift, written by Bauer to the Iowa Synod's pastors, "*An die eh-rwürdigen Pastoren der Iowasynode*," dated November 30, 1874. Before he received an adequate reply and resolution of the issues raised in this document, Bauer died on December 13, 1874.

Furthermore, the subsequent historical materials from the Iowa Synod disclose how the partnership of Bauer with the Iowa Synod continued to be acknowledged and appreciated in the records from the second generation of church and seminary leaders, demonstrated by photos and references to Bauer in Iowa Synod history, at least through the time of the merger of the Iowa Synod into the American Lutheran Church in 1930. However, in materials dating from the middle and later decades of the twentieth century, awareness of Bauer's role and significance for the history of the Iowa Synod and Wartburg Theological Seminary fell steadily into oblivion with infrequent mention of his name, let alone recognition of his actual influence. The name of Loehe eventually came to represent the entire first generation of co-workers in Neuendettelsau after the passing of the second generation of church leaders in the Iowa Synod and faculty at Wartburg Seminary. It took the impulse of the 200th anniversary of Bauer's birth to stimulate recollection of the theological genealogy of this influential ancestor in Lutheran church history in the United States.

Examining the Bauer Correspondence with the Iowa Synod: Eight Themes

Christian Weber has summarized four critical aspects of the Bauer legacy that exerted significant impact upon the church in North America, particularly through his relationship with the Iowa Synod in the mid-19th century: (1) close connection for Bauer between dogmatics and ethics, (2) understanding of the distinctiveness of the particular theological "direction" (*Richtung*) to be imparted through the education of the emissaries (*Sendlinge*) in Germany that was expected to continue in their service in the North America, (3) insistence on formation for "the apostolic life," a way of living (*Lebensführung*), as expected from those pastors educated under Bauer's tutelage, and (4) clear focus on the centrality of Christian mission for the church in North America, including, at least initially, mission to the Native American people (*Heidenmission*).[3]

---

3. Weber, "Weitblickend, konzentriert und ehrlich (1812–74)," 24–28.

These are among the concerns that come to expression in detail through the extant correspondence. The letters disclose matters of a personal nature, for example, the discussion of the death of Bauer's son,[4] as well as matters pertaining to educational cooperation and theological positions. It is clear from the tone of the letters that they are written between persons who know each other and are concerned for one another's well-being, not only personally but theologically. Eight features distinguish this correspondence in relationship to the educational and missionary connections between Bauer and the Iowa Synod, especially in relation to the theological relationships and controversies with the LCMS. In chronological order of their appearance in the letters, the topics include:

1. Financial Support: Setting limits on the level of financial support available for the North American mission work and the requirement that the leaders of the Iowa Synod submit reports for the sake of accountability.

2. Deaconess Initiative: The shifting of Loehe's primary attention away from North American mission work (as a result of the controversy over the doctrine of ministry with the LCMS in Michigan) to concentrate on the development of the deaconess work in Neuendettelsau in the mid-1850s. This gave Bauer increasing responsibility for managing the educational work in partnership with the Iowa Synod.

3. Geographic Distance: The problem of geographical distance faced both by Bauer in Germany and the leaders of the Iowa Synod, which negatively affected Bauer's capacity to understand and advise regarding local developments in the Iowa Synod and complicated his understanding of the many theological controversies, especially between the Iowa Synod and the LCMS.

4. Native American Mission: Initial interest in supporting mission to the American Indians by the Iowa Synod and the eventual reduction of support for this work.

5. Student Preparation: Bauer's stewardship over the sending of students from the *Missionsanstalt* Neuendettelsau to the Iowa Synod,

---

4. Letter dated July 22, 1860. All quoted correspondence is in the Region 5 Archives of the Evangelical Lutheran Church in America, located at Wartburg Theological Seminary in Dubuque, Iowa, USA.

including comments on the readiness of some of these students for certain types of ministry and the need of others for more education.

6. Theological Direction: Acute interest in the theological "direction" (*Richtung*) of the Iowa Synod in relationship to the LCMS, especially based on reports Bauer received from others about the Iowa Synod and his speculation about their meaning. This focus came to expression most critically in the *Denkschrift* composed in November 1874 and was left unresolved by Bauer's death two weeks later.

7. Anniversary Observance: Celebration of the partnership between the institutions in Germany and the Iowa Synod at the twenty-fifth anniversary of the Neuendettelsau North American mission work in 1866.[5]

8. Invitation to Iowa Synod: Bauer's reply to the invitation that he should personally come to the United States for the fifteenth anniversary of the Iowa Synod in 1869.

Commentary will be offered on each of these eight points, based on gleanings from the missionary correspondence of Bauer to the leaders of the Iowa Synod.

Financial Support

Bauer makes very clear the limits that had to be set on the amount of financial support possible for the ongoing mission work of the Iowa Synod and for the support of the teachers school and seminary. On September 20, 1855 Bauer wrote to "the dear brethren in the Lord"" that they were receiving the second half of a payment for the purchase of a seminary building in the amount of $1100, with the request to send a receipt immediately. He describes the significance of this support and indicates the importance that the Iowa Synod take responsibility for its future support:

> Here you have new evidence that we are not neglecting the brothers in Iowa, but rather are promoting their undertaking with the greatest of sacrifices and our own personal, undiminished concern and responsibility, no less so than with any other previous undertaking. We have collected this sum with difficulty and must borrow in part against the payment of interest,

5. For perspective on the Neuendettelsau interpretation of this event, see Weber, "Die Anfänge."

because the first half is not yet entirely repaid. We hope that the brothers will acknowledge such a service. Thereby we have done everything that was possible and well beyond our capacity, so that we would not again be in the position to offer additional support of this kind. The entire capitalization, both the first and second half, should be understood as a donation to the Iowa Synod. We will prepare a payment plan exactly so, that we will give as much support as possible to the seminary. Moreover, the Synod may go freely on its way. We desire no further accountability and expect to make no charges to the seminary, not even for those things which exist within the Iowa seminary. May God grant you grace, that you are in the position to arrive at a favorable purchase, thereby being delivered out of all difficulties![6]

In subsequent years there were several requests communicated by Bauer on behalf of the Committee of the *Centralverein* and other leaders in Neuendettelsau for more frequent and regular reports by the Iowa Synod documenting the use of the support given to the synod and seminary.[7] By the end of January 1862, an agreement had been reached between Bauer and Sigmund Fritschel ("and the other brothers") about sending monthly reports, although it does not appear this agreement was maintained with consistency in the future.

Deaconess Initiative

Bauer makes very explicit that the primary focus of Loehe had now shifted to building up the deaconess institutions:

The deaconess initiative is a burning and shining light, which draws to itself the eyes of thousands and creates blessings for hundreds of suffering people, so that God is loudly praised for that which he is doing here. It is a means by which to give new energy to our entire activity. I write this to you, in order that you to some degree are put in the position, even from a great distance and while you are immersed in your own activity, to discover the correct stance in making a judgment.[8]

6. Bauer to the "Geliebter Bruder," September 20, 1855. All citations are translated by the author.

7. Bauer letter, March 8, 1861, and Bauer to Deindörfer, January 26, 1862.

8. Bauer to "Lieber Bruder," September 20, 1855.

Bauer reflects on the financial demands placed upon the organization by the growing deaconess work, although he communicates clearly that they have not lost interest in the work of the North American "brothers."[9] Bauer also comments briefly in the letters about the request to send deaconesses from Neuendettelsau to Toledo, making clear that certain conditions would need to be met as a prerequisite[10] and eventually that the negotiations regarding the sending of deaconesses were not a matter for the official involvement of the Iowa Synod: "The deaconess ministry is kept separate from all partisan ecclesial questions."[11] This policy appears firmly in place in Neuendettelsau and was to be applied in other places as well, so as not to embroil the deaconess work in unnecessary complications or controversies. Bauer contrasted the different circumstances existing in the working relationships with the deaconess houses in Russia and the less stable situation in North America. Here again, the greater distance to the United States played a significant role in the discussion.

Geographic Distance

As already mentioned, the geographical distance between locations[12] and the lapse in time for communication led not only to complications in understanding, but even to serious theological misinterpretations between Bauer and the Iowa Synod, which were made more complex by the varying opinions rendered to Bauer by different correspondents about what was going on in the Iowa Synod. This challenge was bridged occasionally by direct visits to Germany by leaders or pastors from the Iowa Synod. Improved relations were especially fostered by the fund-raising visit of Sigmund Fritschel to Germany and Russia in 1861.[13]

Native American Mission

While there are early signs of support for continuing the mission to the Native Americans, by the 1860s the partners in Neuendettelsau saw the chief responsibility for the continuation of this work as belonging

9. Bauer to Sigmund Fritschel, January 20, 1856.

10. Bauer/Loehe to Georg Grossmann, March 8, 1861.

11. Bauer to Georg Grossmann, July 21, 1869.

12. Bauer to Sigmund Fritschel, January 20, 1856.

13. Bauer/Loehe to Georg Grossmann, March 8, 1861.

to the Iowa Synod. In one of the earliest letters from Bauer to Sigmund Fritschel, he wrote approvingly of the plans to continue the work among Native Americans through the Iowa Synod:

> Related to your plan to work with the heathen [sic], we offer our approval, if the financial means are adequate. We would not want you to falter into need through such an undertaking, whereby we could not be able to provide the means to sustain it. This is the reason for our delayed reply. As I already remarked to Brother Grossmann, 500 to 600 Gulden are set aside, but we want to see whether the local chapters are also willing to give ongoing support. The matter also has not yet been clarified with the Central Chapter.[14]

By January 1856, Bauer had to communicate the reluctance of the pastors' conference to support further mission work among the American Indians, due to the lack of any earlier progress. While Schmidt had been designated as "missionary to the heathen," the financial means did not appear to be available for continuing to support the work from Germany. Therefore, Bauer placed strong limitations on the possibility of future support:

> I have written that it rests entirely in the hands of the Iowa Synod, if something is to come from this initiative. It [the Synod] must itself undertake the mission among the Indians; we would be able to guarantee nothing in terms of support, if we are not able to receive the requisite reports. It has never occurred to us to want to take over direction from such a distance. This also extends beyond our responsibility as the Society for Inner Mission. We also have no objections, if the Synod connects us with the mission societies for the heathen [sic], or sends us reports about this work to awaken interest. Only so can something come out of the initiative.[15]

On July 11, 1861 Bauer mentioned a gift of 730 Gulden for the "*Heidenmission*."[16] While Bauer recalled the dedicated missionary work of Braeuninger among the Indians in his letter of January 26, 1862, following Braeuninger's tragic death in 1859,[17] the correspondence turned away from this topic. In June 1867 Bauer reported a shift in focus away

14. Bauer to Sigmund Fritschel, March 29, 1855.

15. Bauer to Sigmund Fritschel, January 20, 1856.

16. Bauer to "Dear brother," July 11, 1861.

17. Schmutterer and Lutz, "Mission Martyr on the Western Frontier."

from support for the Native American work in North America to other "inner mission" efforts.[18] Thereafter the topic of mission to the American Indians fell silent.

Student Preparation

As the years unfolded, there was detailed information shared about the students who were to be sent to the Iowa Synod from Neuendettelsau and discussion about either their readiness for pastoral ministry or their need for further education. For example, Bauer wrote about five students (*Zöglinge*), three of whom had completed three years of study already, a fourth 2½ years, and the fifth who had received education in the trade of building construction:

> All of them have a good general education. They are altogether well habituated and ordered and possess reliable, earnest character and sense. They all have sucessfully completed a thorough examination. They are all being given provisions and sent forth at the expense of the Society. At their departure from the Society they have to secure special documentation that they have been given provisions and are sent by the Society. After their departure from the Society, in the case that they change over to other synods, they are expected to repay their entire educational and emmigration expenses.[19]

This communication makes clear the shared goal that students prepared and sent from Neuendettelsau were intended to serve in the congregations and ministries of the Iowa Synod. Only by repaying their educational expenses should they be allowed to serve in another church body. The letter also makes clear the attention devoted to both careful theological preparation and character formation of those who were to serve in pastoral ministry. Another complicating factor was addressed in this and other letters—the requirement that young men in Germany complete military service before a certain age. Negotiating the obligation to complete military service could dramatically influence the timing of the eventual emigration of students.

The correspondence makes frequent mention of the preparation of certain students by name, as well as comments about their educational

18. Bauer to Gottfried Fritschel, June 26, 1867.

19. Loehe and Bauer to Grossmann, March 8, 1861.

preparation and fitness for service.[20] The change in requirements regarding military service led Bauer to suggest the possibility that the school in Neuendettelsau could begin to function as a preparatory seminary (*Proseminar*) for Wartburg Seminary.[21] However, after the establishment of a newly constructed mission house (*Anstalt*) at a different location in Neuendettelsau, the changed living circumstances allowed for the flourishing of the educational and formational process with renewed vigor. In 1869, for example, Bauer wrote about the sending of eight students, each with distinctive abilities and suitableness for different forms of service. At the same time, he remarked about the educational preparation and formation of an additional eighteen students: "You see how God is blessing our initiative and allowing the seeds to sprout."[22]

A few letters also explored the possibilities and requests of other persons to make their way to service in North America: a teacher and his son from Russia (with the name of Israel),[23] a direct request by letter from A. Weise about becoming a pastor in the Iowa Synod,[24] and a complicated case involving the return of a pastor named Flachenecker to service in the Iowa Synod, including the steps that would be necessary for possible reconciliation.[25] The letter fragments about such personal matters are tantalizing, but the outcomes are left unresolved for contemporary readers of the letters.

Theological Direction

Bauer expressed in several letters serious concern about the "direction" (*Richtung*) of the Iowa Synod, based on reports he had received from others and on certain doctrinal decisions approved at meetings of the Iowa Synod (or at least reports he had received about such decisions). He raised alarm wherever he perceived the Iowa Synod might be shifting back to the direction of the LCMS in the controversies over questions

20. Bauer to Sigmund Fritschel and "the other brothers at Wartburg," January 26, 1862; Bauer to Johannes Deindörfer, February 14, 1867.

21. Bauer to Deindörfer, May 5, 1868.

22. Bauer to Johannes Deindörfer, April 23, 1869.

23. Bauer to Johannes Deindörfer, July 11, 1861.

24. A. Weise to the President, February 24, 1868.

25. Bauer to Deindörfer, May 5, 1868.

such as predestination or chiliasm. This is a prominent theme in the correspondence during the 1860s.

Bauer closely followed the documentation of doctrinal positions taken by the Iowa Synod and paid strict attention to reports made to him by others about the synod's theological direction. Of interest to Bauer was the continuation of the distinctiveness of the Iowa Synod's position, determined at the origin of the synod regarding ordination (*Amt*) and "open questions." In separating from the LCMS in 1853, the theologians who founded the Iowa Synod based their theological stance on Loehe's writings about ordination (which was at odds with Walther's "transference" theory[26]) and also defended very emphatically the possibility of "open questions" in theological matters. While it was necessary to have full agreement on essential doctrinal matters in order to enjoy full communion with other Christians and church bodies, there could remain differences in nonessential matters, which did not need to become church dividing. The LCMS firmly rejected this position, claiming a strict Lutheran confessionalism that expected full agreement on all doctrinal points.

New controversies continued to break out between the LCMS and Iowa Synod over the next decades, including over fine points of eschatology, such as chiliasm (the nature of the thousand-year reign of Christ) or the pope as anti-Christ.[27] Bauer occasionally exercised public criticism of the Iowa Synod's doctrinal developments, sometimes without recognizing the consequences this could have for the Iowa Synod's leaders. For example, Bauer wrote in June 1866:

> [Our] comment that the Iowa Synod has not entirely main-
> tained its line, insofar as this is disclosed from its publications,
> gave rise to the occasion that you and the brothers have become
> deeply distressed and it has become a cause of suffering for you,
> insofar as you have been subject to ridicule from the side of Mis-
> souri. If we would have been able to intuit that these comments
> could become so sensitive for the brothers, they would have
> not been published with such severity, but rather, according
> to your wishes, have been communicated privately. If we have

26. Compare to chapter 3.

27. For example, *Was lehrt die Iowa-Synode von der Inspiration der Heiligen Schrift? Aus ihren eigenen Publikationen und anderen Quellen dargestellt* (Twin City Local Conference, n.d.).

thereby failed, it laid far from our intention to bring you into such difficulty.[28]

Bauer insisted that the Iowa Synod maintain consistency in its articulation of doctrinal positions with the views in Neuendettelsau.

Despite their protests, Bauer did bring sharp theological criticism against the Iowa Synod, requesting copies of particular documents for his own examination.[29] Eventually, after further discussion and explanation, the apparent differences became clarified to Bauer's satisfaction.[30] For example, after an exchange of letters about potential doctrinal shifts in the Iowa Synod, Bauer wrote:

> I have been converted from my thoughts. If they have subsequently disquieted you, I am sorry. I simply accept the status quo as God's will. I have won clarity for myself . . . We are able and desire to be nothing other than ingredients for you, as long as you are glad for this contribution and as long as you need us, and as long as we see that this miraculous and rare cooperation is God's will.[31]

Nevertheless, Bauer's paternal concern for the Iowa Synod and its direction (*Richtung*) persisted to the end of his life. Shortly before his death, Bauer composed a *Denkschrift*, in which "he wanted to intervene in the controversies between the Missouri and Iowa Synods."[32] Again, Bauer expressed his fear that the Iowa Synod was losing its distinctiveness and returning to the doctrinal positions of the Missouri Synod. It appears from the correspondence that Bauer had far more concern for common teaching between Neuendettelsau and Iowa than did Loehe, who was devoting his main energy by this time to other activities beyond the mission work in North America, especially to the development of the deaconess institutions. Loehe had long ago handed over responsibility for the preparation of students to Bauer.

In the *Denkschrift* Bauer raised critical questions about points of doctrine in dispute at the time, particularly matters of eschatology, asking for clarification and requesting answers regarding the contested issues. He asked especially about theological statements from a meeting in

28. Bauer to Johannes Deindörfer, June 1, 1866.
29. Bauer to Johannes Deindörfer, May 5, 1868.
30. Bauer to "Präses," July 21, 1869.
31. Bauer, Fragment after August 31, 1870.
32. Rössler, "Friedrich Bauer," 48.

Davenport, Iowa in 1873 that included proposed constitutional revisions (as he understood them). Bauer expressed concern at perceived attempts by Missouri to divide the membership of the Iowa Synod, especially in relation to the meaning of subscription to the Lutheran Confessions. Both Loehe and Bauer had expressed their conviction that the Lutheran tradition needed to remain open to further development as history unfolded, in contrast to the strict confessionalism of Missouri. Bauer wrote:

> We desire a biblical and ecclesial Lutheranism, whereby the symbols maintain their validity, but constitute no obstacle for faithful biblical research according to a rightly understood *analogia fidei*—not a traditionalism, which simply repeats the established doctrinal concept through a false notion of the analogy of faith, blocking all progress in enlightenment and knowledge, in the instance that one appears to fall into conflict with the dominant theological system, as inherited from the past. This allows those who possess an absolutely pure and infallible doctrine to put an obstacle in the way and, through spiritual pride, name all those brothers who stand upon the same faith foundation and confession as heretics and deny them fellowship in an unjust and ungodly way.[33]

This was occasioned by recent reports that Bauer had received from others about emerging developments in the Iowa Synod about contested theological issues (for example, eschatology), which should remain open questions. In this *Denkschrift* Bauer reminded the colleagues in the Iowa Synod of their historical and affectionate relationships, while also asserting his genuine theological concerns.[34]

As Roessler concludes, although Bauer's warnings ultimately were "as we know today, influenced by unsubstantiated concerns,"[35] we need to ask why he was so persistent in raising these issues in the 1860s until his death on December 13, 1874. Clearly, Bauer had invested so much in the preparation of his students (*Zöglinge*)—both their theological education and their formation in what he called "the apostolic life"—that he continued to feel tremendous responsibility for their well-being and faithfulness the rest of his life. Bauer's practice of teaching his students through daily "life together" and his desire that they persist in ancient

33. Bauer, "*An die ehrwürdigen Pastoren der Iowasynode*," November 30, 1874.

34. For an extensive treatment of Bauer's *Denkschrift*, see Liebenberg. "Friedrich Bauers Denkschrift," 189–243.

35. Rössler, "Friedrich Bauer," 48.

apostolic practices (including singleness rather than marriage)[36] reveals his deep investment in their ongoing leadership and the direction (*Richtung*) of the Iowa Synod, as expressed most elaborately in the *Denkschrift*. While it was unfortunate that the fears of Bauer as they came to expression at the end of his life could not be resolved before his death, it is most likely that the differences would have been resolved, had there been time for further correspondence.

Anniversary Observance

Official communication from the Iowa Synod at the twenty-fifth anniversary of the North American mission work in 1866 demonstrates the deep connection and gratitude by the Iowa Synod leaders for their respected teacher and supporter in Neuendettelsau. Bauer wrote that this was a time for examining their past work and freely evaluating their ongoing relationship. This event was held at a time when Bauer had begun to raise certain theological questions about the direction of the Iowa Synod. Nevertheless, the correspondence makes clear his commitment to mutual partnership:

> May the Lord grant us his mind, that we seek nothing other than his glory and that we not shy away from scorn; so we will become always more unified in truth and love. The way of truth is truly narrow and steep, especially in our days, where there is such great confusion and everything wants to go awry.[37]

Bauer here sounded an apocalyptic note regarding the present situation facing the church.

Invitation to Iowa Synod

Bauer was invited to visit North America for the fifteenth anniversary of the founding of the Iowa Synod in 1869, an invitation that deeply moved him and gave him the opportunity to reflect on past achievements:

> Hereby we have been given unambiguous and factual proof, how great, urgent, and upright your integrity to walk hand in hand with us and to work with singleness of mind and spirit toward

---

36. Bauer to "Geliebte Bruder," January 7, 1863.
37. Bauer to Deindörfer, June 1, 1866.

the attainment of the great goal. That goal is none other than to serve the Lutheran church in America and wherever possible to give shape to it, so that longing souls will easily recognize, through its pure and biblically faithful confession, works of love and moderation in all things, signs of God's presence, amid the confusion of ecclesial divisions.[38]

Although Bauer had to decline the invitation, this served as an occasion for expressing his conviction that the current doctrinal controversies had been settled, even if new concerns were emerging about the possible sub-dividing of the Iowa Synod into geographical regions.

Reclaiming Bauer's Contribution to the Loehe Legacy

In conclusion, it is important to reclaim the significance of Friedrich Bauer's influence on the development of the pastors and direction of the Iowa Synod. More than a hundred students who were sent to North America first received theological instruction in dogmatics and ethics, as well as other disciplines, from Bauer as their primary teacher and mentor. Moreover, the correspondence reveals that Bauer's focus on the apostolic life, grounded upon living together in community—theology students and their teachers together under the same roof—was in many ways a legacy derived more from Bauer than from Loehe, since by the mid-1850s, Loehe had turned over almost all theological instruction and formation of students (*Zöglinge*) into Bauer's capable hands.

The history of Wartburg Theological Seminary by William Weiblen is entitled *Life Together*. Often this descriptor is thought to derive exclusively from Loehe (and perhaps subsequently from Bonhoeffer). While Loehe was instrumental in conceptualizing a proposal for a "Lutheran Society for the Apostolic Life"[39] and sought to implement a form of apostolic life through the deaconess institutions, it was Bauer who implemented the idea of the apostolic life in preparing theological students and

38. Bauer to Präses (Grossmann), July 21, 1869.

39. Loehe, "Vorschlag zu einem Lutherischen Verein (1848)," 213–52. Further-more, Loehe, "*Der evangelische Geistliche* (1852/1858)," 147, dedicated the second volume of "Der evangelische Geistliche (1858)" to "the students of the closely connected preparation schools, both the evangelical-Lutheran preachers seminary Wartburg in St. Sebald at the spring, Iowa and the evangelical-Lutheran Mission School in Neuen-dettelsau in Mittelfranken." In "Der evangelische Geistliche," 7–317, there is evidence of the specific teaching Loehe likely imparted to students at the Missionsanstalt re-garding the character of the apostolic life.

candidates for pastoral ministry, an undertaking for which he dedicated all his energy. The particular shape of theological education for "the apostolic life" through intentional Christian community belongs as much to the legacy of Bauer as to Loehe himself.[40] From the very beginning, this was formation for a church in mission.[41] Sensibility for the vitality of the Christian community derived from Bauer's deep commitment to the theological conviction that each person was created in God's image and made to live in communion with God in Jesus Christ and, for his sake, with one another.[42]

The correspondence between Bauer and the leaders of the Iowa Synod from 1851 to 1874 recounts a fascinating chapter in the history of the relationship among the Iowa Synod, Wartburg Theological Seminary, and the *Missionsanstalt* Neuendettelsau. We discover that the early leaders of the Iowa Synod and Wartburg Theological Seminary had close personal relationships with Bauer as their respected teacher and as sponsor of dozens of students who became pastors of the church through Bauer's theological teaching, distinctive form of communal formation for ministry, and personal influence.[43] In contrast, for the second generation of leaders and teachers in the Iowa Synod, while Bauer was honored and remembered as a figure in the history of the synod and seminary, the references to him in the historical narrative become briefer and far more generalized.[44]

By the time of the third and fourth generations in North America, however, and especially after the merger of the Iowa Synod into the American Lutheran Church in 1930 and for the ongoing history of Wartburg Theological Seminary, the historical record has been directed almost entirely to remembering the significance of Loehe. The 200th anniversary of Bauer's birth gave occasion for reclaiming this forgotten ancestor, not only in the history of the church and institutions in Neuendettelsau but also for the history of the Lutheran church in North America, especially the history of Wartburg Theological Seminary. The next chapter explores Bauer's distinctive contributions to the theological curriculum by examining the textbooks he authored.

40. Rössler, "Friedrich Bauer," 20; and Bauer to "Geliebter Bruder," January 7, 1863.

41. Rössler, "Friedrich Bauer," 32.

42. Reiner, "Nachhaltige Wirkung," 207.

43. For example, see the notice of Bauer's death in *Kirchenblatt der evangelisch-lutherischen Synode Iowa* 18 (March 15, 1875) 41–42.

44. For example, Zeilinger, *A Missionary Synod with a Mission*, 16–17.

6

Theological Curriculum
at the *Missionsseminar* Neuendettelsau
in the Nineteenth Century

IN THE PREVIOUS CHAPTER, we have seen how renewed attention recently has been devoted to the contributions of Friedrich Bauer to the Loehe legacy. Although Loehe has come to be portrayed as a religious genius who worked in relative independence from others, this view distorts the actual circumstances—that Loehe was fully interdependent in collaborating with many other partners. Nowhere is this more apparent than in the preparation of candidates for pastoral ministry in North America through the Neuendettelsau *Missionsanstalt* (Mission Institute). Bauer should be considered not only as a co-worker, but as the key figure for guiding the educational process, especially in the period after the *Missionsanstalt* relocated from Nuremberg to Neuendettelsau in 1853 and after the founding of the deaconess work in 1854, which increasingly occupied the attention of Loehe.

Friedrich Bauer as Teacher

Friedrich Bauer contributed scholarly discipline, lesson planning, and an ordered curriculum to the work of *Missionsseminar* (Mission Seminary). He also was responsible for the daily administration of the school. In its early period the course of study at the *Missionsseminar* lasted three years; later, it extended to seven years. The daily schedule began in summer at 5 a.m. and in winter at 5:30 a.m., with bedtime at 10 p.m. The activities of the day included "work and rest, lessons and housework, walks and yard work."[1] The discipline prohibited developing close relationships with women, especially not with deaconesses.

Bauer was especially committed to building common life in a spiritually-centered community among and with the students.[2] As the tension between Bauer and Loehe over the construction of a new building for the *Missionsanstalt* in the 1860s demonstrated, Bauer—even more than Loehe—insisted on the value of theological "life together" (*gemeinsames Leben*) among the theological candidates and their teacher.[3] To this end and in spite of challenging conflict with Loehe about the need for new accommodations, Bauer doggedly pursued living arrangements that would foster life in community, which led to the successful completion of a new building in 1867. During his tenure as *Inspektor* of the *Missionsanstalt*, approximately 190 candidates were sent for service in North America. Those completing their education were sent exclusively to North America until 1875; opportunities for service opened in Australia beginning in 1875, New Guinea and Africa after 1886, and Brazil after 1897.[4]

This chapter concentrates on Bauer's contribution to the theological curriculum that was used for the instruction of theological candidates through the *Missionsseminar*. The focus will be on two texts that were originally designed by Bauer, expanded by Johannes Deinzer, and revised for publication by Martin Deinzer. Each of these men served successively as *Inspektor* for the *Missionsanstalt*: Bauer from 1846 to 1874, J. Deinzer from 1875 to 1897, and M. Deinzer from 1897 to 1917. The texts examined in this chapter are *Christliche Ethik auf lutherische Grundlage* (Christian Ethics on Lutheran Foundations, 1904 edition) and *Christliche Dogmatik auf lutherische Grundlage* (Christian Dogmatics on Lutheran Foundations, 1921 edition).[5]

In addition to these texts, Bauer published the *Glaubenslehre der evangelisch-lutherische Kirche* by Nikolaus Hunnius (1585–1643), which also was clearly foundational from early on as a study text in use by the theological candidates. Bauer reports that the publication of the Hunnius

---

1. Vorländer, "Das Missionsseminar," 22.

2. Nessan, "Friedrich Bauer zum 200," 260–61.

3. Rössler, "Friedrich Bauer," 39–48.

4. Vorländer, "Das Missionsseminar," 23.

5. One limitation of this study is that it does not compare successive versions of these works, in order to differentiate the contributions of each author.

text (original, 1625) was initially commissioned by Loehe in 1844 for Loehe's use in teaching the *Sendlinge* for North America.[6]

> What the old father Nikolaus Hunnius teaches, that is our faith, which we teach to our students, in order that they also teach it again in the congregations of North America. Above all they should learn what defines the common Lutheran faith of all times and lands. Except for the Confessional writings of our church, which naturally take the first place, no book is so well suited for our purposes as the *Glaubenslehre* by old Nikolaus Hunnius.[7]

A second edition appeared in 1850; the volume edited by Bauer in 1870 was the third edition. In his Foreword to the third edition, Bauer acknowledged the use of the Hunnius text in the North American mission work to that date and noted that he has contributed only slight emendations and footnotes to the original text.

Structure of the Texts:
Christliche Dogmatik and *Christliche Ethik*

The table of contents of these two textbooks demonstrate the serious, rigorous, systematic, and comprehensive character of the theological instruction given to theological candidates at the *Missionsseminar* in Neuendettelsau. The title page of each volume indicates it was intended "for the students of the Neuendettelsau *Missionsanstalt.*" Including indexes, *Christliche Dogmatik*[8] and *Christliche Ethik*[9] encompass, respectively, 511 pages and 372 pages. It is fair to assume, based on their foundational relationship to the Hunnius *Glaubenslehre*, that the comprehensiveness of the curriculum belongs to the earliest origins of the school.

 Christliche Dogmatik is structured in four major parts preceded by a prolegomena: theology, patrology, Christology, and pneumatology. This work is subdivided into 225 numbered sections. *Christliche Ethik* is structured in ten major parts preceded by an introduction: (1) the original image of God, (2) the loss of the divine image, (3) the powers which abide in the fallen human being and the remainder of the divine image

---

6. Hunnius, *Glaubenslehre der evangelsch-lutherische Kirche*, i–ii.

7. Hunnius, *Glaubenslehre*, ii–iii.

8. Bauer, Deinzer, and Deinzer, *Christliche Dogmatik*.

9. Bauer, Deinzer, and Deinzer, *Christliche Ethik*.

of God, (4) the law in relation to the restoration of the image of God, (5) the divine image realized in the person of Jesus Christ, (6) rebirth as the reestablishment of the divine image in the human being, (7) implications and influence of the divine image in all life circumstances . . . with constant regard for the community, (8) the individual effects of the divine image in the doctrine of the individual freedom of the single Christian and the church, (9) moral implications of the divine image in the cross and suffering, and (10) the moral implications of hope or the life of hope toward the goal of final consummation. This work is subdivided into eighty numbered sections. With its organizing principle focused on the human person as created in the image of God, the *Christliche Ethik* can be regarded as a theological anthropology that devotes special attention to ethical questions and conclusions.

Both the dogmatics and ethics texts include many features that together constitute a unified concept of the whole of theology. The work is grounded in Scripture, the doctrinal heritage of the church, and Lutheran confessional theology. While there are several references that underscore the influence of Loehe, the text is also conversant with other contemporary theologians, including Bengal, Frank, Hofmann, Kaftan, Luthardt, Thomasius, and Vilmar. The authors engage in deliberate argument with the positions of Kant, Schleiermacher, Strauss, and Ritschl. Moreover, these textbooks devote considerable attention to matters of controversy in the nineteenth century, such as the character of ordination and the pastoral office, open questions, the nature of inspiration, predestination, and the unfolding of the last things (eschatology). The doctrinal position is intentionally located in contradistinction to Roman Catholic, Reformed, and Pietist/Methodist views. It also distinguishes itself at several points from the views of Walther and the Lutheran Church—Missouri Synod (LCMS). These references demonstrate that while these works are structured according to the classical theological *loci*, at the same time, the authors seriously engaged the theological issues of the day as they perceived them.

Sources of Authority: Scripture and Symbols

Foundational to the entire project is the grounding of dogmatics and ethics in the authority of Scripture and the Lutheran confessional writings (Symbols). The Prolegomena of *Christliche Dogmatik* contrasts the religious impulse which is universal to human beings with what can be known through Jesus Christ. Revelation is the "objective" aspect of religion, while faith is the "subjective" aspect. To distinguish their position from philosophical claims that attempt to reduce religion to what is rational, the authors assert that "supernatural revelation is therefore rational, trans-rational, and contra-rational at the same time."[10]

Holy Scripture is the inspired source of divine revelation. The inspiration of Scripture by the Holy Spirit issues forth as the "credibility of the testimony, which derives from [the assertions] themselves."[11] This aims to provide an experiential verification of the witness of Holy Scripture, which is not to be equated with verbal inspiration. While the Holy Spirit provided "direction" (*directio*) and the "suggestion of matters and words" (*suggestio rerum et verborum*) which undergird the verity of salvation history, the authors differentiate their view from a verbal inspiration that would insist on God's literal dictation to the biblical writers.[12] This view allows for the concession that "one must admit the possibility of an error in non-essentials."[13] The interpretation of Scripture takes seriously the literal sense of the text and relates each part to the whole of Scripture to make room for the historical development of doctrine.[14]

Regarding the authority of the Lutheran Confessions, the authors understand their role as the interpretation and application of Scripture to new contexts and challenges. The Lutheran Confessions are the "normed norm" (*norma normata*) and not the "norming norm" (*norma normans*). Thereby, Scripture is afforded the highest authority, while the Lutheran Confessions have derivative authority in relation to their witness to Scripture that emerged at a particular moment in church history. Central to the Lutheran Confessions is the doctrine of justification, especially as articulated in the Augsburg Confession, Small Catechism, and Epitome. Within the Lutheran Confessions, one needs to distinguish between fundamental and non-fundamental articles, holding decisively to the authority of the fundamental articles. Whereas Scripture witnesses to the voice of God, the Symbols witness to the voice of the church. Because the Lutheran Confessions are to be understood as authoritative "insofar

---

10. Bauer, Deinzer, and Deinzer, *Christliche Dogmatik*, 9.

11. Bauer, Deinzer, and Deinzer, *Christliche Dogmatik*, 16.

12. Bauer, Deinzer, and Deinzer, *Christliche Dogmatik*, 22–24.

13. Bauer, Deinzer, and Deinzer, *Christliche Dogmatik*, 25.

14. Bauer, Deinzer, and Deinzer, *Christliche Dogmatik*, 32–34.

as" (*quatenus*) they convey God's word, not "because" (*quia*) they convey God's word, the authors affirm the possibility of "open questions" that are not yet resolved by Scripture or the Symbols.[15]

Citations from the church fathers serve as another source of authority in these works. However, the authors appeal not only to patristic sources to substantiate theological claims, but also sometimes to illustrate a failed theological direction. The most significant sources of the authority of church tradition are the creeds, which are also included among the Lutheran confessional writings.

Theological Themes

The *Loci* of Melanchthon serves as the prototype for all subsequent Lutheran dogmatics. Clearly, the authors also are greatly influenced by the salvation history paradigm for their dogmatic construction, as was conceptualized by theological contemporaries like Hofmann at Erlangen, and by the Lutheran confessional theological tradition, as represented by the nineteenth century theologians Philippi, Thomasius, Vilmar, and Frank.[16]

Evidence for the doctrine of the Holy Trinity derives primarily from the narrative of Scripture rather than other proofs. God's being is related to God's character as it has been revealed in Scripture, especially as God's character is known as love. The properties of the Triune God are discussed in relation to God's knowing, willing, and feeling. God's properties have been established in divine self-limitation, which allows for human freedom, a major theme that is developed in detail in the ethics volume. Grace is an expression of divine patience in relation to human waywardness. The three persons of the Trinity are known through their works as revealed in Scripture: creation, redemption, and sanctification.[17]

The cosmos originates through the creative activity of God, in contrast to pantheism or theories based on some organizing of preexisting matter. The authors allow for the development of creation from simpler to more complex forms over an extended length of time, even as they distinguish the biblical creation stories from the views of Darwin, theosophists, or deists. While God permitted the possibility of evil, this conviction had

15. Bauer, Deinzer, and Deinzer, *Christliche Dogmatik*, 35–39.

16. Bauer, Deinzer, and Deinzer, *Christliche Dogmatik*, 44.

17. Bauer, Deinzer, and Deinzer, *Christliche Dogmatik*, 73–87.

to be affirmed theologically as a necessary aspect of a good creation. The goal of creation is the glory of God and the blessedness of all creatures. The earth has a preferred place among all the worlds created by God.[18] The authors examine angelology at considerable length in relation to the biblical witness, including a discussion of Satan and fallen angels.[19]

Human beings are unique in God's creation due to their capacity for connection with the spiritual world. Humans are unified beings, made in God's image and constituted of body, soul, and spirit. The image of God entails limited freedom and ethical responsibility. While humans were created with the possibility of not sinning (*posse non peccare*), they failed to realize this potentiality. The fall is rooted in the human desire to be like God. Original sin entails that the sin of Adam is imputed and transmitted to all human beings through procreation. While humans may exercise limited free will in external works, the will is entirely bound in relation to God's work of salvation (versus Pelagius). One achievement of Lutheran theology is the overcoming of semi-Pelagianism.[20]

Christology begins with a discussion of predestination and the distinctiveness of the Lutheran view regarding the mystery of divine provision in contrast to the Reformed doctrine of double predestination (which the authors also attribute to certain Lutheran theologians amid the controversies of the nineteenth century). While God knows all, God does not predetermine all. Faith arises from the use of the means of grace. God's redemptive act in Jesus Christ is the center of all history. The dogmatic formulation of the two natures of Christ in the one person, derived from the christological controversies of the early church, documents the orthodox christological position. Special attention is devoted to a discussion of the meaning of *kenosis*, with an explicit contrast made to the views of Thomasius and Hofmann. The work of Christ involves the representative character (*Stellvertretung*) of Christ in making vicarious satisfaction for human sin.[21]

The lengthiest part of the dogmatics involves a discussion of various aspects of pneumatology: the order of salvation, the means of grace, the doctrine of the church and the pastoral office, and eschatology. Reference is made to classical elements in the order of salvation: call, illumination,

18. Bauer, Deinzer, and Deinzer, *Christliche Dogmatik*, 88–93.

19. Bauer, Deinzer, and Deinzer, *Christliche Dogmatik*, 93–107.

20. Bauer, Deinzer, and Deinzer, *Christliche Dogmatik*, 107–39.

21. Bauer, Deinzer, and Deinzer, *Christliche Dogmatik*, 140–214.

regeneration, conversion, and justification. Central to the teaching on the order of salvation is the doctrine of justification, including a discussion of the nature of faith and the relation of faith to good works as the fruit of faith. The means of grace are Word (preaching and absolution) and sacraments (baptism and the Lord's Supper). Baptism of children is biblically warranted and correlates with the practice of confirmation. The words of institution authorize the teaching of the real presence of Christ in the sacrament. The Lutheran position regarding the two sacraments of baptism and the Lord's Supper is defended against both Roman Catholic and Reformed claims.[22]

The Holy Spirit builds up and preserves the church as a community. Pietism endangers the church through the establishment of circles of the pious (*ecclesiolae in ecclesia*), and rationalism threatens to reduce the faith to rational individualism. Maintaining focus on the centrality of the means of grace safeguards the "visible" character of the church. The key feature of church existence is its confessional stance. While the Lutheran church has not arrived at perfection and remains open to future development and fulfillment, something authentic has been attained in the Lutheran tradition.

In this regard, two positions distinguish themselves: the gnesio-Lutheran or old-Lutheran view, as they, not without presumption, call themselves; and, the so-called neo-Lutheran view, to which Loehe and Vilmar belong, which does not view the ideal church as already realized in the period of the Reformation, but rather appeals to the form of the apostolic church and strives toward an ever greater perfection in doctrine and life.[23]

It is the "neo-Lutheran" view of the authors that remains open to a post-Reformation development of doctrine, embraces the possibility of "open questions" (for example, regarding ordination or eschatology), and looks toward future fulfillment. The topics of pastoral ordination (*Amt*) and eschatology (especially a discussion of the events in the end times) are taken up at length in both the dogmatics and the ethics. Here they will be discussed under the heading of "controversies." The ultimate fulfillment of God's creation will involve eternal blessedness with a new heaven and new earth in the heavenly Jerusalem.[24]

22. Bauer, Deinzer, and Deinzer, *Christliche Dogmatik*, 215–342.

23. Bauer, Deinzer, and Deinzer, *Christliche Dogmatik*, 375.

24. Bauer, Deinzer, and Deinzer, *Christliche Dogmatik*, 342–479.

Ethical Themes

The 1904 edition of *Christliche Ethik* was published at the fiftieth anniversary of the move of the *Missionsanstalt* from Nuremberg to Neuendettelsau. The ethical deliberations are grounded in the dogmatic foundations established in the prior work. The authors carefully correlate dogmatic affirmations with ethical considerations.[25] Morality as a human capacity is based on the image of God belonging to divine creation. Human beings exercise ethical responsibility that is conditioned both by nature and environment. The authors understand temperament, age, gender, family, tribe, *Volk*, and context as factors that influence the exercise of human freedom. "Ethics is the scientific exposition of the doctrine of the moral fulfillment of the human being."[26] Christianity grounds ethics in God. Christian ethics is oriented toward final blessedness and is empowered by the work of the Holy Spirit. Ethics describes Christian moral behavior in all life circumstances.[27]

While the theme of freedom is prominent in Luther's own theology (cf. *The Freedom of a Christian*), the influence of Enlightenment views on human freedom appears to elevate the authors' emphasis on the exercise of human freedom in *Christliche Ethik*. The image of God in humans is closely linked to the created spiritual capacity to exercise freedom. The only prohibition given to humans by God at creation involved a moral limit. At its heart, the fall was a result of human transgression against God's command by choosing evil rather than good. The consequences of sin include the onset of death, suffering, and exile from paradise. Sin affects human ethical capacity, leads to shame, and distorts conscience.[28]

All humans inherit the effects of original sin, which entails the loss of original righteousness and the onset of concupiscence. Nevertheless, there abides a remainder of the image of God. Whereas humans have suffered a loss of free will in relation to divine things, there remains a circumscribed exercise of freedom in earthly things. Conscience, as formed by Christian existence, continues to function as a moral guide. However, it is the law of God that preserves humankind after the fall into sin. Ultimately, the image of God is realized in Jesus Christ, whose work includes the restoration of the image of God, especially through the forgiveness

25. Bauer, Deinzer, and Deinzer, *Christliche Ethik*, 15–16.

26. Bauer, Deinzer, and Deinzer, *Christliche Ethik*, 11.

27. Bauer, Deinzer, and Deinzer, *Christliche Ethik*, 1–21.

28. Bauer, Deinzer, and Deinzer, *Christliche Ethik*, 22–38.

of sin and the work of the Holy Spirit through the means of grace. Faith, hope, and love are chief among salvation's goods for the Christian life. Sanctification involves leaving behind the old, sinful self and living according to Christ's command to love the neighbor. The godly life is not so much the path of individual piety as it is the call to live for the sake of neighbors.[29]

Again, the focus on the exercise of human freedom as expressed in neighbor love, although central to Luther's ethics, may owe more to the *Zeitgeist* of the Kantian tradition than the authors would have been able to admit. A major portion of the ethics volume is devoted to the specific ways that Christians live out the ethical life in community with neighbors, such as attending to the spiritual and bodily needs of others through our earthly callings in social existence and through social institutions. The Bible witnesses to the meaning of neighborliness through the life and ministry of Jesus. The central callings through which Christians serve neighbors include ethical obligations in marriage, family, *Volk*, and state. The authors explore in detail the substance of these moral obligations, including a discussion of the legitimate authority of the state and an excursus on the possible right to revolution.[30]

The church, which receives its clearest expression among those bodies with confessions (above all, the Lutheran Confessions!), is the most perfect form of human community. In the exercise of freedom by an individual Christian in the church, one must distinguish between those things God clearly has commanded and those things that are permissible. The ethical life consists of making choices between the good, the better, and the best. One does well to refrain from opting for the permissible, if this would negatively affect the well-being of the neighbor. Pietism is tempted to make prohibitions about those things that rightly belong to the permissible (for example, theater, playing games, or dancing). In exercising Christian freedom, one is guided by the Word of God, conscience, reasoning, and the law. However, sin always threatens to undermine human pursuit of the good. Therefore, we are continually dependent on divine direction, for example, through pastoral guidance or the appropriate use of ascetical practices (for example, fasting, charity, Scripture reading, or

29. Bauer, Deinzer, and Deinzer, *Christliche Ethik*, 38–150.

30. Bauer, Deinzer, and Deinzer, *Christliche Ethik*, 150–233.

meditation). Above all, Christians receive guidance through the observance of Sunday worship in accordance with Acts 2:42.[31]

One of the most moving passages in the ethics deals with the meaning of the cross and suffering in the Christian life. Suffering takes many forms, such as martyrdom, opposition to the world, testing, and discipline. The causes of suffering are varied, such as the world, the flesh, and the devil. Most challenging are those forms of suffering that are sent by God! The rule of suffering is to follow God's will. The dangerous consequences of suffering include falling away, depression, melancholy, and despair. God's presence in suffering can strengthen faith and give prospect of release. Christians are called not to flee from suffering but to surrender to God's purposes, repent, discover patience, and learn the sufficiency of God's grace. God's Word lends strength in times of suffering.[32]

The final ethical challenge is death. It is natural to experience loss and grief in the face of death and to receive comfort in one's time of fear. Daily prayer and the accompaniment of others provide strength when death approaches. Scripture witnesses to the ultimate Christian hope, the resurrection of the dead, and the second coming of Jesus Christ. When the Christian life arrives at its ultimate goal, the battle between spirit and flesh will come to an end, and we will arrive at eternal blessedness. The church is being prepared as the eternal bride of the Lamb when Christians will participate in the final glory, holiness, and blessedness of the New Jerusalem.[33]

Controversies

Just as church history has been punctuated by many controversies, the nineteenth century also offered many occasions for theological debate, argument, controversy, and division. The dogmatics and ethics texts make regular reference to the doctrinal controversies of the past to provide guidance to the church in navigating challenges to theological understanding in the present. The authors orient the reader to past controversies (for example, the ancient trinitarian or christological debates) as well as many controversies of the Reformation era.

---

31. Bauer, Deinzer, and Deinzer, *Christliche Ethik*, 233–311.

32. Bauer, Deinzer, and Deinzer, *Christliche Ethik*, 311–30.

33. Bauer, Deinzer, and Deinzer, *Christliche Ethik*, 330–57.

These theological works should be located in relation to the controversies of the sixteenth century, which informs their theological direction. Clearly, the authors position themselves in opposition to the Roman Catholic views which first generated the Protestant Reformation: indulgences, works righteousness, the authority of the papacy, the definition and number of sacraments, or the nature of the priesthood. The guiding theological principle is justification by grace through faith in Christ alone. At the same time, these texts are written in the wake of the Prussian Union that reinvigorated resistance to Reformed theology, for example, in relation to double predestination or the nature of Christ's presence in the Lord's Supper.

There are also well-defined differences in relation to the post-Reformation emergence of Pietism, including its tendencies to undervalue the means of grace as dispensed through the institutional church or its exaggerated attention to certain expressions of personal holiness. Finally, there are explicit criticisms of rationalism and the influence of Enlightenment thinkers who threatened to reduce religion to reason apart from revelation. For all these reasons, one might categorize these works as a contribution to Lutheran apologetics.

The most extensive discussion of controversial themes, however, are related to the burning issues of the nineteenth century.[34] One can note the nuancing of positions also among different Lutheran parties, for example, the earlier reference to the differences between "gnesio-" and "neo-Lutherans." Clearly, these works are conversant with the theological debates raging in North America in the middle to late nineteenth century. The authors mention explicitly and repeatedly theological differences between their views and those of Walther and the LCMS. Among the central issues in this debate were the authority for ordination (*Amt*), the status of open questions, predestination, and teaching about the last things (eschatology).

Bauer defends Loehe's views on ordination as published in his book, *Aphorisms on the New Testament Offices and their Relationship to the Congregation* (1849).[35] This controversy is discussed at length in the dogmatics[36] and mentioned again in the ethics,[37] where the views of Loehe

34. The issues raised between the Iowa Synod and the LCMS at the end of the nineteenth century are documented in Fritschel and Fritschel, *Iowa und Missouri*.

35. Loehe, *Aphorisms on the New Testament Offices*.

36. Bauer, Deinzer, and Deinzer, *Christliche Dogmatik*, 379–99.

37. Bauer, Deinzer, and Deinzer, *Christliche Ethik*, 240–41, 296.

are explained and defended. A closely related issue involves defense of the teaching about "open questions." This was consistent with the neo-Lutheran position regarding confessional subscription, which argued that only agreement in essential matters was necessary for church unity, while differences of opinion are allowable in non-essentials.[38] "Open questions are those, about which the church has not yet agreed, or, not yet had the occasion to address."[39] The dogmatics text also affirms the teaching about open questions in relation to the question of chiliasm.[40]

Intense debate over the doctrine of predestination is documented in the dogmatics. Eleven pages of text are devoted to refuting what is described as the shared viewpoint of the Reformed tradition and the LCMS, including extensive references to the theological arguments of Walther.[41] In effect, the authors argue against a strong version of (double) predestination, through which God determines the destiny of both the elect and the damned. Such a view threatened to undermine the efficacy of the means of grace as God's established instruments for generating faith. Moreover, such a strong version of predestination displaced the centrality of the cross and resurrection of Jesus Christ as God's saving deed. Neither the Roman Catholic view (that elevated the human role in salvation) nor the Reformed view (that marginalized God's salvation in Jesus Christ) was acceptable. The authors of the dogmatics allow room for the mystery of God to prevail in the face of exaggerated claims about God's power to predestine.

A final issue receiving disproportionate attention in both the dogmatics and ethics texts involves eschatology and mapping out of the last things. The nineteenth century was rife with speculation about the signs of the end times and the second coming of Christ. In North America vitriolic polemic was exchanged between pre-millennialists and various types of post-millennialists about ordering events of the end times. This controversy is reflected in the detailed analysis by the authors regarding what was to transpire before the final consummation of history. No less than seventy pages of the dogmatics is written about eschatology, much of this discussion an interpretation of apocalyptic biblical passages to elaborate the unfolding sequence of events prophesied by God. The seven

---

38. Bauer, Deinzer, and Deinzer, *Christliche Dogmatik*, 39–40.

39. Bauer, Deinzer, and Deinzer, *Christliche Dogmatik*, 377.

40. Bauer, Deinzer, and Deinzer, *Christliche Dogmatik*, 416.

41. Bauer, Deinzer, and Deinzer, *Christliche Dogmatik*, 142–53.

central themes are: (1) preaching of the Gospel to all peoples, (2) the conversion of Israel, (3) the general apostasy, (4) the appearance of the anti-Christ, (5) the first return of Christ, (6) the first resurrection, and (7) the thousand-year reign of Christ. Each of these themes is discussed in detail regarding God's revealed plan for the end times.[42] By devoting so much attention to these speculations, the authors demonstrate the extent to which they were influenced by the temper of their times.

Conclusion

A close reading of *Christliche Dogmatik* and *Christliche Ethik* illustrates the rigorous, systematic, and comprehensive character of the theological instruction given to theological candidates at the *Missionsseminar* in Neuendettelsau. This theological training was deeply grounded in the Bible, patristic sources, and the Lutheran Confessions. Candidates also became knowledgeable in the art of apologetics, learning how to engage the theological controversies of their times.

Those prepared through the course of study documented in these textbooks and sent to North America (or other mission destinations) received a solid theological and ethical foundation for taking up their ministries as pastors and teachers of the church, or in preparation to complete their education at theological institutions in their new countries. Wartburg Theological Seminary received from Neuendettelsau the brothers, Sigmund and Gottfried Fritschel, who served both as mission pastors in the Iowa Synod and the two primary faculty members of the seminary until the end of their lives. The instruction they brought to their students was grounded in the theological curriculum of the *Missionsseminar* that they received under the instruction of Bauer and Loehe in the 1850s.[43]

The theological curriculum of the *Missionsseminar*, as exemplified in these texts, provided a model and source for the development of the *Lutheran Dogmatics* of J. Michael Reu (1869–1943), which was used as a dogmatics text not only in his own teaching career at Wartburg Theological Seminary from 1899 to 1943 but also by his successors until 1960.[44] Reu's *Dogmatics*, organized around the human being's communion with

---

42. Bauer, Deinzer, and Deinzer, *Christliche Dogmatik*, 426–77.

43. Fritschel, *Biography of Drs. Sigmund and Gottfried Fritschel.*

44. Reu, *Lutheran Dogmatics.*

God, shares a parallel formal structure with the *Christliche Dogmatik* (Bauer/J. Deinzer/M. Deinzer), makes comparable appeals to biblical and confessional authority, and echoes the organizing paradigm of salvation history. Most striking is the comparable method for grounding dogmatics and ethics in Scripture. The influence of the theological curriculum, including these two textbooks, taught at the Neuendettelsau *Missionsseminar* had long-lasting significance for the teaching of dogmatics and ethics in North America and other global mission partner churches. The next chapter examines in detail the development of theological education in North America by those influenced by Bauer's theological commitments, especially his commitment to theological formation in community. The ethos and theology of Wartburg Theological Seminary from the nineteenth century to the present was deeply influenced not only by Loehe but also by the labors of Bauer.

7

The Theology of Wartburg
Theological Seminary

PREVIOUS CHAPTERS HAVE GIVEN close examination to the contributions of Wilhelm Loehe and Friedrich Bauer to the Iowa Synod and the institutions they founded and fostered. Now, we turn attention to the history and theology of Wartburg Theological Seminary. To provide an accurate description of "the" theology of a single seminary over the course of its entire history is a daunting undertaking. A seminary is constituted by an immense number of living participants who contribute to its communal life—students, alumni, staff, and professors—to say nothing about those persons and events that influence its life from the outside. Each of these participants brings original theological perspective and agency to the collective enterprise. Moreover, these living participants are not always consistent over time nor are they always coherent. (Why do they keep changing their minds?) Meanwhile, the content of an institution's theology is influenced by concrete historical circumstances, large and small, that decisively shape what is thought and taught. All of this means that making claims about the content of a "seminary's" theology is a complex and abstract business. In short, conclusions remain preliminary and proximate.

Nevertheless, those who know Wartburg Theological Seminary often speak of a Wartburg "ethos." Those who stand apart from the Wartburg tradition note an identifiable character in Wartburg graduates. I myself consider Wartburg as a kind of Mother House—a Lutheran "order" to which one belongs for life, long after the day of graduation or departure from the immediate community. Despite the difficulty of the task, this chapter draws together several threads that contribute to the fabric of a theology of Wartburg Theological Seminary.

Salzmann on "The Theology of Wartburg Seminary"

In an address to the Iowa District of the American Lutheran Church on June 23, 1954 at the occasion of Wartburg's centennial, Professor Samuel Salzmann presented on the "The Theology of Wartburg Seminary."[1] It was subsequently published in the Centennial Edition of the *Wartburg Seminary Quarterly* in November 1954. Salzmann served as Professor of Practical Theology at Wartburg from 1934 to 1963. He taught preaching and Christian education, among other subjects. Because of his credentials and, not least of all, because of his relationship as son-in-law to Michael Reu (who is sometimes referred to singularly as "Wartburg's theologian"), Salzmann provides a fascinating lens through which to catch a snapshot of the theology of Wartburg Seminary in the middle of the twentieth century. Salzmann's vantage point, eleven years after Reu's death, provides retrospective on the Reu era (1899–1943) at the very time that Wartburg opened to new post-World War II horizons. Salzmann summarized the theology of Wartburg Seminary under three aspects: a theology of the church, a theology of the Word, and a theology of God as a God of history.

Theology of the Church

Interestingly, Salzmann chooses this as the first characteristic of Wartburg's theology. The founders of Wartburg were a part of the "renewal of faith at the beginning of the nineteenth century," a reaction to the forces of rationalism.[2] This renewal was "a spontaneous return to the almost-forgotten gospel of the grace of God in Jesus Christ, so the theology which it brought forth was the theology not of individual leaders but of the church."

The confessions of the church took a prominent place in this renewal. The Iowa Synod, which the founders of Wartburg helped to ground, held closely to the "Lutheran symbols" but—and this is a point Salzmann

---

1. Salzmann, "The Theology of Wartburg Seminary," 11–23.

2. For this and the following quote, see Salzmann, "The Theology of Wartburg Seminary," 12.

emphasizes more than once—never viewed the Lutheran Confessions in a sectarian way. In the fierce theological controversies of the nineteenth century, the Wartburg faculty "stood not for a theology that accommodated itself to the changing opinions of the times, not for a theology that changed with the change of personnel on the Faculty, not for the theology of some influential leader, but for a theology that was based on the faith of the Church."[3]

As a theology of the church, Wartburg's theology was "functional." This meant that the seminary was concerned about congregational preaching, worship, and education in its teaching and publications. It also incorporated a focus on "foreign mission." Wartburg sought to guide the worship and devotional life of congregations. Here Salzmann made special reference to Wilhelm Loehe and the impact of his worship book, *Agende*, on both the worship life of German-speaking congregations and the development of the English language *Common Service* book of 1888. In this and other ways, Wartburg contributed to the "cultivation of the devotional life" in the church.[4]

Theology of the Word

Salzmann stresses the centrality of the study of Scripture in the seminary curriculum. This can be ascertained not only from the various courses, but also from the prominence given to the Bible as the foundation for all that is taught. The approach to exegesis at Wartburg is neither "Lutheran

3. Salzmann, "The Theology of Wartburg Seminary," 13. The controversies named by Salzmann were over "the doctrine of the Word, of the Ministry, of Last Things, of Church Fellowship or of the Right Use of the Confessions."

4. Salzmann wrote: "Those who knew some of the early members of our Faculty, Grossmann, the Fritschels, Reu, tell of the saintly lives they led. When I came to St. John's thirty-seven years ago, people were still telling of Sigmund Fritschel's charity among the poor. What they asked of others they first practiced themselves. The first constitution of the Synod provided that applicants for membership had first to pass through a period of probation lasting six months or more during which they were to prove the sincerity of the profession of a holy life before they could be received. The fraternal kiss was used when pastors came together in conference or synodical meetings. Bible study hours and prayer meetings were encouraged. A half hour of quiet devotion upon rising, prayer when the clock struck twelve, prayer at the setting of the sun were established customs in the Seminary. To this day classes are opened with prayer. While such outward expressions of piety have largely passed away, the cultivation of the spiritual life has remained." Salzmann, "The Theology of Wartburg Seminary," 15.

traditionalism" nor "the eclectic exegesis of sects."[5] Rather the Scripture is interpreted as a living Word of God that "equips the student . . . to discover the grand unity and purpose which binds all the books of Holy Scripture together." The approach used to interpret the Bible at Wartburg is also applied to the Lutheran Confessions. The Confessions "bring all the light of Scriptures to bear upon certain doctrines" and "give us the assurance that the Holy Spirit always fulfilled and always will fulfill the Savior's promise to His Church."[6]

Dogmatics, as taught at the seminary, is rooted in Scripture, as illustrated by the dogmatic system of Dr. Reu. This approach to dogmatics has its origin in Luther and Melanchthon and has been revived by theologians of the nineteenth century (Bengel, Hofmann, Delitsch, and Oehler). "It must be a dogmatics that flows from the Scriptures as the brook flows from its spring, as plain and simple and full of life as the Scriptures themselves. We must not begin by leading the student before the complete and ready building of saving truth. We must begin by leading him into the Scriptures, and with the aid of exact, grammatical-historical exegesis help him see how a truth was revealed gradually in God's dealing with His people through the centuries, so that finally he finds it expressed in the Confessions."[7] This theology of the Word also grounds what is taught in the area of practical theology at Wartburg, for example, in preaching and Christian education.

Theology of God as a God of History

God acts in history. This is what we learn about God by paying attention to Scripture. God is revealed gradually in the historical process. Over the course of history, God reveals ever new insights. Both the Bible and the Confessions must therefore be read according to their historical contexts. This approach to revelation makes Wartburg ready to consider certain matters as "open questions."[8] Because the Bible and the Confessions do not give detailed answers to every question, one must be ready to entertain

5. For this and the following quote, Salzmann, "The Theology of Wartburg Seminary," 16.

6. Salzmann, "The Theology of Wartburg Seminary," 17.

7. Salzmann, "The Theology of Wartburg Seminary," 17–18.

8. For this and the following quote, Salzmann, "The Theology of Wartburg Seminary," 21.

the possibility that non-fundamental issues allow for more than a single interpretation: "A spirit of tolerance in such minor matters has always characterized the theology of our Seminary."

The God who is revealed in the Scripture is a Living God, "the transcendent, eternal, almighty, living Lord" who "enters into this dying, degraded, enfeebled, hopeless world" and is made "known to me as the ultimate reality, confronts me, me personally in it as one person confronts another, deals with me on His own terms, not mine, judges me, lays claim on me, and in turn, offers me Himself, His heart, His love, so that I can make Him more perfectly my own, and become more sure of Him than of anything that I might be able to know with my senses and comprehend with my understanding."[9] In sum, God is a God of the Gospel, not law. The greatest of all divine works is the incarnation. The church is nothing other than the "continuation in history of the life and work of Jesus Christ the risen Lord . . . Christ must be continuing to dwell and work in any Christian group that still makes use of His means of grace."[10] This conviction has made Wartburg open to ecumenical relationships.

Salzmann's address proposed three core theological commitments that characterize the theology of Wartburg Seminary in its first hundred years. Based on these, several questions arise: What needs to be added to his account? Do these categories continue to depict Wartburg's theology today? Are there new themes that have emerged in the last half-century? If so, should we evaluate these new accents as gains or losses? We turn next to such questions.

The Fritschel Era (1854–1900)

Wartburg Seminary was founded by *Sendlinge* (emissaries) sent out with basic theological preparation provided by Wilhelm Loehe and his colleague, Friedrich Bauer. Loehe cared about the spiritual well-being of the German emigrants settling in America and desired that they hear the Word, receive the sacraments, and be instructed in the Lutheran tradition. Pastors and teachers had to be prepared to minister to them in their

9. Salzmann, "The Theology of Wartburg Seminary," 21. The original language was not inclusive.

10. Salzmann, "The Theology of Wartburg Seminary," 22. He went on to write: "Hand in hand with loyalty to the truth as they saw it, the members of our Faculty have always cherished and nourished the spirit of ecumenicity long before that word became a watchword in the Church throughout the world."

new home. Seeing this emergency situation, Loehe and Bauer organized a school for basic theological instruction to those who were ready to go to America as pastors and teachers. The founders of Wartburg Seminary— Georg Grossmann, Johannes Deindoerfer, and Sigmund Fritschel, along with Gottfried Fritschel who arrived a little later—received their initial theological formation from Loehe and Bauer. Through these founders, Wartburg Seminary maintained a close connection to Neuendettelsau and to the theology of Loehe.

The main features of Loehe's theological matrix, especially his accent on mission, influenced the history of Wartburg Seminary to this day, beginning with the Fritschel era. Both Sigmund and Gottfried Fritschel, as the primary faculty of Wartburg Seminary for over thirty years at its inception, received training directly from Loehe and Bauer through the program developed at Neuendettelsau. Sigmund Fritschel first came to Iowa in July 1854, and Gottfried Fritschel followed in May 1857. Due to the financial pressures that forced Sigmund into several contingency appointments, the two brothers were not united as faculty members at Wartburg until August 1858. Both brothers gave frequent testimony to Loehe's influence on their outlook.[11] This collaboration continued until Gottfried's death on July 13, 1889.[12]

Sigmund and Gottfried Fritschel served as professors at the seminary, and were also active administrators in the Iowa Synod, representatives of the seminary and synod to other Lutheran church bodies, authors and publishers of the *Kirchen-Blatt* (and later the *Kirchliche Zeitschrift*), preachers, and organizers of numerous Lutheran congregations. Although each brother brought unique accents, in what follows the work of the *par nobile fratrum* ("noble pair of brothers") will be considered in the singular.[13] Their contributions to the theology of Wartburg Seminary will be summarized with three central points: confessional fidelity, pastoral theology, and church planting.

11. Ottersberg, "The Brothers Fritschel," 4.

12. Sigmund Fritschel died on April 26, 1900.

13. Weiblen, *Life Together*, 7–10; Fritschel, *Biography of Drs. Sigmund and Gottfried Fritschel*, 10.

Confessional Fidelity

The Iowa Synod and Wartburg Seminary were embroiled in controversy from the moment of inception. The departure from Michigan and the end of the common work with the Lutheran Church—Missouri Synod was the consequence of controversy over the doctrine of ministry.[14] Moreover, in the latter half of the nineteenth century, the Fritschels engaged in debate over many other theological controversies on behalf of the Iowa Synod: open questions, chiliasm, the anti-Christ, Sunday worship, usury, and especially predestination. Periodical articles, tracts, and books contributed to a fierce discussion of these issues.[15]

The understanding of the Lutheran Symbols and the meaning of Confessional subscription was at the heart of the matter. Sigmund Fritschel described the difference with the theological opponents of the Iowa Synod:

> Accordingly, there is a distinction to be made between the *dogmas, properly speaking, and other parts of the Symbols;* as e.g. the frequent exegetical, historical and other deductions, illustrations and demonstrations. Only the former, i.e. the dogmas, constitute the Confession, whilst the latter partake of this dignity only indirectly, inasmuch as they define the dogmas more clearly. What the Symbols state and intend *as a confession,* the articles and doctrines of faith, this it is, to which the Synod is bound, not because they are the Church's decisions in controversies that have come up, but because they present the saving truth and doctrine of the Scripture. The Church is bound to accept these doctrines which constitute the Confession in their totality, *without exception,* whilst the demand of doctrinal conformity by no means includes *all unessential* opinions which *are only occasionally* mentioned in the Symbols.[16]

The Iowa Synod operated according to a confessional hermeneutic that included both reading them in their historical context and distinguishing between what is dogma/doctrine and what is "unessential." The latter conviction was the basis for the consistent assertion by the Fritschels that there are matters that remain "open questions," and that full agreement on such questions is not necessary for church fellowship. The bitter

14. Schaaf, "The Controversy about *Kirche* and *Amt,*" 121–62.

15. Fritchel and Fritschel, *Iowa und Missouri.*

16. Fritschel, "The German Iowa Synod," 66. On page 62, he describes the viewpoint of the Iowa Synod as "a strictly confessional as well as ecumenical Lutheranism."

controversies with the LCMS are largely attributable to disagreements about confessional interpretation.

The Fritschels never sacrificed the expectation of confessional fidelity. For example, in the relationship of the Iowa Synod with the General Council, they insisted on a fuller measure of confessional agreement as the basis for church fellowship. The Iowa Synod position came to be articulated in the Galesburg Rule, which states: "Lutheran pulpits for Lutheran pastors only, and Lutheran altars for Lutheran communicants only.[17] However their insistence on confessional fidelity made a distinction between the center and the periphery of confessional truth.

Pastoral Theology

The theology represented by the Fritschels was for the sake of the formation of pastors of the church. While the seminary was located at St. Sebald (1857–1874), the professors lived in close community with the students who were being formed for pastoral service. Later at Mendota, Illinois, and Dubuque, the professors continued to be primarily engaged as teachers preparing their students for pastoral ministry. The curriculum was designed to form graduates as faithful preachers and teachers of the Gospel and effective in pastoral responsibilities. The only textbook authored by Sigmund Fritschel, entitled *Pastorale,* was published posthumously by his nephew and based on notes Fritschel prepared for his students. The book deals with the meaning of pastoral call, ordination, and a variety of pastoral acts.[18] Sigmund taught especially in the areas of Old Testament exegesis, dogmatics for first-year students, and pastoral theology. Gottfried taught dogmatics for the upper levels, symbolics, church history, and especially exegesis.[19] All of these subjects were oriented toward the preparation of those who would be serving the church as pastors.

Church Planting

The massive immigration from Germany to the United States in the 1840s and 1850s set the stage for the founding and rapid growth of the Iowa Synod. According to census figures, 1,386,293 persons of German

17. Fritschel, *Biography of Drs. Sigmund and Gottfried Fritschel,* 60.
18. Fritschel, *Pastorale.*
19. Fritschel, *Biography of Drs. Sigmund and Gottfried Fritschel,* 88.

nationality migrated to the United States during these years, many to Iowa and neighboring states. Beginning with Wartburg Seminary's origins at Dubuque and encompassing the entire period of activity of Sigmund and Gottfried Fritschel at St. Sebald, Mendota, and after the return to Dubuque, both faculty and seminarians initiated in a vigorous program of church planting. Setting out on weekends by foot, coach, or train, they established preaching stations in the radius of reachable locations from the seminary. Moreover, graduates of Wartburg Seminary were the founding pastors of numerous congregations in Iowa and surrounding states. The rapid growth of the synod was the result of diligence in church planting by professors, students, and graduates of Wartburg Seminary. Justifiably, the Iowa Synod was described at its seventy-fifth anniversary as "a missionary synod with a mission."[20]

These three characteristics—confessional fidelity, pastoral theology, and church planting—epitomize the theological commitments of Sigmund and Gottfried Fritschel. To a large extent, these commitments were carried into the future by the next generation of Fritschels who served on the faculty: Max and George, whose efforts were joined by the most well-known and prolific theologian in the history of the seminary, J. Michael Reu.

The Reu Era (1900–1940s)

The next generation of faculty included Max Fritschel, son of Sigmund, who served forty-eight years as professor and director of Wartburg Seminary, and George Fritschel, son of Gottfried, who served thirty years as professor of church history and published several books on Lutheran church history. Both carried forward the legacy of their fathers in preparing pastors for the ministry of the Iowa Synod.

Teaching on the Wartburg faculty together with these colleagues during the first decades of the twentieth century was J. Michael Reu, the person for whom the library at Wartburg Theological Seminary has been named. Johann Michael Reu (1869–1943) was born in Diebach, Germany and trained for pastoral ministry at the mission institute founded by Loehe in Neuendettelsau.[21] He came to the United States in 1889, serving for ten years as pastor first at Mendota and then at Rock Falls, Illinois.

20. Zeilinger, *A Missionary Synod with a Mission.*
21. Drachenberg, "J. Michael Reu," 40–43.

In 1899, Reu was called as professor to Wartburg Seminary at Dubuque, Iowa where he taught until the end of his life. A self-taught theologian, Reu became a prominent figure who exercised major influence on seminary students, laity, and the larger church. For many reasons, he is identified as the most renowned professor and prolific theologian in the history of Wartburg Seminary.

Over a teaching career that spanned forty-four years, from 1899 to his death in 1943, Reu taught virtually every subject in the seminary curriculum. Moreover, the range of topics is reflected in the extensive bibliography of books, articles, and reviews (most shorter pieces were published in the *Kirchliche Zeitschrift*). The Reu corpus includes a total of sixty-six books and a reported 3,631 book reviews. The influence of Reu on the formation of pastors for the church, however, did not end with his death. His printed lectures on dogmatics continued to be used in the classroom at Wartburg into the early 1960s, while his published writings have continued to draw attention to the present. Three distinguishing marks that represented Reu's theology forcefully shaped the theology of Wartburg in the first half of the twentieth century: a scriptural theology, grounded in Lutheran heritage, and directed toward the purpose of Christian education.

Scriptural Theology

For Reu the Bible was clearly the primary source of authority for theology as interpreted through the lens of the Lutheran Confessions. Even the casual reader can note the extensive references to biblical passages and the careful interpretation of particular texts throughout his published writings and printed lectures. Reu, like others shaped by nineteenth century German dogmatic theology, exuded confidence that there was a unified biblical theology.[22] God has been revealed over the course of history to have certain durable traits. The Scriptures testify to the consistent pattern of divine activity in the world. The task of Christian systematic theology is to exposit these themes and categorize the knowledge revealed through God's Word.

The paradigmatic example of his approach is the method and content of what affectionately came to be called "Reu's Dogmatics," revised

22. For example, Luthardt, *Kompendium*, 104–131; von Hoffman, *Der Schriftbeweis*.; and Thomasius, *Christi Person und Werk*.

and reprinted in numerous editions during the years of his teaching ministry and beyond.[23] The organizing idea of Reu's *Lutheran Dogmatics* is "Communion with God."[24] Each locus of Christian doctrine is examined and articulated with reference to the interpretation of specific biblical texts. Inadequate interpretations are refuted in constructing a sound dogmatic system, built upon the solid foundation of Holy Scripture. The force of Reu's theology was so profound that his successor, Emil Matzner, continued to lecture on dogmatics by reading verbatim from Reu's text until 1960, eighteen years after Reu's death. For nearly sixty years, students at Wartburg Seminary were formed theologically for ministry by this decidedly scriptural theology.

Lutheran Heritage

The second major characteristic of Reu's contribution was his cultivation of Lutheran history and theology. Reu was convinced that the Lutheran tradition was the purest expression of true teaching. He wrote in his *Lutheran Dogmatics*: "The real nature of the Christian religion is maintained far more genuinely in the faith and confession of the Lutheran Church."[25] Reu produced for students and the church a host of books that aimed to instill appreciation for and appropriation of the Lutheran heritage: *Dr. Martin Luther's Small Catechism With a Selection of Short Scripture Texts, Hymns, and Prayers;*[26] *Thirty-five Years of Luther Research;*[27] *Life of Luther;*[28] *Augsburg Confession: A Collection of Sources with an Historical Introduction;*[29] *Luther's German Bible: An Historical Presentation Together with a Collection of Sources;*[30] and *The Smalkald Articles.*[31] Reu's magnum opus was devoted to remembering and appropriating the

23. For example, J. Michael Reu, *Lutheran Dogmatics.*

24. This organizing principle bears striking similarity to the work of other nineteenth century German theologians, ironically even Schleiermacher's theme of the "feeling of absolute dependence on God."

25. J. Michael Reu, *Lutheran Dogmatics,* 7.

26. Chicago: Wartburg Publishing House, 1919.

27. Chicago: Wartburg Publishing House, 1917.

28. Dubuque: Wartburg Seminary, 1938.

29. Chicago: Wartburg Publishing House, 1930. For the 400th anniversary of the Augustana.

30. Columbus: Lutheran Book Concern, 1934.

31. Dubuque: Wartburg Seminary, 1937.

Lutheran and Reformation heritage. Over decades he assembled an amazing collection of catechisms published in Germany during the sixteenth century. A total of nine volumes were published as *Quellen zur Geschichte des kirchlichen Unterrichts*.[32] The jewel among all the various catechisms was Luther's own *Small Catechism*. For this project Reu was awarded a doctorate in theology from the University of Erlangen in 1910. Thereby, he became "Dr. Reu."

The cultivation of Lutheran heritage for students and the larger church was a commitment Reu shared with other faculty colleagues, particularly with George Fritschel who published several volumes dedicated to Lutheran history.[33] With Reu as editor, the publication of the journal *Kirchliche Zeitschrift* also demonstrated the commitment of the Wartburg faculty to reclaim the Lutheran tradition for the next generation.

Christian Education

Reu and the other members of the Wartburg faculty were engaged in the preparation of pastors for service in the church. Reu taught courses in dogmatics, homiletics, and catechetics, producing major texts on these topics.[34] Reu produced a theory of catechetics and also prepared teacher training materials and curriculum for all ages, seeking to instill throughout the church a love for Scripture and the Lutheran heritage.[35] He was deeply committed to Christian education both for children and adults. Many of his writings are aimed at the education of the laity. Reu's initiative in continuing education for clergy is also noteworthy. The Luther Academy was a summer continuing education event hosted on the Wartburg Seminary campus that Reu and President Emil Rausch founded in 1937. This is one of the earliest documented events of its kind, which continues to this day as the Luther Academy of the Rockies. Among all his ventures in Christian education, none was more influential than the dissemination and use of what came to be called "Reu's Catechism."[36] This

32. Gütersloh: C. Bertelsmann, 1904–1932.

33. Fritschel, *Geschichte der lutherischen Kirche in Amerika*; Fritschel, *The Formula of Concord*; and Fritschel, *Quellen und Dokumente*.

34. Reu, *Homiletics* and Reu, *Catechetics*.

35. For example, Reu, *How I Tell Bible Stories*, the extensive materials published as *Wartburg Lehrmittel* beginning in 1911, and as *Wartburg Lesson Helps* beginning in 1916.

36. Reu, *Luther's Small Catechism*.

congregational resource was first published in 1906 and went through twelve printings, the last in 1964. Many confirmands in the 1960s and 1970s used Reu's catechism for their Christian education.

Salzmann's description of the theology of Wartburg Seminary in 1954 reflects the central commitments of Reu, his father-in-law. The formidable shadow of Reu was cast long into the future, even as new themes gradually began to emerge.

Post-World War II (1940s–1960s)

The period after the Second World War was an age of significant transition for theological education in general and Wartburg Seminary in particular. The G. I. Bill facilitated a dramatic influx of students during the late 1940s and 1950s. This time became the pinnacle of church going for Protestants in the United States. The suburbs were expanding, and attending church was part and parcel of what it meant to be a good American. The funding of home missions was at its height. At Wartburg Seminary, this was also a period of transition from the era dominated by Reu's influence. While professors like Salzmann and Matzner provided continuity based on the theology of Reu, new themes and accents began to emerge. In this period, three of the most significant characteristics were new approaches to biblical foundations, new methods of pastoral formation, and unprecedented ecumenical breakthroughs.

Biblical Foundations

In biblical studies, as in every other aspect of seminary study, the approach of Reu continued to influence the curriculum. However, this was a time when biblical scholarship was rapidly changing with a host of new voices and approaches being introduced including at Wartburg. In the New Testament, for example, the scholarship of Bultmann, Jeremias, Fuchs, and Käsemann from Germany, and Dodd and V. Taylor from England exerted major influence on the field. The historical-critical approach to biblical interpretation was taken with increasing seriousness at Wartburg. One way this began to unfold was through the teaching of professors at Wartburg College who first introduced students—including those subsequently attending Wartburg Seminary—to new developments in biblical study. Alfred Haefner, Ray Martin, Frank Benz, and Edwin Schick were among those college teachers who contributed to expanding the breadth of biblical scholarship at Wartburg Seminary. Moreover, seminary faculty also began to approach biblical texts using the historical-critical method, notably Bodensieck, Leo, and Englebrecht.

Pastoral Formation

Because this was a time of immense growth for the church, with church membership normative in American society, the seminary was fully engaged in preparing pastors for service in congregations. This meant the introduction of new and more extensive methods of pastoral formation. Three approaches were implemented quite early at Wartburg in comparison to other theological schools. First, Professor William Hulme (who like Martin and Schick taught first at Wartburg College before being called to the seminary) introduced the study of pastoral counseling. This was an emerging field at the time, and Wartburg Seminary was at the forefront. Second, also under the stimulus of Hulme, students at the seminary began to participate in Clinical Pastoral Education. This innovative form of theological education eventually became a required element of the Master of Divinity curriculum. The clinical process and focus on professional standards for pastoral care set new standards in the field. Third, Wartburg began to implement a regular model of internship into the curriculum. Professor William Streng was at the cutting edge of the movement to require a year of internship in the Master of Divinity program. These three innovations have dramatically transformed the shape of theological study not only at Wartburg but across the face of theological education.

Ecumenical Breakthrough

Given Wartburg Seminary's grounding in German Lutheranism, the new wave of ecumenical activity beginning in the 1950s and culminating in the 1960s was unprecedented and earthshaking. One harbinger of ecumenical cooperation on the international horizon was the service of Julius and Justine Bodensieck as liaison between the Allied Military Government and the churches of Germany in the wake of the devastation after the Second World War. This built constructive relationships between Wartburg and international partners that set a tone for the ecumenical work that would follow. Another very significant, albeit intra-Lutheran ecumenical venture, was the merger of Trinity Lutheran Seminary in Blair, Nebraska from the Danish Lutheran tradition with Wartburg Seminary in 1956. Professors Paul Nyholm, Theodore I. Jensen, and Ethan Mengers brought gifts from Danish Lutheranism to enrich the theological milieu.

The ecumenical movement received dramatic impetus through the decisions of the Second Vatican Council of the Roman Catholic Church from 1962 to 1965. The theological schools of Iowa were among the first to implement change and innovation because of these deliberations. In 1961 Jerry Folk was the first Wartburg Seminary student to enroll in a course at the Aquinas Institute of Theology, the Dominican seminary located at that time in Dubuque.[37]

> In the summer of 1964, a first prominent marker of change was reached—and after only a few years. The three seminaries in Dubuque and the School of Religion at the University of Iowa formed the *Association of Theological Faculties in Iowa*. Courses were shared by students and new ecumenical programs were offered. Clusters of seminaries in Berkeley and Boston were beginning to educate together—but Dubuque was among the first in North America, among the first in the world. In December 1962, after the first session of Vatican II, Archbishop James Byrne of Dubuque was the first Roman Catholic bishop ever to speak in a Lutheran seminary in North America.
>
> Stimulated by ecumenism, the three Dubuque seminaries—Presbyterian and Methodist, Roman Catholic, Lutheran—developed new programs in theological education. Ecumenism was for each school a creative liberation; ecumenism showed how to be a more effective seminary, a school for theology and ministry in the contemporary world.[38]

In June 1965, the Association of Theological Faculties in Iowa was formed as a joint venture of the School of Religion faculty at the University of Iowa, Aquinas Institute of Theology, University of Dubuque Theological Seminary, and Wartburg Theological Seminary. Ecumenical worship and educational events came to typify life at the seminaries in Dubuque. Among the Schools of Theology in Dubuque, ecumenical cooperation led to a single library administration for the three schools, total integration of the required courses in the biblical disciplines, and full cross-registration

---

37. O'Meara, "Times of Change," 12.
38. O'Meara, "Times of Change," 13.

among course offerings. This ecumenical breakthrough in theological education meant an ever richer spectrum of theological voices began to be influential at Wartburg, such as Pannenberg, Tillich, Barth, Prenter, and Rahner to name but a few.

Contemporary Period (1970s–present)

By far the most important and wide-ranging change to Wartburg Seminary's theology in the contemporary period derives from the impact of women students and women professors in the life of the school.[39] The entire seminary was transformed by the gifts contributed to theological study by the women called to teach and study at Wartburg. The first woman theologian to become professor was Norma Cook Everist, paving the way for many others. New angles of vision have been introduced and feminist perspectives have enriched the overall theological enterprise. Both in the classroom and through publications by women theologians, the theological perspective expanded by viewing the world through the lenses of women. Wartburg has been involved in a long process of becoming a community of women and men together in equal partnership. Perhaps the most concrete example of the commitment to the full inclusion of women in the life of the seminary was the adoption of the Inclusive Language Policy.

Another significant factor in the contemporary period has been the globalization of theological education. This became a major focus by the Association of Theological Schools and was embraced by the Wartburg faculty. In the 1980s and early 1990s, members of the faculty participated in a globalization project that took most of them on immersions in various global contexts. Even more transforming was the impact of international students on the Wartburg ethos, symbolized by the flags of the various countries adorning the refectory walls. Such initiatives led Wartburg to describe itself as a "global community." This global emphasis and the shift toward the full participation of women in the seminary inform three central characteristics of Wartburg's theology in the contemporary period: the focus on biblical and theological wisdom, community ethos, and missional purpose.

---

39. Everist, *And the Women Came.*

Biblical and Theological Wisdom

This stands as one of the central tenets of the "Twelve Pastoral and Dia-conal Practices" adopted by the Wartburg faculty in the first decade of the new millennium.[40] The emerging approach to biblical interpretation is distinguished by a stronger focus on particular texts, allowing each text speak for itself without such heavy reliance on a uniform biblical theology as in previous generations. This approach resonates with appreciation for "socio-rhetorical" methods of interpretation.

The theological wisdom of the contemporary period remains deeply rooted in the Lutheran tradition. In the words of the Twelve Pastoral and Diaconal Practices, Wartburg's theology "articulates the Gospel in a way that is heard as Gospel." It is "publicly Lutheran and Gospel-centered." What is most innovative about recent theology at Wartburg is the focus on the ethical implications of Lutheran theology for social action, the pairing of "Justification and Justice." The Gospel of Jesus Christ sets us free for serving neighbors. The biblical and theological wisdom at Wartburg became informed by liberationist themes, deriving from the efforts of the Namibia Concerns initiative for the freedom of Namibia, feminist theology, and other contextual theologies situated in locations of oppression.

Community Ethos

The ongoing communal commitments of Wartburg Seminary are captured in the title of William Weiblen's short history of the school, *Life Together at Wartburg Theological Seminary*.[41] This community ethos finds many expressions in faculty life, including the emergence of interdisciplinary teaching across the curriculum and de-emphasis on academic divisions. The Wartburg faculty has been noted for its collaborative undertakings, such as the publication of a faculty book,[42] a creative resource in response to the church's evangelism strategy,[43] and

40. "Twelve Pastoral and Diaconal Practices," https://www.wartburgseminary. edu/12-pastoral-diaconal-practices/. Together these practices provide a succinct summary of the recent theological commitments and statement of educational outcomes by the Wartburg Theological Seminary faculty.

41. Weiblen, *Life Together*.

42. Everist, *The Difficult but Indispensable Church*.

43. Everist and Nessan, *Forming and Evangelizing People*.

a journal issue based on the Twelve Pastoral and Diaconal Practices.[44] Furthermore, the seminary has become known as a mutual teaching and learning community, where students not only learn from professors but also from one another, and professors learn from students and each other. The use of small group pedagogy highlights the importance of students discovering their own theological voices. The community ethos has been deepened by an emphasis on "spiritual practices" both within the required curriculum and in the life of the seminary as a whole.

Missional Purpose

The *missio Dei* (mission of God) begins at worship, where the primary actor is the Triune God. This mission is extended through the regular gathering for worship in the Loehe chapel and in the congregations served by Wartburg students and graduates. Assembling together for worship is central for our participation in God's mission. In recent decades, the faculty and curriculum of Wartburg Seminary has been informed and transformed by the multicultural and interreligious context in which ministry occurs. The United States context is characterized by a rich diversity of cultures (for example, Europe, Latin America, Africa, and Asia) and increasingly by religious pluralism.

The three centers at Wartburg Seminary reflect the school's missional purpose, by focusing on rural ministry (Center for Theology and Land), youth and family (Center for Youth Ministries), and the global church (Center for Global Theologies). For ten years the Master of Arts in Theology, Development, and Evangelism stressed a holistic approach to mission that characterizes the history of Wartburg Seminary. Both community development and evangelizing belong to the mission of God in the world. In the words of the seminary mission statement: "The community embodies God's mission by stewarding resources for engaging, equipping, and sending collaborative leaders who interpret, proclaim, and live the gospel of Jesus Christ for a world created for communion with God and in need of personal and social healing."

The missional purpose of the seminary is expressed in the variety of forms of service for which students and graduates are prepared. While Wartburg continues the tradition of preparing ordained pastors for Word and Sacrament ministry, the seminary is increasingly preparing deacons

44. Everist and Nessan, "Twelve Pastoral Practices."

for Word and Service ministry. All forms of service must support and foster the ministry of all the baptized. Therefore, Wartburg Seminary has also implemented Learning for Life courses and certificates in intensive and online formats to support the formation of all the baptized for ministry in the arenas of their daily lives. The leadership of pastors and deacons is ultimately to equip the entire church for participation in God's mission in the world.

Discontinuities and Continuities in the Theology at Wartburg Theological Seminary

What are the innovations and the constants that mark the theology of Wartburg Seminary over its history? Because of the fluidity of theological currents, it is not surprising that there are both discontinuities and continuities for interpreting the Wartburg tradition. Three expressions of discontinuity are noteworthy, especially in relationship to the commitments articulated by Salzmann at the seminary's centennial celebration.

The first discontinuity involves the *diversity of sources for theology*. Whereas Salzmann spoke of a theology of "the" church, a deeper awareness of diversity and complexity within the church's oneness has emerged. The perspectives of women, as well as men, have become sources for theological reflection. Likewise, theology today draws upon a rich diversity of ecumenical, interreligious, cross-cultural, and global sources that is unprecedented in previous generations at Wartburg Seminary. The church is a multi-faceted jewel with rich and diverse resources that inform the theological enterprise.

A second discontinuity relates to *new methods of interpretation*. Salzmann described the theology of Wartburg Seminary as a "theology of the Word." As noted with special reference to Reu, a presumption formerly existed about a single and unified theology within the Scriptures. Emergent within biblical and historical study, a variety of methods are now practiced in relation to theological study, many related to the social sciences. The Bible is interpreted as consisting of a multitude of theologies coexisting within the one canon of Scripture. For example, increased attention has been given to sociological and political readings that deepen the significance of God's Word for the world. This is consistent with a more thoroughgoing historical interpretation of the Lutheran

Confessions according to the social and political contexts of the sixteenth century.

A third discontinuity pertains to increasing awareness of the *complexity of the world*. Salzmann wrote about a theology of the God of "history," meaning history in the singular. Critical scholarship now acknowledges that history is always written from a distinctive viewpoint. Depending on one's presuppositions, there are many histories, even of the same events. Theology at Wartburg seeks to face the challenge of attending to history from a variety of perspectives which include gender, sexual orientation, culture, race, and class.

However, more important than these discontinuities are the formidable continuities in theological commitment that link various periods at Wartburg Seminary. These threads are woven into the fabric of Wartburg from Loehe and the Fritschels through Reu and Salzmann to the present.

First and chief among these is the *missional theology* inherent in the life of the seminary from the very beginning. The words of the Wartburg mission statement say it very well: "Wartburg Theological Seminary serves Christ's church through the Evangelical Lutheran Church in America by being a worship-centered community of critical theological reflection where learning leads to mission and mission informs learning." Mission was the heartbeat of Loehe's theology; furthermore, a sense of mission propelled the Fritschels, Reu, and their co-workers in the Iowa Synod to prepare pastors for service in the church and to participate in church planting. This core missional theology continues to propel Wartburg Seminary in its ministry today.

Congregations are centers for God's mission in the world. Worship is the locus for God's own mission to the world in Word and Sacrament. This *missio Dei* is carried out in diaconal ministry and by the ministry of all the baptized through their daily work in the world. The mission of God is international in scope and enhanced by global partnerships that enable mutual transformation. This mission is grounded in the core evangelical impulse that centers all else: the Gospel of Jesus Christ.

Second, Wartburg has preserved over the generations a distinctive *ecclesial identity*. The theology of Wartburg Seminary has been consistently *pro ecclesia*, that is, for congregations and for the whole church. In an era of individualistic and even schismatic approaches to the church, this commitment to ecclesial partnership becomes even more distinctive. This characteristic can be traced back to Wartburg's earliest years with the commitment to "open questions," which has allowed the theological community to abide even in the face of disagreements. There need not be agreement on every aspect of Christian teaching and practice to remain in communion with one another. Unity about the core essentials, beginning with justification by grace through faith in Jesus Christ alone, suffices for church unity.

"Life together" is an apt phrase to describe ecclesial existence at Wartburg. This life together has been incarnated since the construction of the Castle with the cornerstone laid in 1914. By the genius of the architecture that joins chapel to refectory, worship and community life are bound together in the very limestone. Referring again to Weiblen's history, *Life Together at Wartburg Theological Seminary* is worship-centered. It is fostered by Wartburg's campus, and the sense of being one community has been cultivated even through digital learning and distance education programs. It is nurtured by educational practices that promote mutuality in teaching and learning. It is oriented toward forming leaders for Christian faith communities, particularly congregations. It is for a church in mission through its varied expressions, centered in the Gospel of Jesus Christ for the forgiveness of sins and directed toward a world in need of personal and social healing.

Finally, Wartburg remains committed to a *theology of the living God*, who accompanies the people of God through the dynamic journey of life. The living Triune God travels with us as persons, congregations, and seminary community. The living Triune God becomes manifest in the world in diverse contexts and cultures, as expressed through the various flags which fly in the seminary refectory, representing the countries from which Wartburg Seminary students have come. The living Triune God seeks to incorporate all people within the embrace of an inclusive love, abounding in mercy and grace. The living Triune God has been revealed in Jesus Christ who continues to encounter us today—revealed as the Crucified One in every place of suffering and revealed as the Risen One, giving ever-new reasons for hope.

8

The Loehe Legacy and
the Church of the Future

As with the church in the present, the church of the future is constructed out of the fragments of the past. Only God can create something out of nothing, *ex nihilo*. Human communities—and here we also count the community of church—are always constrained to imagine and construe the shape of the future with reference to what has gone before us. We are limited as human agents by our own personal experiences and accustomed patterns, in which we can be highly invested as the only way forward. The value of education—and, through the chapters of this book, in studying church history—is to expand our horizons to know, appreciate, critically evaluate, and reclaim those fragments of the past that are most promising for fashioning the church of the future.

This book explores the history and legacy of Wilhelm Loehe from historical and theological perspectives. In this final chapter, we imagine how to draw upon this history as a living legacy for the construction of a vital church in the future. We focus less on the past and more on the significance of the Loehe legacy for the emergent church, both for congregational life and theological education. We will explore seven dimensions of the Loehe legacy: mission, worship, equipping others, *diakonia*, open questions, reclaiming the missionary, and character formation based on the repetitions and crucibles of our lives. We will imagine how these themes can contribute dynamically to the vitality of the future church.

Dimension One: Mission

Mission originates from the Triune God, who sends Jesus Christ by the power of the Spirit to gather the church community through worship into life-giving relationships, in order to send forth the people of God to love and serve neighbors in every arena of daily life. Families, schools, workplaces, local communities, and global relationships provide the arenas where Christians have opportunities to serve the neighbors God gives us.[1] Georg Vicedom, a Neuendettelsau missionary, wrote a ground-breaking work called *The Mission of God* in 1960, which articulated the significance of the Loehe legacy for the mission of the church in our times.[2] Vicedom, building on the 1952 Willingen Conference, creatively pointed out that the primary agent of mission is the God who sends Jesus Christ and Holy Spirit to bring forth the kingdom as God's ultimate purpose for human salvation.

> The mission is work that belongs to God. This is the first implication of *missio Dei*. God is the Lord, the One who gives the orders, the Owner, the One who takes care of things. [God] is the Protagonist in the mission. When we ascribe the mission to God in this way, then it is withdrawn from human whims. Hence we must show that God wants the mission and how [God] conducts it.[3]

While the church serves as an agent in God's mission, the efforts of the church are not primary but rather are subsequent and obedient to God as the divine Director of Evangelical Mission. With this seminal insight, the Loehe legacy has born incredible fruit for re-conceptualizing the entire field of missiology in an era where previous mission models have been severely criticized, because of their complicity with nineteenth and twentieth century colonialization and imperialism.

1. Nessan, "Universal Priesthood," 8–15.

2. Vicedom, *The Mission of God*. Long before the subsequent work of David Bosch about the "mission of God" in the book, *Transforming Mission*, Vicedom formulated and developed the foundational concept of *mission Dei* in the Loehe tradition, which has played a seminal role in the "missional church" literature and movement of our times.

3. Vicedom, *The Mission of God*, 5.

Outer Mission

Loehe and his colleagues distinguished mission activity into two types, outer and inner. Whereas inner mission was understood to address those who are already baptized members of the church, outer mission was directed to those persons outside of the Christian community. For example, in Loehe's lifetime outer mission was directed in North America to American Indians and inner mission to the emigrants from Germany gathering into congregations and in need of Christian instruction. This distinction remains useful in our present context, though more nuanced and complex than implemented in previous generations.

Outer mission encompasses not only those in remote places, where people may have never before heard the Gospel, but those committed to other religions, including great traditions like Hinduism, Buddhism, Judaism, and Islam; those who call themselves "spiritual" but not "religious," which means they keep distance from religious institutions; the increasing numbers of those who identify as "Nones," those claiming no religious affiliation; those who espouse atheism as their studied worldview; and even those many persons who may once have been involved in the Christian church but are no longer active or affiliated. Outer mission involves developing competence for building trustful relationships and constructive engagement with those in each of these emergent categories.[4]

Such dialogical involvements summon forth not less but more grounding in one's own Christian faith, trusting that Jesus Christ is not only with us as we enter into these relationships but that Jesus Christ has already been present and working in the lives of those with other viewpoints, even if that presence has been inchoate and incognito, not only to us but perhaps also to them.[5] This reflects the conviction that the mission of God in Jesus Christ has been active and alive at all times, among all people, and in all places, whether acknowledged or not. Because God is God of all history and peoples, God is the universal creator, redeemer, and holy presence. The church does not bring Jesus Christ to others; Jesus Christ has already been working in the entire cosmos, including in every local place on earth and in relation to every particular person, each one

---

4. See Daniel, *Tired of Apologizing for a Church I Don't Belong To*; Drescher, *Choosing Our Religion*; Packard and Hope, *Church Refugees*; McGrath, *The Twilight of Atheism*; and Tickle, *The Great Emergence*.

5. Panikkar, *The Unknown Christ of Hinduism*.

made in God's divine image.[6] Whenever we engage in outer mission, we do so with the expectancy of discovering what God in Christ has already been doing in the lives of those we encounter. This perspective of appreciative inquiry about the traces of God's involvement is a dramatically different paradigm from one that assumes that members of the church are the first and only ones to "bring" Christ to others. The outer mission of God is so comprehensive that we count all persons, even those expressing opposition against God, as already falling within the loving divine embrace of Christ whose arms are extended in welcome from the cross.

Inner Mission

Although this usage has been more common in German missiology than in North America, inner mission is an extremely fruitful concept to be retrieved for the renewal of Christian mission in our time. Often when we engage in discourse about missionary matters, our reference is almost exclusively to what the members of the church are doing in relation to those who are "outside" the church. By making the distinction between outer and inner mission, however, we are reminded that the mission of God needs to be understood as an ongoing activity within the church as much as it is also a divine activity among those who claim no church connection. God the Missionary continues to establish, renew, and deepen life-giving relationships with those already baptized members of the body of Christ, so that they might be drawn ever more closely into divine belovedness and sent forth as agents of that divine love. Inner mission begins with the means of grace employed by God to mediate the gifts and presence of Christ, including the Word, baptism, affirmation of baptism, Holy Communion, prayer, and the Christian community itself.[7]

What does our Missionary God finally want for us, both for church members or for all people? "I came that they may have life, and have it abundantly" (John 10:10). When we consider all the metaphors employed in the New Testament to describe what God in Christ is seeking to accomplish among us—kingdom, salvation, redemption, reconciliation, atonement, forgiveness, and many others—each of these involves

6. Vicedom, *The Mission of God*, 15.

7. Regarding the Christian community as a means of grace, see Bliese and Van Gelder, *The Evangelizing Church*, 45–46.

relationships. God's mission is to establish life-giving relationships with each of us as particular human beings (created in God's image), with all human beings together in human community, and in harmony with the creation itself (earth, waters, and sky with all their creatures). This is the meaning of shalom: abundant life-giving relationships, beginning with the Triune God and extended to every human being, every living creature, and all of creation.[8]

Life-giving relationships are not only that which God desires to offer us; life-giving relationships are the deepest longing of the human heart. There is a striking correspondence between Christian theology and research about what finally makes people happy.[9] While we are socialized to believe that things like wealth, status, and health are the most important factors in human happiness, the key element in long-term human happiness involves the quality of one's relationships and involvements in human community. Certainly, happiness is predicated on certain other things, especially basic sufficiency in what is necessary for physical survival—food, water, shelter, safety, and health care among them. However, social scientific research has consistently demonstrated one compelling finding: "Human beings are social creatures, and the quality of our relationships is inextricably linked with our own physical and mental well-being."[10] There is a striking convergence between the central claim of Christianity about love as the greatest of all gifts (1 Cor 13:13) and what ultimately makes for human happiness.

The inner mission of the church is to so mediate the love of God in Christ to fill our hearts, permeate our being, increase it manifold, and multiply it abundantly, making the cup of our lives to overflow (Ps 23:5). As members of the body of Christ are drawn into the depths of God's love, they become means of grace for one another in "the mutual conversation and consolation" of the saints (*The Smalcald Articles* Part 3, Article 4). Immersed in this love, they are sent to live the Great Commandment: "You shall love the Lord your God with all your heart, and with all your soul, and with all your mind. This is the greatest and first commandment. And a second is like it: 'You shall love your neighbor as yourself'" (Matt 22:37–39). These are the neighbors God gives us to serve in each arena of

8. Nessan, *Shalom Church.*

9. Mineo, "Good Genes Are Nice, but Joy Is Better."

10. Gregoire, "The 8 Most Important Things We've Learned About Happiness."

our daily lives: family, school, workplace, local community, citizenship, and global engagement.

Dimension Two: Worship

Every generation faces its own call to renew the vibrant worship of the living God. Loehe answered that call by returning to ancient sources for the construction of a creative liturgical order, the Loehe *Agende*, which he employed locally in Neuendettelsau and through publication for use by Lutheran congregations in North America. In recent decades Lutheran churches in North America have engaged in vigorous deliberation about the nature and purpose of Christian worship. Many have jettisoned the historic liturgy in favor of "contemporary" forms which intend to appeal to the unchurched and "seekers" through "praise music" led by praise bands, spontaneous interaction by worship leaders, innovative "creedal" statements, messages focused on practical guidance for life from the Bible, and meeting in unconventional worship spaces. While such experiments have generated interest and purported success, particularly among well-circumscribed demographic groups, many theological questions remain about the degree to which such methods have acquiesced to consumer culture and thereby undermined formation in the historic Christian faith.

By contrast, denominational efforts among ecumenical (mainstream) Protestant church bodies—as with the Roman Catholic Church—have sought to reclaim the value of the historic liturgical *ordo*, while at the same time providing resources for contextualizing the liturgy through various musical settings and alternatives for constructing the worship order. Liturgical scholarship has identified four significant dimensions of Christian liturgy: the transcultural, contextual, counter-cultural, and cross-cultural.[11] In many contemporary worship experiments, for example, primary attention has been given to the contextual, often at the expense of the other dimensions, especially the counter-cultural and cross-cultural. In the North American context, this means that contemporary worship has often adopted the style of entertainment, seeking to attract through consumer appeal, rather than honoring the other historic dimensions of liturgical worship. The Loehe legacy compels us in this

---

11. Lutheran World Federation, "Nairobi Statement on Worship and Culture."

generation to recover and renew the centrality of Word and Sacrament at the center of the church's life and mission.

Proclaiming the Word

In Chapter 1 we explored Loehe's own commitment to and practice of excellence in preaching. A church schooled in the Loehe tradition remains grounded in its conviction about the efficacy of the proclaimed Word as a means of grace for bringing Jesus Christ to the world. As we consider the requisites of proclamation in the twenty-first century, we must devote attention to the traditional practices of preaching and teaching Scripture within the gathered congregation, as these remain vital, and also to proclamation that employs new modes of interpersonal communication, including the mediation of God's angels through social media and other forms of electronic communication.[12]

Effective preaching and teaching the Word of God requires a comprehensive hermeneutical approach that honors both the ancient speaking of biblical texts among their original hearers and the recasting of these texts in authentic ways for contemporary hearers. This hermeneutic requires diligence from the interpreter/proclaimer to attend responsibly both to the exegetical process and the task of reading the contemporary context with skill and acumen, so that the living Word of God resonates across the generations with dynamic power, performing law and gospel in our own speaking and hearing. The full hermeneutical circle encompasses two movements: studied effectiveness in retrieving the meaning of biblical texts in their original contexts and wisdom for interpreting the dynamic contexts affecting who we are as human beings today.

The interpreter/proclaimer of God's Word operates with the fundamental conviction that God is both the One who spoke in previous generations through the biblical texts and the Living One who promises to speak again today to hearers of the Word.[13] The method of retrieving the meaning(s) of biblical texts in their original speaking involve four considerations: attending to the text itself, including authorship and redaction; exploring the original audience of a text, including its location in space and time; the occasion for the composition, including its intended purpose, genre, and rhetoric; and studying the world of

---

12. Thompson, *The Virtual Body of Christ.*

13. Nessan, "Interpreting the Bible Lutheranly," 11–35.

the text, including language, cultural factors, religious milieu, and the historical field. In a parallel way, the following four considerations belong to authentic interpretation in any contemporary context: reading historical context, including language, cultural factors, religious milieu, and historical field; examining purpose, genre, and rhetoric for effective communication; knowing as much as possible about the audience, including attention to their location in place and time; and reflecting on one's existential involvement and personal commitments as interpreter/proclaimer of the Word. The goal of proclamation is to create dynamic resonance between the original speaking of the biblical text and the message to contemporary hearers, and to minimize dissonance, which results from inadequate or inauthentic interpretation based on these two hermeneutical movements.

A new challenge and opportunity for proclamation today involves the use of electronic media as means of grace for the work of the Holy Spirit in communicating God's Word as law and gospel. Each form of electronic communication offers opportunities for proclamation of the Gospel of Jesus Christ, from the long-established forms of email, instant messaging, and social media to the latest applications. There many aspects to this brave new world and the Loehe legacy provides precedent. Here we can only comment on one facet: digital teaching and learning in service of the Christian faith.

In many quarters, we hear the frustrating cry of ministers who are unable to gather a group of people together face-to-face for Christian education due to enormous demands on people's schedules. The church, however, has the innovative possibility to gather people for in-depth study of the Bible and Christian faith through the development and use of digital teaching and learning methods, either asynchronously or in hybrid form including synchronous elements. Increasingly, we are discovering how to deliver highly effective social learning (life-giving relationships!) through the practices of "teaching by design" in a "collaborative and globally-networked pedagogy."[14]

While theological schools, such as Wartburg Seminary, have innovated with new methods of distance learning, enormous possibilities also exist for introducing new forms of proclamation and worship into the repertoire of local congregations.[15] Digital teaching and learning

14. Lester, *Understanding Bible by Design*; and Loewen, *Effective Social Learning*.

15. Stache and Nessan, "Adventures into Digital Teaching, Learning, and Formation," 20–45.

communities offer congregations, interested church members, and those
beyond the church opportunity to participate in a challenging and formative encounter with profound life questions from a Christian perspective. As Loehe was extraordinarily innovative in developing new forms
of theological education in his time by establishing an "emergency seminary" to prepare and form teachers and pastors for North America, the
Loehe legacy provides precedent for imagining and developing creative
new experiments for engaging God's Word for Christian formation and
proclamation.

Doing Liturgy

Loehe believed that God is the primary actor, who encounters us in
Word and Sacrament at worship and brings us Jesus Christ. Loehe was
a renewer of liturgical worship, who researched ancient sources and developed his own reconstruction of the worship rite. As we draw upon the
Loehe legacy for the renewal of worship in our time, we urgently need to
recover and become articulate about a dynamic theology of worship that
connects every aspect of the liturgy with formation for the Christian life.

Each of the historic elements of the liturgy involves the worship of
God by the gathered people and the formation of the worshipping congregation in Christian life practices, inspired by God in Christ through
the power of the Holy Spirit.[16] Confession and absolution are an exchange
between the Triune God and the gathered people by which forgiveness is
bestowed for Christ's sake to the penitent. Each worship element fosters
a corresponding Christian life practice; in this case, learning how to say
you are sorry and grant forgiveness to others in daily life for Christ's sake.
Hymns of praise sung to God are simultaneously the song of the gathered
people to glorify God and formation in learning to be thankful toward
God as a way of life. The praying of the *Kyrie* ("In peace let us pray to the
Lord") invites God to grant peace to the whole world, well-being to the
church of God, and unity to all; at the same time, it forms those who pray
this prayer to become themselves the peace of God to others. Hearing the
Word of God read and preached at worship is not only a message of law
and gospel to the congregation in the moment, but also instructive for
a way of life oriented to God's Word every day. Confessing the historic
creeds of the ecumenical church centers the assembly in its own identity,

16. Nessan, *Beyond Maintenance to Mission*, chapter 4.

while also preparing the people of God to witness to this faith in the midst of the world, even as the confession of Christian faith guided the martyrs of previous generations.

Intercessions as prayed to God at worship not only invite God's interventions in that for which we pray, but also function for those who pray as a mission statement. In daring to ask God in Christ to attend to these petitions, those who pray them are also devoted to their fulfillment through their life commitments. The Great Thanksgiving rehearses the people of God to place the death and resurrection of Jesus Christ at the center of their daily thanksgivings. As we come together with the saints of every time and place to the Lord's Table, we receive the body and blood of Christ in order that we become the body of Christ for the life of the world. Here is a meal where there is amazing welcome and mercy for all as Christ's body and blood are received in bread and wine. The benediction and sending of the congregation with "Go in peace. Serve the Lord," provide both a blessing and a commission from the Triune God. The church is sent for sharing the good news and being generous to the poor with this charge: to live according to the collective character that has been etched upon you as members of the body of Christ at worship![17] At worship the church is formed and scattered for mission into all arenas of daily life to serve the neighbors God gives us in our families, schools, workplaces, local communities, and around the globe.[18]

"Doing liturgy" is practiced when we gather for worship in a sanctuary and also functions as formation for being the body of Christ in all involvements of daily life. The worshipping congregation gathers in order to become the liturgy and perform it every day for the life of the world. "I appeal to you therefore, brothers and sisters, by the mercies of God, to present your bodies as a living sacrifice, holy and acceptable to God, which is your spiritual worship. Do not be conformed to this world, but be transformed by the renewing of your minds, so that you may discern what is the will of God—what is good and acceptable and perfect" (Rom 12:1–2). At worship, God in Christ by the power of the Holy Spirit operates on us to transform our lives as we are transmogrified into the very body of Christ. Doing liturgy is who we are!

17. Nessan, *Shalom Church*, chapter 3.
18. DuBois, *The Scattering*.

Dimension Three: Equipping

Equipping the baptized through catechization is one of the most critical educational tasks of the church. Teaching and forming people in the fabric of one holy catholic apostolic faith is the Great Work of the generations. This Great Work is even more urgent in our post-Christian era, when the traditional methods of catechizing (Sunday school, Vacation Bible school, confirmation instruction, and Bible study) show signs of disintegration through pressures on people's time from overscheduled lives and competition due to consumer lifestyles. Parents no longer automatically see the value of Christian education for children as it competes for precious time with other activities that appear to be of greater importance. Many adults, especially younger generations, are exhausted by the pace and stress of their lives and choose alternative Sunday activities, convinced these will be more conducive to their personal welfare. The church faces enormous challenges in its efforts to equip the next generation for Christian existence.

Church leaders need laser focus about intentionally equipping church members in the logic of the Christian faith. If people choose not to attend events designed for Christian education, ministers need to reimagine how the rhythm of their days are filled with opportunities to equip God's people for discipleship. Pastoral conversations, social media, email correspondence, newsletter articles, and web page communications need to be informed by the question: "What does this have to do with Jesus Christ and following him?" If few are willing to gather for Christian education opportunities, ministers need to re-construe all meetings in the church as occasions for educating and equipping for Christian faith. This is what it means to be a "minister of the Word" in our age—the minister of the Word is the one called always and on every occasion to make connections between what we are doing and the significance of God's Word, Jesus Christ. Just as the church has undertaken an amazing journey in liturgical renewal in recent decades, now is a *kairos* for the renewal of what it means to be a teaching and equipping church. Two themes emerge as pertinent from the Loehe legacy: confessing and practicing the Christian faith.

Confessing (Orthodoxy)

"Confessing the Gospel of Jesus Christ" can no longer be considered the sole, or even primary, responsibility of those called as pastors but must become the shared responsibility of all the baptized. In the Affirmation of Baptism service, Christians promise to "proclaim the good news of God in Christ in word and deed." Equipping the baptized for discipleship in our post-Christian age involves building capacity for speaking the good news of God in Christ to other people. In the New Testament, the words translated as "gospel" (*euangelion*) and "proclaiming" (*euangelizomai*) both refer to verbal communication, speaking the promises of Christ one person to another. Paul describes the essential role of the spoken word as a means of grace for creating faith in hearers: "So faith comes from what is heard, and what is heard comes through the word of Christ" (Rom 10:17).

Instead of emphasizing a concentrated focus on equipping Christians to share the story of Jesus and his love with others, the church has too often turned evangelism into an umbrella category that encompasses every form of publicity: advertising, brochures, tracts, bumper stickers, or web pages. While each of these means of communication can be of value, we are misled to equate them with evangelism. For this reason, it is useful to reclaim the original meaning by referring to "evangelizing" rather than to "evangelism" in describing this primary and indispensable Christian practice of speaking the faith. Whereas evangelism encompasses various forms of publicity, evangelizing is very specific: speaking Christ to others.

This does not mean reverting to a formulaic approach to evangelical communication, whereby Christians are taught to memorize and share a packaged message. Instead evangelizing begins with "evangelical listening"—deep listening to the stories of others, building life-giving relationships as we listen, and only then sharing the promises of God in Christ with others according to their particular situation. This approach requires Christians to be aware of the many ways in which the Gospel can be communicated to others. In the New Testament the gifts of Christ are described in many ways (as love, mercy, generosity, forgiveness, life, reconciliation, peace, joy, shared suffering, hope, etc.), so Christian evangelizing needs to be adept at correlating what we hear through evangelical listening with a very specific expression of God's promises matching the needs of that person.[19]

---

19. Everist, *Seventy Images of Grace in the Epistles*.

Confessing the Gospel according to its evangelical character (justification by grace through faith in Christ alone) has been described as
"the article upon which the church stands and falls." Every Christian generation is called to confess this Gospel at the center of its proclamation.
With the decline of Christianity in North America in recent decades, the
responsibility for sharing the Gospel belongs not only to those called
to serve as "professional" ministers of the Word but especially to *all the
baptized* who are living at the forefront of God's mission in the arenas of
daily life. The baptized need to be equipped intentionally for speaking the
good news to others by implementing a variety of evangelizing practices
designed to increase their capacity. These include fostering evangelizing
speech through modeling by church leaders, building small group ministries that foster speaking about one's Christian faith, developing men-
toring programs that focus on sharing of faith stories between trained
mentors and their mentees, and introducing the practice of testimony by
church members into worship services.[20] Professional ministers thereby
are called to give increased attention to their role in leading and equipping others. Equipping the body of Christ to confess means increasing the
proficiency of church members to follow 1 Pet 3:15–16: "Always be ready
to make your defense to anyone who demands from you an accounting
for the hope that is in you; yet do it with gentleness and reverence."

Practicing (Pietism)

Pietism arose as a renewal movement to connect Christian faith with the
entirety of one's life.[21] The leaders of the Pietist movement observed how
Christian faith had become compartmentalized into certain times of the
week and through conventional religious practices, mostly associated
activities organized by the institutional church. By contrast, the Pietist
movement sought the full integration of Christian existence into every
aspect of life. To accomplish this agenda, Pietism engaged in two strate-
gies: (1) imprinting the pattern of the Christian life on believers through
practices like Bible reading, prayer, singing hymns, and small group meetings, and (2) drawing direct connections between Christian discipleship
and everyday life. While Pietism sometimes became distorted by those
who exercised judgment against those whose faith and lives were deemed

20. Bliese and Van Gelder, *The Evangelizing Church*, 129–32.
21. Olson and Winn, *Reclaiming Pietism*.

less than holy, the basic impulse of classical Pietism was sound: Christian faith makes a claim upon the whole person and the whole of life.

Like Orthodoxy and Pietism, confessing the faith through evangelizing and practicing Christian faith in daily life belong inseparably together. We are called to "proclaim the good news of God in Christ *in word and deed*." Practicing the Christian faith involves coherence and explicit connections between what we do "at church" (the gathering) and what we do "outside of church" (the sending). Establishing this coherence begins with affirming that Christian existence has a pattern. That pattern is Jesus Christ. God in Jesus Christ by the power of the Spirit works to imprint the way of Jesus Christ on our lives. This is the meaning of discipleship.[22]

Jesus Christ calls us to follow him. The teachings, ministry, death and resurrection of Jesus Christ reveal the pattern of the Christian life, the way of discipleship. The church serves as the agent of God in Christ by the power of the Holy Spirit to etch the way of Jesus Christ as a pattern for our lives through worship, preaching, teaching, and spiritual practices. At worship, in Christian education, and through our life together in Christian community, the pattern of Jesus Christ is etched upon our lives. God is involved in nothing less than restoring to us the fullness of the image of God according to the image of Jesus Christ.

We are invited and called to live out the pattern of Jesus Christ in daily life. This same pattern that has been inscribed on us at worship, through Christian education (especially Bible study), and by our life together in Christian community[23] is the pattern we bring to all the arenas of our daily lives. Because our identity is rooted in the person and way of Jesus Christ, we represent Jesus Christ as we minister to others in word and deed. Christian existence is who we are, not only what we do. The disconnection between "churchified" life and daily life can occur from either direction: either by not understanding that church is about patterning our very lives on Jesus Christ or by not extending the pattern of Jesus Christ into all our roles and relationships.

The Christian life is not about "being good." The Christian life is about serving as "little Christs."

> As our heavenly Father has in Christ freely come to our aid, we
> also ought freely to help our neighbor through our body and its
> works, and each one should become as it were a Christ to the

22. Williams, *Being Disciples.*

23. The classic text is Dietrich Bonhoeffer, *Life Together and Prayerbook of the Bible.*

other that we may be Christs to one another and Christ may be the same in all, that is, that we may be truly Christians.[24]

This is baptismal existence: daily dying and rising with Christ. God in Jesus Christ puts to death everything in us that is not of Christ; God in Jesus Christ raises up in us everything that is of Christ. The church is called to equip the members of the body of Christ to "be Christ" for the sake of the world through our words (confessing/evangelizing) and our deeds (practicing/serving).

Dimension Four: Diakonia

Jesus Christ is a diaconal minister. One of the most apt and accurate descriptions of the ministry of Jesus Christ is the ministry of Word and Service. From many angles the New Testament testifies to the servanthood of Jesus: "The greatest among you will be your servant" (Matt 23:11). Jesus came to proclaim the kingdom of God (Mark 1:14–15), the ministry of the Word, and Jesus came to serve others, the ministry of Service: "It will not be so among you; but whoever wishes to be great among you must be your servant, and whoever wishes to be first among you must be your slave; *just as the Son of Man came not to be served but to serve, and to give his life as a ransom for many*" (Matt 20:26–28).

That Jesus Christ would become incarnate in the form of a servant was God's plan from eternity: "Let the same mind be in you that was in Christ Jesus, who, though he was in the form of God, did not regard equality with God as something to be exploited, but emptied himself, *taking the form of a slave*, being born in human likeness" (Phil 2:5–7a). Not only Paul ("Let the same mind be in you . . ."), but Jesus Christ himself commands all his followers to live as ministers of Word and Service.

> After he had washed their feet, had put on his robe, and had returned to the table, he said to them, "Do you know what I have done to you? You call me Teacher and Lord—and you are right, for that is what I am. So if I, your Lord and Teacher, have washed your feet, you also ought to wash one another's feet. For I have set you an example, that you also should do as I have done to you. Very truly, I tell you servants are not greater than their master, nor are the messengers greater than the one who sent

24. Martin Luther, "The Freedom of a Christian (1520)."

them. If you know these things, you are blessed if you do them"
(John 13:12–17).

Jesus Christ ordains his followers to Word and Service ministry by the washing of feet. The basin and towel are signs of Word and Service ministry for the whole church. What if all followers of Jesus Christ were to take him at his Word, making foot-washing a sacrament within our church? Love as the spiritual gift and the washing of feet with water as the material sign, all at Jesus' command. How would our church be transformed? Word and Service at the heart of the matter! The *diakonia* of all believers!

Diakonia of All Believers

As the New Testament makes clear, Word and Service ministry is not only the ministry of Jesus Christ, it is the ministry Jesus Christ entrusts to the whole church: "For we do not proclaim ourselves; we proclaim Jesus Christ as Lord and ourselves as your slaves for Jesus' sake" (2 Cor 4:5). Word and Service ministry, made explicit by those serving in diaconal ministry, deacons and deaconesses, is really the nature of ministry itself as entrusted by God to the *laos*, the whole people of God in Christ Jesus. Diaconal ministry, as marvelously articulated and renewed by Loehe through the ministry of deaconesses, is at the heart of all ministry, the *diakonia* of all believers.

The reinvigoration of the vocation of all the baptized is inextricably linked to the capacity of the church to reimagine diaconal ministry. No theme from the Reformation has more potency to contribute to the renewal of the church in the next generation than the universal priesthood of all believers.[25] Whereas the ecclesial status quo has institutionalized ("churchified") Christian existence by equating what happens through the institutional church as Christianity per se, Luther described faith as "a living, daring confidence in God's grace so certain that you could stake your life on it one thousand times."[26]

This vibrant and dynamic understanding of faith means that the life of the baptized is not something confined to what happens in a church building, no matter how important worship, preaching, teaching, and sacraments remain for the formation of Christian identity and mission. Rather, Christians are sent to live out their faith with living, daring

25. Nessan, "Universal Priesthood," 8–15.
26. Luther, "Prefaces to the New Testament," 370–71.

confidence into all the arenas of daily life where God gives us neighbors to serve—in families, schools, workplaces, local communities, and civic engagement for the common good.[27] We stand at a juncture where the decline in church affiliation in the United States is gaining momentum. People, especially young people, are genuinely searching for meaning and ways of authentic service to others, but they do not perceive what the church has to offer as a living, daring confidence on which to stake their lives.

One crucial issue involves how we understand the relationship between the ministry of pastors and the ministry of all the baptized. How might we reimagine Word and Sacrament ministry in relation to the ministry of Word and Service, and diaconal ministry as the ministry of the whole people of God, a *diakonia* of all believers? Word and Sacrament ministry exists as a ministry of service "to equip the saints for the work of ministry, for building up the body of Christ" (Eph 4:12). How do Word and Sacrament ministers contribute to this service? By proclaiming the Word and stewarding the sacraments so that the *laos* (laity, whole people of God) are *set free from* everything that prevents them from becoming the persons they were created to be. And how do Word and Service ministers contribute? Deacons minister by proclaiming the Word and by their service to others so that all the *laos* are *set free for* living out the ordination of their own baptism in all the arenas of daily life—family, school, workplace, local community, and civil society.

Word and Sacrament ministry must be renewed among us finally as a ministry oriented toward God's purposes of equipping a diaconal church in service to others for the life of the world. The ministry of Word and Service is neither a threat to nor a competition with Word and Sacrament ministry. Instead, Word and Sacrament ministry finds its fulfillment only when exercised as a contribution toward the vibrancy of a diaconal church, sent and scattered for the ministry of Word and Service in all the arenas of life.

Deacons

With this vision for the diaconal ministry of all believers—that is, the neighborliness of all believers—the role of those called as deacons (diaconal ministers) becomes as crucial for the church today as it was in the

27. See resources provided by the Life of Faith Initiative, www.lifeoffaith.info.

life of the earliest church or for the ministry of Loehe in the nineteenth century. The heart of diaconal ministry involves a dynamic exchange between church and world. *Diakonia* means service. Deacons are called to bring the crying needs of the world to the attention of the church and to equip the church for addressing holistically the aching needs of society. Diaconal ministry, a ministry of Word and Service, has two key features: (1) the *exemplary function* to model the character of the ministry of all baptized persons at the interface of church and world, and (2) the *catalytic function* to equip intentionally all members of the body of Christ to claim their baptismal vocation of service to neighbors in their daily lives.

The role of diaconal ministers within the church exists as *sign and catalyst* for what every follower is called by Jesus Christ to become: a minister of Word and Service. Those serving in the office of deacon fulfill a two-fold role on behalf of a diaconal church. First, through the exercise of their own charismatic gifts in diverse specializations, they demonstrate the character of Word and Service ministry as they are sent by the church from worship into the world to serve neighbors and then bring the needs of the world to the attention of the church. Second, through their ministry, deacons function as catalysts among the whole people of God, equipping others for service in order that the church becomes diaconal at the very heart of its identity and mission. The time has come to renew the deaconate as both a historic and inherently necessary office within the Christian church. Diaconal ministry involves the ongoing reformation of the entire church to become Word and Service ministry to the world in the name of Jesus Christ, the *diakonia* of all believers.[28]

All ministry in the name of Jesus Christ is an expression of this diaconal calling. As the apostles necessarily raised up deacons for the ministry of Word and Service in the early church (Acts 6:1–6), there is an inextricable connection between Word and Service ministry and Word and Sacrament ministry. This connection, however, is not a matter of hierarchy and subservience but rather one of complementarity and mutual enrichment. Ministers of Word and Sacrament have the opportunity to become articulate interpreters and strong advocates for the office of deacons in their ministries of Word and Service, for the sake of the transformation of the post-Christendom church into a missional church fully engaged in diaconal servanthood in all arenas of daily life. Word and Sacrament ministry finds its genuine purpose only in alignment with

28. Nessan, "The Neighborliness (Diakonia) of All Believers," 143–46.

Word and Service ministry, since it is diaconal ministry for which Jesus Christ has prepared and sent the church into the world from the beginning. The church of Jesus Christ becomes vital for the life of the world as it is completely oriented toward equipping the *diakonia* of all believers.

Dimension Five: Open Questions

The Iowa Synod and Augustana Synod were arguably two traditions that contributed the most well-integrated and catholic understandings of the church among the predecessor bodies that flowed into the Evangelical Lutheran Church in America.[29] One of the most intriguing and needful contributions to ecclesiology from the Loehe legacy is the principle of "open questions." This principle, which has been examined in this book as deriving from Loehe and developed by the leaders and theologians of the Iowa Synod, anticipates one of the key hermeneutical moves of the later ecumenical movement.

In 1893 Sigmund Fritschel described the Iowa Synod as representing "a strictly confessional as well as ecumenical Lutheranism."[30] During the twentieth century, building ecumenical consensus was fostered wherever the process shifted focus away from concentrating exclusively, or even primarily, on those beliefs that divide and separate, and instead devoted principle attention to shared convictions that are core to Christian faith. This involves making a distinction between matters which are central and those which may be considered peripheral, even *adiaphora*.

Regarding the Iowa Synod's method of allowing "open questions," the church historian J. L. Neve wrote:

> Iowa, from the very beginning, acted according to the principle that in matters of faith it is essential to agree in case church-fellowship is to take place, but that doctrinal points, which are not doctrines of faith, must not affect fellowship of faith and church-fellowship. They must be considered "open questions." By this not a theory but a general principle concerning the treatment of differences within the Church in regard to church-fellowship is laid down.[31]

29. Ottersberg, "The Evangelical Lutheran Synod of Iowa and Other States, 1854–1904."

30. Fritschel, "The German Iowa Synod," 62.

31. Neve, *A Brief History of the Lutheran Church in America*, 290.

By contrast, the Lutheran Church—Missouri Synod (LCMS) demanded complete agreement on each point of doctrine, as demonstrated in the controversy with Loehe over ordination and the many controversies waged with the Iowa Synod in the nineteenth century. "Iowa, however, insisted that this principle had always been a confessional declaration of the Lutheran Church, and that the Lutheran Church has always acted according to this principle. Another practice would end in sectarianism, and would be un-Lutheran, since it was just as wrong to add to the confessions as it was to detract from them."[32] Here we discover two contrasting hermeneutical methods for interpreting the Lutheran Confessions, a difference that has persisted to the present. The principle of "open questions" remains a lasting contribution of the Loehe legacy to ecumenical understanding, whose articulation deserves more recognition and consideration regarding points of theological controversy today.

The Ultimate

In his *Ethics,* Dietrich Bonhoeffer described the importance in Christian theology of distinguishing, yet without separating, the "ultimate" from the "penultimate." The ultimate pertains to the doctrine of justification by grace through faith in Jesus Christ alone, while penultimate matters always must be viewed in relation to the ultimate.

> What is the penultimate? It is all that precedes the ultimate—the justification of the sinner by grace alone—and that is addressed as penultimate after finding the ultimate. At the same time it is everything that follows the ultimate, in order again to precede it. There is no penultimate as such, as if something or other could justify itself as being in itself penultimate; but the penultimate becomes what it is only through the ultimate, that is, in the moment when it has already lost its own self-sufficiency. The penultimate does not determine the ultimate; the ultimate determines the penultimate . . . From this follows now something of decisive importance, that the penultimate must be preserved for the sake of the ultimate. Arbitrary destruction of the penultimate seriously harms the ultimate.[33]

32. Neve, *A Brief History of the Lutheran Church in America,* 291. The author cites the Augsburg Confession, article 7 regarding the *satis est* ("it is enough").

33. Bonhoeffer, *Ethics,* 159–60.

By placing justification at the very center of Christian faith and teaching, Bonhoeffer sought to secure Jesus Christ as the center around whom all other matters revolve and in relation to whom all other questions are relativized.

Agreement about Jesus Christ as the ultimate source of our justification before God was crucial for unity in the Christian faith and served to distinguish, in the midst of the church struggle in Germany between the Confessing Church and the German Christians, those who succumbed to compromise with the Nazi machinations in church politics. Bonhoeffer summoned the church to vigilance about the costly discipleship of Jesus Christ against yielding to "cheap grace."[34] By distinguishing without severing the relationship between the ultimate and penultimate, Bonhoeffer effectively acknowledged the existence of a "hierarchy of truths," a term later employed to guide the church in its interpretation of doctrine and involvement in ecumenical relations.[35]

The Penultimate

To describe a point of doctrine as "penultimate" does not suggest that it is unimportant. Discerning the province of the penultimate has great significance for understanding the coherence of the Christian faith and especially for engaging in the deliberation of ethical issues. The church needs to give its best analysis of and reflection upon penultimate matters, in order to represent Christian teaching faithfully and the Christian life with integrity. However, designating certain matters as penultimate allows the church to respect differences of interpretation on a range of issues without putting at risk justification, the ultimate, as the basis for church unity.

In the heated controversies between the Iowa Synod and LCMS in the nineteenth century, Loehe and his followers crafted a hermeneutical approach to the Lutheran Confessions that distinguished between the ultimate claims of dogma and penultimate matters. Speaking about the doctrinal stance of the Iowa Synod, Sigmund Fritschel wrote:

> On account of this historical view of the Symbols, the Iowa Synod does not see in them a code of law of atomistic dogmas of equal value and equal weight, but an organic expression of

34. Bonhoeffer, *Discipleship*, 53–56.
35. McBrien, "The Hierarchy of Truths."

the living connection of the faith of the Church. Accordingly, there is a distinction to be made between the *dogmas, properly speaking, and other parts of the Symbols;* as e.g. the frequent exegetical, historical and other deductions, illustrations and demonstrations. Only the former, i.e. the dogmas, constitute the Confession, whilst the latter partake of this dignity only indirectly, inasmuch as they define the dogmas more clearly . . . The Church is bound to accept these doctrines which constitute the Confession in their totality, *without exception,* whilst the demand of doctrinal conformity by no means includes *all unessential* opinions which *are only occasionally* mentioned in the Symbols.[36]

The key to implementing the principle of open questions in theological debate and ecumenical relationships involves not only agreement about the principle itself, but also consensus regarding which particular theological or ethical questions can be counted as penultimate (and therefore in need of interpretation only in relation to the ultimate). The great breakthroughs in recent church history, leading to ecumenical rapprochement and especially the adoption of full communion agreements, witness to the fruitfulness of the hermeneutical method anticipated and implemented by the representatives of the Loehe legacy in the Iowa Synod. Given the sharp polemics and polarization of viewpoints in our time, especially regarding controversial ethical questions, the church can draw upon the wisdom of open questions as it engages in such discussions. Jesus Christ is the ultimate source of life, who provides justification by grace through faith in him. Holding to this center sets us free for reasonable discourse and mutual respect when engaging penultimate matters.

Dimension Six: Reclaiming the Missionary

The word "missionary" is out. Due to manifest abuses confusing Christian evangelism with Western cultural imperialism and denominationalism, through many of the missionary efforts by European and North American churches in the nineteenth and early twentieth centuries, this is not without good reason.[37] Attitudes conveying cultural superiority, ethnocentrism, imposition of Western categories, English as the normative language, and the inferiority of other cultures too often were

36. Fritschel, "The German Iowa Synod," 65–66.
37. Bosch, *Transforming Mission,* 291–97.

considered the norm. Negative instances of the work of such missionaries, those who failed to carefully examine and identify their cultural
assumptions, are plentiful and sometimes egregious.[38] This assertion is in
not intended to discredit the faithful service of those who have served as
missionaries in global contexts and done so with cultural sensitivity. It is
rather to acknowledge that in modern history, churches regularly failed
to operate with an approach that respected the need to incarnate the
Christian message within the cultural matrix of other peoples. In recent
times, much has been gained by employing the accompaniment model of
missionary collaboration, a method which intentionally involves mutual
partnership and enrichment.[39]

The church needs to reclaim a missionary impulse for the sake of
theological education in the present historical moment.[40] If we are indeed dwelling in a post-Christian era, when we can no longer take for
granted even the most rudimentary familiarity with biblical and Christian teachings among people in the West, then we are living in an explicitly missionary situation analogous to the first centuries of Christian
history.[41] While the word "mission" is trendy—even many secular orga-
nizations now seem to have "mission statements"—and the neologism
"missional" has become commonplace, using the word "missionary" may
invite misunderstanding, if not resistance. This creates a dilemma for
those interpreting the Loehe legacy, because theological education according to this legacy, including its embodiment at Wartburg Theological
Seminary, has been consistently missionary both in theological commitments and pastoral-diaconal engagement. This chapter aims to reclaim
the seven-fold matrix of the Loehe legacy for the contemporary church,
including arguing for the recovery, reinterpretation, and renewal of the
missionary concept to address the challenges facing church and society
in the twenty-first century.

If Loehe's theology is like the beating of the human heart, the dia-
stolic (inward) moment is worship and the systolic (outward) moment is
mission. At worship, the people of God encounter Jesus Christ in Word
and Sacrament as they confess their faith and are taken up into the *missio Dei*, and then are propelled into the world as agents of the Gospel's

38. For a literary depiction, Kingsolver, *The Poisonwood Bible*.

39. Evangelical Lutheran Church in America, *Global Mission in the Twenty-First
Century*.

40. Nessan, "Mission and Theological Education," 176–93.

41. Hall, *The End of Christendom*.

mission. It is fully consistent with Loehe's theology that two of the most extensive studies of his thought in recent times have emphasized the missionary character of his contributions.[42] Christian Weber refers to the Loehe legacy in describing the church's call to mission:

> It is very urgent for the church to start moving. The church must get away from self-centered thinking and protecting its ownership. It needs to find a global and missionary perspective . . . In Loehe's words: "For mission is nothing but the one church of God in its movement, the actualization of the one universal, catholic church." This is the vision of Loehe. He drew a picture with words. The church is like a huge pilgrimage ascending a mountain. The first pilgrims have already reached the top. But the top is covered with clouds and cannot be seen from afar. At the end of the pilgrimage, people of all nations and colors join in. The pilgrims are a unity because they share the way.[43]

Every Christian generation faces the dilemma of how to appropriate faithfully the traditions of the past and address the mission challenges of the present. The term "missionary," for the compelling reasons already named, has been criticized and fallen into disfavor. There are clear signs, however, that we have entered an age where the recovery and reclamation of the missionary concept is crucial. Moreover, the characteristics of contemporary postmodern and post-Christian society necessitate clear missionary convictions, not in relationships with people from other countries but primarily in relation to the complex secular and religious milieu here in the North American context.[44]

One definition of the postmodern condition involves the disintegration of all metanarratives that bind together social existence.[45] In a situation where there remain no universally valid truths to make the social fabric coherent, the vacuum is filled by multiple versions of reality. Each subculture operates according to its own language game, values, rituals, and lifestyle. When these subcultures collide, especially in defense of their ultimate loyalties, the situation becomes conflicted, even explosive. In the best cases, cultural diversity offers an opportunity for the mutual enrichment of all parties, yet too often tensions lead to competition, if

42. Weber, *Missionstheologie bei Wilhelm Loehe*; and Ratke, *Confession and Mission, Word and Sacrament.*

43. Weber, "The Future of Loehe's Legacy," 96–102.

44. Hall, *The End of Christendom.*

45. Lyotard, *The Postmodern Condition*, 39–41.

not outright hostility. By contrast, in the worst cases of polarized political discourse, we feel we have entered a "post-truth" era. We live in an historical period when the volatility of "tribalism" has become all too evident.[46]

What does it mean that our present age is characterized as post-Christian or post-Christendom? The former paradigm of Western civilization, in which Christianity was assumed to provide the religious fabric of culture, is no longer valid. Consider the widespread biblical illiteracy of the general population, to say nothing of church members. Allusions to the most central biblical stories no longer convey meaning. Basic Christian practices, such as prayer, are not transmitted from parent to child in the home. There remains no sacred time during the week, not even Sunday mornings, when church activities are privileged over other activities. The significance of Christian holy days has been successfully co-opted by consumer appropriations of Christmas and Easter. The compartmentalization of Christian faith as separate from daily life is commonplace.

At such a challenging moment in Christian history, it is imperative for church leaders to recover and reclaim the church's missionary identity. What are the central features of the missionary mindset needed in our context? First, we need a deep understanding of the faith tradition in which we stand. This involves clarity about the centrality and the efficacy of the Gospel of Jesus Christ. It entails personal appropriation of key theological doctrines of the tradition. Given the multicultural and multi-religious complexity of our context, this theological posture needs to be characterized by deep appreciation for the diverse voices that have contributed to the formation of the tradition, both in Scripture and in Christian history. These diverse sources provide rich resources in our missionary enterprise of interpreting the faith, including awareness of the value of dissenting voices—and even heretical opinions—from the Christian past.

Second, the missionary mindset envisioned here involves a profound capacity to listen. This means listening not only to the words spoken by others but the way their words constitute a worldview. Careful and active listening attends to the nuances of emotion and values expressed by others. The other person is honored, not threatened, by this manner of listening. One is attentive to the religious implications of what is heard and seeks to explore the ultimate concern in, with, and under what is said. A

---

46. Zelman, *Our Beleaguered Species.*

cultivated capacity to listen employs methods of cultural and theological analysis to understand and interpret what has been heard. This approach to listening takes time—time to test one's emerging hypotheses so that other perspectives might be invited to affirm or clarify their accuracy. One must develop long-term relationships rather than seek instant gratification as we build relationships of mutual trust through active listening.

Third, this form of missionary work understands itself as service to the holistic well-being of the other person and the community to which the other belongs. It imagines the world communally, not individualistically. Missionary service "is not envious or boastful or arrogant or rude. It does not insist on its own way; it is not irritable or resentful . . ." (1 Cor 13:4–5). Missionary service is lived out in acts of love that attend to those things that contribute to the restoration of relationships in community. The missionary embodies the promise of the Gospel by attending to those most in need and dedicating service to them. God's partiality for the least is modeled by the missionary. Concern for the wholeness of the entire community, beginning with the most vulnerable members and including the creation itself, reflects God's own desire for the shalom of God.[47] Missionary service is not a matter of weakness, but of gentle strength, risking one's own comfort and safety, in order to challenge policies and structures that put one's neighbor at risk.

Finally, this missionary approach entails the ability to translate our faith tradition into other "languages." Here we are not referring to conventional languages, like German or Spanish, although the mission of the church is seriously hampered by the inability of its leaders to communicate with the burgeoning Latinx population. Rather, we mean the ability to speak in the multiple languages of culture (for example, the language of youth, contemporary music, or social media) and to translate into multiple religious languages (for example, the languages of New Age, civil religion, Buddhism, or Mormon). Rooted in the inherited Christian tradition, the new missionary must be a broker of cultures and religions, creative in interpreting and translating the Good News into languages that are understandable to the ears, hearts, and minds of those whose lives are versed in their own very particular cultural and religious tongues.

The heritage of the Iowa Synod, including the institutions of Wartburg Theological Seminary and Wartburg College (and those leaders and congregations formed in this heritage), preserves a missionary identity

---

47. Nessan, *Shalom Church*, chapter 1.

that has evolved organically from Wilhelm Loehe and been embodied contextually in each succeeding generation, serving as a living legacy for the future church. Rather than abandoning the missionary concept, the time is here for its revival. Not only can we embrace the task of "engaging, equipping, and sending collaborative leaders who interpret, proclaim and live the gospel of Jesus Christ for a world created for communion with God and in need of personal and social healing," but even more aspire that each person formed in the Loehe legacy be sent forth with the self-understanding and vocation of a missionary.[48] In short I propose this motto: "Every minister a missionary."

Dimension Seven: Character Formation by Repetition and Crucibles

How are we formed as persons and communities in the Christian faith? Character becomes etched upon us by those things that we repeat again and again in our lives until they become habits and by how we enter into and endure the crucibles that overtake us in living our lives. Both means are effective in imprinting the Loehe legacy.

First, the Loehe legacy is about the repetition of the deep patterns of Christian existence through shared practices. Chief among these practices are participation in the liturgy, hearing God's Word, and regular engagement in spiritual practices that form who we are as persons. The Loehe legacy has always included intentional focus on the centrality of liturgy for encountering God in Christ and thereby transforming one's life into worship (Rom 12:1–2). Closely related, the Loehe legacy has valued the proclamation and hearing of God's Word as formative for Christian existence, grounding us in the person and way of Jesus Christ, who is God's living Word. Both worship and proclamation are means of grace, whose repetitions over time form our identity through the enactment of the elements of the liturgy and the proclaimed Word. These repetitions are then taken up into one's own devotional life through prayer, Bible reading, singing hymns, and other spiritual practices. Such repetitions constitute the rhythm of the Christian life to immerse us in the depths of the historic Christian faith as preserved in the Loehe legacy.

Second, our existence as Christian persons is tested as by fire through the crucibles that come upon us as we live our broken lives amid a finite

48. Wartburg Theological Seminary Mission Statement.

and sinful world. Inevitably our lives are marked by experiences of deep sadness, loss, and grief. We experience the effects of human waywardness, alienation, sickness, and death, as well as other consequences that belong to the chances and changes of life. For Loehe, such experiences included the ordeal of extended waiting to receive his call as a pastor, the death of his young wife, difficulties in the lives of his children, dissent within the Bavarian Lutheran Church, controversies with his mission partners in North America, and conflict with close colleagues in Neuendettelsau. Loehe himself was profoundly affected by the crucibles known to human beings in this world.

At the same time, Loehe demonstrated how such crucibles may, by God's faithfulness under the sign of the cross, become the occasion for living by faith in service to neighbors in need. Loehe had acute sensitivity to human suffering as demonstrated by pastoral care for the members of his parish, compassion for the misery of the German immigrants in North America, concern for American Indians, and commitment to care for the needs of the sick, aged, disabled, and other marginalized persons through the training of deaconesses and the organization of diaconal institutions.

The Loehe legacy provides historical perspective and living resources for the contemporary church to reconstitute Christian existence today. We revitalize ecclesial life by cultivating new and imaginative repetitions of historic Christian practices and by entering into Christian solidarity with others as they—and we—endure the crucibles that beset all human life. We pray this legacy, as it has been lived out among persons, congregations, and institutions shaped by Wilhelm Loehe, may provide a compass for orienting the future of a church that seeks to be aligned with the mission of the Triune God.

Appendix A

Loehe's Legacy and the Apostolic Calling of Wartburg Theological Seminary for the Church and World in the Twenty-First Century[1]

BY ANN L. FRITSCHEL, CRAIG L. NESSAN,

AND WINSTON D. PERSAUD

NEUENDETTELSAU? A PLACE WILHELM Loehe never desired to live, commenting that he would not even want his dog to be buried there. Yet this village has become to this day a center for the gathering and sending of "apostles" for mission to the global church. These are the two central impulses of the Loehe legacy and the apostolic calling of Wartburg Theological Seminary (WTS) in the twenty-first century: (1) gathering for life together in the worshipping, teaching, and learning community, and (2) being sent forth from this community in witness and service to others for the life of the world.

What is the attraction and ongoing significance of the Loehe legacy? Seven core characteristics demonstrate remarkable continuity between the vision and practice of Wilhelm Loehe, the nineteenth-century pastor, and the life of WTS in its more than 160 years of history.

First, the Loehe legacy is *worship-centered*. Loehe reformed liturgical practice according to historic forms and renewed worship for the church in the nineteenth century, understanding that in worship God was at work accomplishing God's mission for the life of the world. At

1. Originally written in 2010 at the request of the President for the Board of Directors of Wartburg Theological Seminary.

WTS worship remains the centering practice of our life together in Jesus Christ.

Second, the Loehe legacy is *communal*. Loehe gathered people around worship into a community of life-giving relationships that stretched from Neuendettelsau to the ends of the earth. At WTS each new generation of students is initiated into bonds of friendship that are formed in life together of mutual conversation around worship, community, and classroom and that leads to a sending into witness and service to others.

Third, the Loehe legacy is rooted in *Lutheran pietism*. Loehe was deeply committed both to the Lutheran confessional heritage and to Christianity as a living faith. Wartburg Theological Seminary holds together two impulses that are often rent asunder in the life of the church: commitment to historic Lutheranism, centered on justification by grace through faith in Christ alone, and the expression of this faith in personal faith and integrity through lives devoted to justice.

Fourth, the Loehe legacy allows for *open questions*. While Loehe held core Lutheran commitments to justification as articulated in Scripture and the confessional writings, he also maintained an ecclesiology that allowed Christians to have different opinions on non-essential matters. At WTS this characteristic has fostered a way of being church that is clear about ultimate matters but respectful of difference in penultimate matters.

Fifth, the Loehe legacy is *diaconal*. Loehe founded in Neuendettelsau a host of diaconal institutions to serve the needs of the most vulnerable members of society. WTS has prepared students for diaconal service not only as pastors but as deaconesses, diaconal ministers, chaplains, associates in ministry, and active laity, always with an eye on service to the needs of others.

Sixth, the Loehe legacy is *missional*. For Loehe, worship and community life were never ends in themselves, but rather the centering activity for being sent into the world in service to God's mission. WTS understands itself as serving God's mission by sending leaders forth from its communal formation process as leaders for faith communities who "proclaim and interpret the gospel of Jesus Christ to a world created for communion with God and in need of personal and social healing."

Seventh, the Loehe legacy is *global*. Although located in the out-of-the-way setting of Neuendettelsau, Loehe cultivated a global vision of God's mission, reaching out to North America, Australia, Brazil,

Tanzania, and Papua New Guinea. WTS continues to cultivate a global ministry by receiving, preparing, and sending students from and for the global church.

The WTS Mission Statement articulates well how the Loehe legacy continues to come alive in the school: *Wartburg Theological Seminary serves the mission of the Evangelical Lutheran Church in America by being a worship-centered community of critical theological reflection where learning leads to mission and mission informs learning. Within this community, Wartburg educates women and men to serve the church's mission as ordained and lay leaders. This mission is to proclaim and interpret the gospel of Jesus Christ to a world created for communion with God and in need of personal and social healing.* Our mission statement is known and shared by all the members of this community; it focuses the purpose of our life together. The Twelve Pastoral and Diaconal Practices further articulate the shape of the WTS' curriculum and formation process in fulfilling our mission.

The WTS "way" of forming valued leaders involves the fostering of intentional relationships among students, faculty, and staff in life together through worship, convocations, student-advisor interactions, faculty team-teaching, small-group pedagogy, J-term immersions, contextual education, and community life. The Wartburg "way" has received enthusiastic affirmation through both reaccreditation reports from the school's accrediting agencies *and* the practice of assessment undertaken by the seminary. ELCA bishops and churchwide leaders especially affirm the values of ecclesial partnership, collegiality, and reading context as fostered by the communal formation process of WTS. The mission of WTS closely relates times of *gathering* as teaching and learning community and the *sending* forth into witness to and service of God's mission in the world.

The mission frontier of the twenty-first century presents new and dramatic challenges to the Loehe legacy as WTS seeks to respond faithfully and effectively to its apostolic calling. It is imperative that "learning leads to mission and mission informs learning" abides as the central feature of Wartburg's apostolic calling as it considers new partnerships and unprecedented changes across the landscape of theological education. WTS has been a school located in the heartland of the United States, which has in each generation claimed a global scope for its mission. It has been a center for gathering together gifted people, joining them to worship-centered community, grounding them in biblical and theological wisdom, and sending them forth as valued leaders at God's mission frontiers. Those Wartburg Theological Seminary sends forth as missionaries (*Sendlinge*) from this place of formation are equipped with a theology centered in the Gospel of Jesus Christ, steeped in biblical wisdom, sharing a global vision, demonstrating a spirit of collegiality, breadth of hospitality, skills in collaborative leadership, and a deep commitment to the mission of the Triune God in the world.

Appendix B

Wilhelm Loehe

Sources and Literature in English

Compiled by the Author

Primary Books

Loehe, Wilhelm. *Aphorisms on the New Testament Offices and their Relationship to the Congregation—On the Question of the Church's Polity (1849)*. Translated by John Stephenson. Fort Wayne, IN: Repristination, 2008.

———. *Dialogue on Luther's Small Catechism*. Rajahmundry: Braun, 1908.

———. *Liturgy for Christian Congregations of the Lutheran Faith*. 3d ed. Edited by J. Deinzer. Translated by F. C. Longaker. Introduction by Edward T. Horn, 1902. Reprint, London: Forgotten, 2018.

———. *Loehe on Mercy: Six Chapters for Everyone, the Seventh for the Servants of Mercy (1858–1860)*. Translation of *Von der Barmherzigkeit* by Holger Sonntag. Preface by Matthew C. Harrison. St. Louis: LCMS World Relief and Human Care, 2006.

———. *Of the Divine Word as the Light Which Leads to Peace*. Defiance, OH: Papenhagen & Deindoerfer, 1903.

———. *The Pastor: The Pastoral Theology of Wilhelm Loehe*. Edited by Charles P. Schaum. Translated by Wolf Dietrich Knappe and Charles P. Schaum. St. Louis: Concordia, 2015.

———. *Questions and Answers to the Six Parts of the "Small Catechism" of Dr. Martin Luther*. 2d ed. Edited and translated by Edward T. Horn. Columbia, SC: Duffie, 1893. Reprint, Fort Wayne, IN: Repristination, 1993; Windham, 2013.

———. *Seed-Grains of Prayer: A Manual for Evangelical Christians*. Chicago: Wartburg, 1914. Reprint, Fort Wayne, IN: Emmanuel, 2010; and Watseka, IL: Just and Sinner, 2016.

———. *Three Books about the Church*. Translated and edited by James L. Schaaf. Philadelphia: Fortress, 1969.

————. *Three Books Concerning the Church, Offered to Friends of the Lutheran Church, for Consideration and Discussion.* Translated by Edward T. Horn. Reading, PA: Pilger, 1908.

————. *The Word Remains: Selected Writings on the Church Year and the Christian Life.* Edited by Michael N. Frese and John T. Pless. Fort Wayne, IN: Emmanuel, 2016.

Primary Articles

Loehe, Wilhelm. "Lutheran Emigrants to North America: A Letter to the Readers of the *Sonntagsblatt*." Translated by Erika Bullmann Flores as transcribed by James L. Schaaf in his dissertation. *Noerdlingen Sonntagsblatt* 11 (January 10, 1841) 9–14.

————. "Of Confession to the Father Confessor." *Una Sancta* 31 (Fall 1997) 11–12.

————. "Preface to the *Agende Fuer Christiliche Gemeinden des Lutherischen Bekenntnisses*." *Logia* 17 (Holy Trinity 2008) 31–38.

————. "The Sacrament of Repentance." *Una Sancta* 10.2 (1951) 1–11.

————. "The Sacrament of Repentance (Holy Absolution)." *Una Sancta* 10.3 (1951) 10–23.

————. "A Sermon on the Sunday of the Holy Trinity." *Logia* 17 (Holy Trinity 2008) 13–17.

————. "Why Do I Declare Myself for the Lutheran Church?" *Logia* 17 (Holy Trinity 2008) 27–29.

Secondary Books

Bickel, A. M., *Our Forgotten Founding Father: A Biography of Pastor William Loehe.* Napoleon, OH: Bickel, 1997.

Blaufuss, Dietrich, ed. *Wilhelm Loehe: Erbe und Vision.* Gütersloh: Gütersloher, 2009.

Blaufuss, Dietrich, ed. *Wilhem Loehe: Theology and History.* Neuendettelsau: Freimund, 2013.

Blaufuss, Dietrich and Corzine, Jacob, eds. *Wilhelm Loehe and Christian Formation.* Neuendettelsau: Freimund, 2016.

Forster, Walter O. *Zion on the Mississippi: The Settlement of the Saxon Lutherans in Missouri 1839–1841.* St Louis: Concordia, 1953.

Fry, George C. *Wilhelm Loehe in Perspective.* n.p., 1977.

Geiger, Erika. *The Life, Work, and Influence of Wilhelm Loehe (1808–1872).* St. Louis: Concordia, 2010.

Heintzen, Erich H. *Love Leaves Home: Wilhelm Loehe and the Missouri Synod.* St. Louis: Concordia, 1973.

Hock, Albert Llewellyn. *The Pilgrim Colony: The History of Saint Sebald Congregation, The Two Wartburgs, and the Synods of Iowa and Missouri.* Minneapolis: Lutheran University Press, 2004.

Hunnius, Nicolaus. *Epitome Credendorum.* Preface by Wilhelm Loehe. Translated by Paul Edward Gottheil. Nuremberg: Sebald, 1847.

Mauelshagen, Carl. *American Lutheranism Surrenders to Forces of Conservatism.* Athens: University of Georgia, 1936.

Mayer, Herbert T. *A Reader in the History of Pastoral Care.* St. Louis: n.p., 1980.

Maxfield, John A. *Wilhelm Loehe and the Nineteenth-Century Revival of Lutheran Confessionalism and Mission*, St. Louis: Concordia Historical Institute. Luther Academy/ Northville, SD: Logia, 2012.

Nessan, Craig L. *The Theology of Wartburg Theological Seminary: 1854-2004*. Dubuque, IA: n.p., 2005.

Ratke, David C. *Confession and Mission, Word and Sacrament: The Ecclesial Theology of Wilhelm Loehe*. St. Louis: Concordia Publishing, 2001.

Schober, Theodore. *Wilhelm Loehe Biography*. Translated by Bertha Mueller. N.p., 1959.

———. *Wilhelm Loehe: Witness of the Living Lutheran Church*. Translated by Bertha Mueller. n.p.

Schober, Theodore, Bertha Mueller, and Frederick Sheely Weiser. *Treasure Houses of the Church: The Formation of the Diaconate Through the Lutherans Wilhelm Loehe, Hermann Bezzel and Hans Lauerer*. N.p., 1961–1965.

Stuckwisch, D. Richard. *Johann Konrad Wilhelm Loehe, Portrait of a Confessional Lutheran*. Bynum, TX: Repristination, 1994.

Weiblen, William H. *Life Together at Wartburg Theological Seminary, 1854-2004*. Sesquicentennial Edition. Craig L. Nessan, ed. Dubuque, IA: n.p., 2006.

Wiederaenders, Robert C. *Correspondence of Wilhelm Loehe in American Repositories*. Dubuque: Archives of The American Lutheran Church, Wartburg Theological Seminary, 1969.

Chapters in Books

Conser, Walter H. *Church and Confession: Conservative Theologians in Germany, England, and America, 1815-1866*, 57–72. Macon, GA: Mercer University Press, 1984.

Honold, Matthias. "Deaconesses in Nursing Care: International Transfer of a Female Model of Life and Work in the 19th and 20th Century." In *Deaconesses in Nursing Care: International Transfer of a Female Model of Life and Work in the 19th and 20th Century*, edited by Susanne Kreutzer and Karen Nolte, 65–77. Stuttgart: Steiner, 2016.

Schattauer, Thomas H. "The Reconstruction of Rite: The Liturgical Legacy of Wilhelm Loehe." In *Rule of Prayer, Rule of Faith: Essays in Honor of Aidan Kavanagh, O.S.B.*, edited by Nathan Mitchell and John F. Baldovin, 243–77. Collegeville, MN: Liturgical, 1996.

Schmutterer, Gerhard M. and Charles P. Lutz. "Mission Martyr on the Western Frontier: Can Cross-Cultural Mission Be Achieved?" In *Church Roots: Stories of Nine Immigrant Groups that Became the American Lutheran Church*, edited by Charles P. Lutz, 117–42. Minneapolis: Augsburg, 1985.

Nessan, Craig L. "Loehe in America, Two Historical Trajectories in the Missouri and Iowa Synods." In *Wilhelm Loehe (1808-1872) Seine Bedeutung fur Kirche und Diakonie*, edited by Schoenauer, Hermann, 103–17. Stuttgart: Kohlhammer, 2008.

Pless, John T. "Wilhelm Loehe and the Missouri Synod." In *Wilhelm Loehe (1808-1872) Seine Bedeutung fur Kirche und Diakonie*, edited by Schoenauer, Hermann, 119–34. Stuttgart: Kohlhammer, 2008.

Wittenberg, Martin. "Wilhelm Loehe and Confession: A Contribution to the History of *Seelsorge* and the Office of Ministry within Modern Lutheranism." In *And*

Every Tongue Confess: Essays in Honor Of Norman Nagel on the Occasion of His Sixty-fifth Birthday, edited by G. Krispin and J. Vieker, 113–50. Chelsea, MI: Book Crafters, 1990.

Dissertations

Carroll, Roy William. "Place, Praise and Faith: A Study of Architecture and Music in the Worship Life of the Lutheran Church." PhD diss., University of Iowa, 1999.

Frank, Victor C. "The Work of Wilhelm Leohe in North America." PhD diss., Concordia Seminary (St. Louis), 1932.

Goebel, Hans Volkert. "An Analysis of Wilhelm Loehe's Theology of Worship with Special Emphasis upon His Contribution to European and American Lutheranism." BD thesis, Lutheran Theological Seminary at Gettysburg, 1965.

Greenholt, Homer Reginald. "A Study of Wilhelm Loehe, His Colonies, and the Lutheran Indian Missions in the Saginaw Valley of Michigan." PhD diss., University of Chicago Divinity School, 1937.

Heintzen, Erich Hugo. "Wilhelm Loehe and the Missouri Synod, 1841–1853." PhD diss., University of Illinois (Urbana), 1964.

Hofrenning, James. "A Study of the Ecclesiology of the Newly Merged American Lutheran Church in Order to Determine to What Degree It Reflects the Theological Position of Wilhelm Loehe and Ole Hallesby Regarding the Doctrine of the Church." PhD diss., New York University, 1964.

Jahr, Arnold H. "Loehe's Contributions to Lutheranism in America." BD thesis, Wartburg Theological Seminary, Dubuque, 1939.

Korby, Kenneth Frederick. "The Theology of Pastoral Care in Wilhelm Loehe with Special Attention to the Function of the Liturgy and the Laity." PhD diss., Concordia Seminary (St. Louis), 1976.

Krueger, John W. "Discipline, Community, and Sacrifice in Wilhelm Loehe's Design for a Catechism of the Apostolic Life." STM thesis, Wartburg Theological Seminary, 1990.

Miesner, Willis. "Wilhelm Loehe and His Controversy with the Missouri Synod." BD thesis, Concordia Theological Seminary (Springfield), 1968.

Reents, John H. "Loehe's Works for the Lutheran Church in America Up to 1853." BD thesis, Wartburg Theological Seminary, 1933.

Schaaf, James L. "Wilhelm Loehe's Relation to the American Church: A Study in the History of Lutheran Mission." PhD diss., Heidelberg, 1961.

Schattauer, Thomas H. "Announcement, Confession, and Lord's Supper in the Pastoral-Liturgical Work of Wilhelm Loehe: A Study of Worship and Church Life in the Lutheran Parish at Neuendettelsau, Bavaria, 1837–1872." PhD diss., University of Notre Dame, 1990.

Stuckwisch, Rick. "The Liturgical Theology of Johannes Konrad Wilhelm Loehe: Confessional Lutheran Liturgiologist." STM diss., Concordia Theological Seminary (Fort Wayne), 1994.

Tietjen, John H. "The Ecclesiology of Wilhelm Loehe." STM thesis, Union Theological Seminary, New York, 1954.

Walker, Kevin G. "A Translation of Wilhelm Loehe's *Zugabe to Unserer Kirchliche Lage*: His Meditative Effort in the Church and Ministry Controversy between the

Buffalo Synod and the Missouri Synod, with a Brief Intoduction and Historical Timeline." MDiv thesis, Concordia Theological Seminary (Fort Wayne), 2002.

Secondary Articles

Blaufuss, Dietrich. "Loehe Preaches the Psalms." *Logia* 17 (Holy Trinity 2008) 7–11.

———. "Saint and Heretic: Wilhelm Loehe in German Historiography since 1872." *Currents in Theology and Mission* 33 (April 2006) 105–12.

———. "Wilhelm Loehe and Enlightenment Movement." *Currents in Theology and Mission* 39 (February 2012) 56–57.

Briese, Russell John. "Wilhelm Loehe and the Rediscovery of the Sacrament of the Altar in Nineteenth-Century Lutheranism." *Lutheran Forum* 30 (1996) 31–34.

Conser, Walter H. "Wilhelm Loehe and the Revolution of 1848." *Logia* 17 (Holy Trinity, 2008) 39–43.

Chung, Paul S. "Confession and Global Mission: Contextualizing Wilhelm Loehe." *Currents in Theology and Mission* 39 (February 2012) 38–44.

Fenton, John W. "Wilhelm Loehe's *Hauptgottesdienst* (1844) as Critique of Luther's *Deutsche Messe*." *Concordia Theological Quarterly* 64 (April 2000) 127–48.

Gaiser, Frederick. "Witness and Worship: The Legacy of Loehe." *Word & World* 24 (Spring 2004) 119–97.

Geiger, Erika. "The Biography of Wilhelm Loehe: Insights into His Life and Work." *Currents in Theology and Mission* 33 (April 2006) 87–92.

Goebel, Hans. "Wilhelm Loehe and the Quest for Liturgical Principle." *Una Sancta* 22.4 (1965) 20–32.

Graebner, August L. "Johann Michael Gottlieb Schaller: A Biography." Translated by Walter R. Roehrs. *Concordia Historical Institute Quarterly* 54 (Spring 1981) 2–29.

Hellwege, John. "Wilhelm Loehe: American Lutheranism's Distant Father." *Concordia Historical Institute Quarterly* 83 (Spring 2010) 2–17.

Hopf, Friedrich Wilhelm. "Wilhelm Loehe as Witness for the Sacrament of the Altar." Translated by August J. Engelbrecht. *Wartburg Seminary Quarterly* 11 (June 1948) 3–8; (September 1948) 3–9.

Huggins, Marvin. "Help from the Homeland." *Lutheran Witness* 116 (1997) 11.

Kantzenbach, Friedrich Wilhelm. "Wilhelm Loehe—100 Years Later." *Springfielder* 35 (December 1971) 191–96.

Klein, Ralph W. "Wilhelm Loehe and His Legacy." *Currents in Theology and Mission* 33 (April 2006) 82–86.

Kleinig, Vernon. "Lutheran Liturgies from Martin Luther to Wilhelm Loehe." *Concordia Theological Quarterly* 62 (April 1998) 125–44.

Koble, Brandon W. "Wilhelm Loehe's Dinah: Against Useful Lusts." *Logia* 27 (Epiphany 2018) 17–21.

Kothmann, Thomas. "Wilhelm Loehe as Religious Instructor." *Currents in Theology and Mission* 39 (February 2012) 5–12.

Korby, Kenneth F. "Loehe's Seelsorge for His Fellow Lutherans in America." *Concordia Historical Institute Quarterly* 45 (November 1972) 227–46.

———. "Wilhelm Loehe and Liturgical Renewal." *Essays and Reports of the Lutheran Historical Conference* 5 (1974) 57–84.

Loehe, Max. "Wilhelm Loehe: Neuendettelsau Influence in the Lutheran Church of Australia." *Springfielder* 35 (December 1971) 183–90.

Loest, Mark A. "Loehe's Michigan Colonies: Then and Now." *Currents in Theology and Mission* 39 (February 2012) 58–64.

Lohrmann, Martin J. "Loehe and the Ministerium of Pennsylvania: Wilhelm Loehe's Reception Among Contemporaries in the Eastern United States." *Currents in Theology and Mission* 39 (February 2012) 72–80.

———. "A Monument to American Intolerance: The 'Open Questions' of Loehe's Iowa Synod in Their American Context." Seminar paper, Lutheran Theological Seminary at Philadelphia, 2007.

Ludwig, Frieder. "Mission and Migration: Reflections on the Missionary Concept of Wilhelm Loehe." *Word & World* 24 (Spring 2004) 157–64.

Marzolf, Dennis. "Loehe in *Logia*." *Logia* 17 (Holy Trinity, 2008) 5.

Meyer, Carl S. "Johann Konrad Wilhelm Loehe—In Memorium." *Concordia Theological Monthly* 43 (July–August 1972) 442–45.

Mundinger, Gerhard H. "Wilhelm Loehe." *Concordia Historical Institute Quarterly* 70 (Spring 1997) 2–19.

Naumann, Cheryl, D. "Lutheran Deaconesses in North America: Assessing Loehe's Influence." *Currents in Theology and Mission* 39 (February 2012) 21–27.

Nessan, Craig L. "Friedrich Bauer (1812–1874) Hidden Giant of Neuendettelsau." *Lutheran Quarterly* (Winter 2012) 395–411.

———. "Loehe and His Coworkers in the Iowa Synod." *Currents in Theology and Mission* 33 (April 2006) 138–44.

———. "Loehe in America: Two Historical Trajectories in the Missouri and Iowa Synods." *Logia* 17 (Holy Trinity 2008) 19–26.

———. "Missionary God, Missionary Congregations." *Dialog: A Journal of Theology* 40 (Summer 2001) 112–17.

———. "Missionary Theology and Wartburg Theological Seminary." *Currents in Theology and Mission* 31 (April 2004) 85–95.

———. "Wilhelm Loehe in Deindoerfer's History of the Iowa Synod." *Currents in Theology and Mission* 39 (February 2012) 65–71.

Nessan, Craig L. and Thomas H. Schattauer. "Wilhelm Loehe: Theological Impact and Historical Influence." *Currents in Theology and Mission* 39 (February 2012) 2–4.

Nichol, Todd W. "Wilhelm Loehe, The Iowa Synod and the Ordained Ministry." *Lutheran Quarterly* 4 (Spring 1990) 11–29.

Ottersberg, Gerhard. "Response to Dr. Schaaf's Paper ('Wilhelm Loehe and the Ohio Synod')." *Lutheran Historical Conference* 5 (1974) 102–7.

———. "Wilhelm Loehe." *Lutheran Quarterly* 4 (1952) 170–90.

Pless, John T. "The Missionary Who Never Left Home." *The Lutheran Witness* 127 (February 2008) 11–13.

———. "Wilhelm Loehe and the Missouri Synod: Forgotten Paternity or Living Legacy?" *Currents in Theology and Mission* 33 (April 2006) 122–37.

———. "Wilhelm Loehe: His Voice Still Heard in Walther's Church" *Concordia Theological Quarterly* 75 (July/October 2011) 311–28.

Ratke, David C. "The Church in Motion: Wilhelm Loehe, Mission, and the Church Today." *Currents in Theology and Mission* 33 (April 2006) 145–56.

———. "The Eccelssial Vision of Wilhelm Loehe." *Lutheran Forum* 33 (Fall 1999) 29–33.

———. "Wilhelm Loehe and the Catholicity of the Church." *Pro Ecclesia* 9 (Summer 2000) 261–84.

———. "Wilhelm Loehe and His Significance for Mission and Ministry." *Word & World* 24 (Summer 2004) 136–44.

———. "Wilhelm Loehe and Worship, Mission, and Renewal." *Cross Accent* 14, no. 3 (2006) 32–37.

Sasse, Hermann. "Walther and Loehe: On the Church." *Springfielder* 35 (December 1971) 176–82.

Schaaf, James L. "Father from Afar: Wilhelm Loehe and Concordia Theological Seminary in Fort Wayne." *Concordia Theological Quarterly* 60 (January–April 1996) 47–73.

———. "Paul August Baugmart: Loehe's Third Sendling." *Lutheran Historical Conference* 15 (1994) 92–112.

———. "Wilhelm Loehe and the Missouri Synod." *Concordia Historical Institute Quarterly* 45 (1972) 53–67.

———. "Wilhelm Loehe and the Ohio Synod." *Essays and Reports of the Lutheran Historical Conference* 5 (1974) 85–101.

Schattauer, Thomas H. "The Loehe Alternative for Worship, Then and Now." *Word & World* 24 (Spring 2004) 145–56.

———. "Loehe's *Agende* in America." *Currents in Theology and Mission* 29 (February 2012) 13–20.

———. "Sunday Worship at Neuendettelsau under Wilhelm Loehe." *Worship* 59 (1985) 370–84.

———. "'Sung, Spoken, Lived': Worship as Communion and Mission in the Work of Wilhelm Loehe." *Currents in Theology and Mission* 33 (April 2006) 113–121.

Schlichting, Wolfhart. "Educational Horizons in Wilhelm Loehe: Pointing to Holy Communion as an Introduction to Living Justification." Translated by Dietrich Wolf. *Logia* 25 (Epiphany 2016) 25–31.

Schmalenberger, Jerry L. "Chasing Loehe's Ghost." *Lutheran Partners* 14 (March–April 1998) 370–84.

Schmelder, William. "A Synod is Born." *Lutheran Witness* 116 (1997) 8–14.

Schwarz, Hans. "Wilhelm Loehe in the Context of the Nineteenth Century." *Currents in Theology and Mission* 33 (April 2006) 93–104.

Schultz, Klaus Detlev. "Wilhelm Loehe's Missiological Perspective." *Currents in Theology and Mission* 39 (February 2012) 28–37.

Steele, Elizabeth and Sally L. Kerr. "The Diaconate: Loehe's Legacy of Service to the Neighbor." *Word & World* 24 (Spring 2004) 165–70.

Stephenson, John R. "Wilhelm Loehe, an Ecumenical Lutheran? From 'Nein' through 'Jein' to a Qualified 'Ja.'" *Currents in Theology and Mission* 39 (February 2012) 45–51.

Streng, William D. "Where Have All the Heroes Gone?" *The Lutheran Standard* 12 (April 4, 1972) 11.

Suelflow, August R. "Centennial of the Neuendettelsau Deaconess Institute, 1845–1954." *Concordia Theological Monthly* 25 (Spring 1954) 672–74.

Sundberg, Walter. "Wilhelm Loehe on Pastoral Office and Liturgy." *Word & World* 24 (Spring 2004) 190–97.

Trachte, Larry. "Wilhelm Loehe, Disciple." *Currents in Theology and Mission* 33 (April 2006) 157–59.

Wangelin, William R. "Loehe's Lens: Wilhelm Loehe's Critique of Democratic Principles in the Missouri Synod during the Revolutions of 1848/49." *Concordia Historical Institute* 86 (Summer 2013) 30–47.

Weber, Christian. "The Future of Loehe's Legacy." *Currents in Theology and Mission* 31 (April 2004) 96–102.

Weiser, Frederick S. "Wilhelm Loehe: Lutheran Pioneer in Communal Ministry." *Una Sancta* 21 (1964) 43–51.

Wilson, H. S. "Embracing Global Christianity: A Missiological Challenge." *Currents in Theology and Mission* 33 (April 2006) 160–73.

Reviews and Lectures

Friedrich, Edward C. Review of *Love Leaves Home: Wilhelm Loehe and the Missouri Synod*, by Erich H. Heintzen. *Wisconsin Lutheran Quarterly* 70 (October 1973) 293–94.

Klug, Eugene F. Review *Confession and Mission, Word and Sacrament: The Ecclesial Theology of Wilhelm Loehe*, by David C. Ratke. *Concordia Historical Institute Quarterly* 75 (Fall 2002) 187–88.

MacKenzie, Cameron A. Review of *The Life, Work, and Influence of Wilhelm Loehe (1808–1872)*, by Erika Geiger. *Concordia Historical Institute Quarterly* 85 (Spring 2012) 62–63.

Mattes, Mark C. Review of *Wilhelm Loehe: Erbe und Vision*, Dietrich Blaufuss, ed. *The Journal of Ecclesiastical History* 62 (January 2011) 193–94.

Mattes, Mark C. Review of *Wilhelm Loehe und Bildung*, Dietrich Blaufuss and Jacob Corzine, eds. *Lutheran Quarterly* 32 (Spring 2018) 112–14.

Nessan, Craig L. Review of *Drei Buecher von der Kirche. 1854, Studienausgabe*, by Wilhelm Loehe, Dietrich Blaufuss, ed. *Lutheran Quarterly* 22 (Spring 2008) 87–88.

Nessan, Craig L. Review of *The Pastor*, by Wilhelm Loehe. *Currents in Theology and Mission* 43 (April 2016) 33.

Ottersberg, Gerhard. "Wilhelm Loehe and Wartburg Theological Seminary." *Lecture on 100th Anniversary of Loehe's Death*, Wartburg College, Waverly, Iowa, 1972.

Pless, John T. Review of *The Pastor*, by Wilhelm Loehe. *Concordia Theological Quarterly* 80 (July–October 2016) 374–75.

Tews, Christian C. Review of *Wilhelm Loehe: Theologie und Geschichte*, Dietrich Blaufuss, ed. *Concordia Historical Institute Quarterly* 88 (Fall 2015) 74–75.

Weber, Christian. "The Future of Loehe's Legacy." Address delivered at Wartburg Theological Seminary, Dubuque, Iowa, October 30, 2001.

Bibliography

Baepler, Walter A. *A Century of Grace*. St. Louis: Concordia, 1947.

Bär, Stefan, ed., *Was mir Loehe bedeutet: Stimmen zu Wilhelm Loehe aus heutiger Sicht*. Fürth: Wilhelm-Loehe-Gedenkstätte, 2010.

Bauer, Friedrich, et al. *Christliche Dogmatik auf lutherische Grundlage*. Neuendettelsau: Missionsanstalt, 1921.

———. *Christliche Ethik auf lutherische Grundlage*. Neuendettelsau: Missionsanstalt, 1904.

Bliese, Richard H., and Craig Van Gelder, eds. *The Evangelizing Church: A Lutheran Contribution*. Minneapolis: Augsburg Fortress, 2005.

Bonhoeffer, Dietrich. *Discipleship*. Edited by Geffrey B. Kelly and John D. Godsey. Translated by Barbara Green and Reinhard Krauss. Dietrich Bonhoeffer Works 4. Minneapolis: Fortress, 2001.

———. *Ethics*. Edited by Clifford J. Green. Translated by Reinhard Krauss, Charles C. West, and Douglas W. Stott. Dietrich Bonhoeffer Works 6. Minneapolis: Augsburg Fortress, 2005.

———. *Life Together and Prayerbook of the Bible*. Edited by Geffrey B. Kelly. Translated by Daniel W. Bloesch and James H. Burtness. Dietrich Bonhoeffer Works 5. Minneapolis: Fortress, 2004.

Bosch, David J. *Transforming Mission: Paradigm Shifts in Theology of Mission*. Maryknoll, NY: Orbis, 1991.

Bouman, Walter. "The Unity of the Church in 19th Century Lutheranism." PhD diss., Heidelberg University, 1957.

Brand, Eugene, "The Lord's Supper According to the Lutheran Tradition in North America." In *Coena Domini II: Die Abendmahlsliturgie der Reformationskirchen vom 18. Bis zum frühen 20. Jahrhundert*, edited by Irmgard Pahl, chapter 8. Freiburg: Academic Press, 2005.

Braun, F. *Zum diamentenen Jubilaeum der Evangelisch-Lutherischen Synode von Iowa und anderen Staaten 1854–1929*. Chicago: Wartburg, 1929.

Briese, Russell John. "Wilhelm Loehe and the Rediscovery of the Sacrament of the Altar in Nineteenth-Century Lutheranism." *Lutheran Forum* (30 May 1996) 31–34.

Buehring, P. H. *The Spirit of the American Lutheran Church*. Columbus: Lutheran Book Concern, 1940.

Chung, Paul S. *Christian Mission and a Diakonia of Reconciliation: Justification and Justice*. Minneapolis: Lutheran University Press, 2008.

———. "Confession and Mission: Contextualizing Wilhelm Loehe." In *Wilhelm Loehe: Theology and History*, edited by Dietrich Blaufuss. Neuendettelsau: Freimund, 2013.

Daniel, Lillian. *Tired of Apologizing for a Church I Don't Belong To: Spirituality without Stereotypes, Religion without Ranting*. New York: Faith Words, 2017.

Deindörfer, Johannes. *Geschichte der Evangelischen-Lutherischen Synode von Iowa und anderen Staaten*. Chicago: Wartburg, 1897.

Drachenberg, Herbert R. "J. Michael Reu on the Word of God and Lutheran Unity." STM thesis, Wartburg Theological Seminary, 1971.

Drescher, Elizabeth. *Choosing Our Religion: The Spiritual Lives of America's Nones*. New York: Oxford, 2016.

DuBois, Dwight L. *The Scattering: Imagining a Church that Connects Faith and Life*. Eugene, OR: Wipf & Stock, 2015.

Evangelical Lutheran Church in America-Global Mission Unit. *Global Mission in the Twenty-first Century: A Vision of Evangelical Faithfulness in God's Mission*. Chicago: ELCA, 1999.

The Evangelical-Lutheran Synod of Iowa. *Agende für christliche Gemeinden des lutherischen Bekenntnisses: Auf Grund der Agende von Wilhelm Loehe*. Chicago: Wartburg, 1919.

Everist, Norma Cook, ed. *The Difficult But Indispensable Church*. Minneapolis: Fortress, 2002.

———. *Seventy Images of Grace in the Epistles . . . That Make All the Difference in Daily Life*. Eugene, OR: Cascade Books, 2015.

Everist, Norma Cook and Craig L. Nessan, eds. "Twelve Pastoral Practices for the Life and Mission of the Church." *Currents in Theology and Mission* 38 (October 2011).

———. *Forming and Evangelizing People: Perspectives and Questions for Use in the Church*. Dubuque: Wartburg Theological Seminary, 2005.

Everist, Norma Cook, and Sandy Berg. *And the Women Came: The Stories of the First 125 Women at Wartburg Seminary*. Dubuque: Wartburg Theological Seminary, 1983.

Forster, Walter O. *Zion on the Mississippi: The Settlement of the Saxon Lutherans in Missouri 1939–1841*. St. Louis: Concordia, 1953.

Fritschel, George J. *The Formula of Concord*. Philadelphia: Lutheran Publication Society, 1916.

———. *Geschichte der lutherischen Kirche in Amerika*. Gütersloh: C. Bertelsmann, 1896.

Fritschel, George J., ed. *Quellen und Dokumente zur Geschichte und Lehrstellung der evangelische-lutherische Synode von Iowa und anderen Staaten*. Chicago: Wartburg, n.d.

Fritschel, Herman L. *Biography of Drs. Sigmund and Gottfried Fritschel*. Milwaukee: n.p., 1951.

Fritschel, Sigmund. "The German Iowa Synod." In *The Distinctive Doctrines and Usages of the General Bodies of the Evangelical Lutheran Church in the United States*. Philadelphia: Lutheran Publication Society, 1893.

———. *Pastorale*. Edited by George J. Fritschel. Dubuque: Wartburg Seminary, 1918.

Fritschel, Sigmund and Gottfried Fritschel. *Iowa und Missouri: Eine Verteidgung der Lehrstellung der Synode von Iowa gegenueber den Angriffen des Herrn Prof. Schmidt.* Chicago: Wartburg, n.d.

Gebhardt, Walter and Matthias Honold. "Internationale Beziehungen der Diakonie Neuendettelsau im historischen und aktuellen Kontext I." In *Tradition und Innovation: Diakonische Entwicklungen am Beispiel der Diakonie Neuendettelsau,* edited by Hermann Schoenauer, 47-57. S Diakoniewissenschaft 9. tuttgart: Kohlhammer, 2004.

Geiger, Erika. *The Life, Work, and Influence of Wilhelm Loehe, 1808-1872.* Translated by Wolf Dietrich Knappe. St. Louis: Concordia, 2010.

Gregoire, Carolyn. "The 8 Most Important Things We've Learned About Happiness in The Past 10 Years." *The Huffington Post* (December 6, 2017). http://www.huffingtonpost.com/2015/05/23/science-of-happiness_n_7154918.html.

Hall, Douglas John. *The End of Christendom and the Future of Christianity.* Valley Forge, PA: Trinity, 1997.

Heintzen, Erich H. *Prairie School of the Prophets: The Anatomy of a Seminary 1846-1976.* St. Louis: Concordia, 1989.

Hock, Albert Llewellyn. *The Pilgrim Colony: The History of Saint Sebald Congregation, the Two Wartburgs, and the Synods of Iowa and Missouri.* Minneapolis: Lutheran University Press, 2004.

Honold, Matthias, "Deaconesses in Nursing Care—International Transfer of a Female Model of Life and Work in the 19th and 20th Century." In *Deaconesses in Nursing Care: International Transfer of a Female Model of Life and Work in the 19th and 20th Century,* edited by Susanne Kreutzer and Karen Nolte, 65-77. Stuttgart: Steiner, 2016.

Hunnius, Nikolaus, *Glaubenslehre der evangelsch-lutherische Kirche.* Edited by Friedrich Bauer. Nördlingen: Beck, 1870.

Jenner, Harald. *Von Neuendettelsau in alle Welt: Entwicklung und Bedeutung der Diakonissenanstalt Neuendettelsau/Diakonie Neuendettelsau 1854-1891/1900.* Neuendettelsau: Diakonie Neuendettelsau, 2004.

Kingsolver, Barbara. *The Poisonwood Bible: A Novel.* San Francisco: HarperFlamingo, 1998.

Koller, Wilhelm. *Die Missionsanstalt in Neuendettelsau: Ihre Geschichte und das Leben in Ihr.* Neuendettelsau: Missionshaus Verlag, 1924.

Korby, Kenneth Frederick. "The Theology of Pastoral Care in Wilhelm Loehe with Special Attention to the Function of the Liturgy and the Laity." PhD diss., Concordia Seminary, St. Louis, 1976.

Kothmann, Thomas. "Wilhelm Loehe als Erzieher, Religionslehrer und Katechet." In *Wilhelm Loehe: Theology and History,* edited by Dietrich Blaufuss, 205-53. Neuendettelsau: Freimund, 2013.

Kressel, Hans. *Wilhelm Loehe als Prediger.* Gütersloh: Bertelsmann, 1929.

Lester, G. Brooke. *Understanding Bible by Design: Create Courses with Purpose.* Minneapolis: Fortress, 2014.

Liebenberg, Roland. "Testament eines biblischen Lutheraners: Friedrich Bauers Denkschrift und Anschreiben und die Synode von Iowa." In *Friedrich Bauer (1812-1874): Pionier in der Weltmission, Wegbereiter des Duden,* edited by Claudia Jahnel and Hermann Vorländer, 189-243. Neuendettelsau: Erlanger, 2013.

————. *Wilhelm Loehe (1808–1872): Stationen seines Lebens.* Leipzig: Evangelische Verlagsanstalt, 2011.

Liebenberg, Roland, et al., eds. *Diakonissen fuer Amerika: Sozialer Protestantismus in internationaler Perspektive im 19. Jahrhundert.* Translated by Ruth Gänstaller, Wolf Knappe, and Craig L. Nessan. Leipzig: Evangelische Verlagsanstalt, 2013.

Lindberg, Carter. "Introduction." In *The Pietist Theologians*, edited by Carter Lindberg. Oxford: Blackwell, 2005.

Loehe, Wilhelm. *Aphorisms on the New Testament Offices and Their Relationship to the Congregation.* Translated by John R. Stephenson. Malone, TX: Repristination, 2008.

Loehe, Wilhelm. "Das zehnte Jahr der Diakonnissenanstalt Neuendettelsau (1865)." In *Wilhelm Loehe Gesammelte Werke*, volume 4:17–421. Neuendettelsau: Freimund Verlag, 1962.

Loehe, Wilhelm. "*Der evangelische Geistliche (1852/1858).*" In *Wilhelm Loehe Gesammelte Werke*, volume 3.2:7–317. Neuendettelsau: Freimund Verlag, 1958.

Loehe, Wilhelm. *Diakonissenspruch.* Translated by Craig L. Nessan. http://diakonissen-neuendettelsau.de/Was-Diakonissen-in-Neuendettel.564.0.html.

————. "Die lutherische Auswanderer in Nordamerika: Eine Ansprache an die Leser des Sonntagsblattes." In *Wilhelm Loehe Gesammelte Werke*, 4:16–19. Neuendettelsau: Freimund, 1962.

————. *Liturgy for Christian Congregations of the Lutheran Faith.* Translated by F. C. Longaker with introduction by Edward T. Horn. Newport, KY: n.p., 1902.

————. *Loehe on Mercy.* Translated by Holger Sonntag with preface by Matthew Harrison. St. Louis: Board for World Relief and Human Care, 2007.

————. *Seed-Grains of Prayer: A Manual for Evangelical Christians.* Translated by H. A. Weller. Columbus: Wartburg, 1912.

————. *Three Books about the Church.* Translated and edited by James L. Schaaf. Philadelphia: Fortress, 1969.

————. "Vorschlag zu einem Lutherischen Verein für apostolisches Leben samt Entwurf eines Katechismus des apostolischen Lebens (1848)." In *Wilhelm Loehe Gesammelte Werke*, 5.1:213–52. Neuendettelsau: Freimund, 1954.

Loewen, Nathan. *Effective Social Learning: A Collaborative, Globally-Networked Pedagogy.* Minneapolis: Fortress, 2015.

Lohrmann, Martin J. "A Monument to American Intolerance: The Iowa Synod's 'Open Questions' in Their American Context." in *Wilhelm Loehe: Erbe und Vision*, edited by Dietrich Blaufuss, 294–306. Gütersloh: Gütersloher, 2009.

————. "Loehe and the Ministerium of Pennsylvania." *Currents in Theology and Mission* 39 (February 2012) 72–79.

————. "Prairie Royalty: Auguste von Schwartz (1807–1877) and the Baltic Noblewomen Who Supported the Iowa Synod." *Journal of the Lutheran Historical Conference*, forthcoming.

Luthardt, Christoph Ernst. *Kompendium der Dogmatik,* 14th Edition. Leipzig: Doerffling & Franke, 1914.

Luther, Martin. *Freedom of a Christian.* Translated by Mark D. Tranvik. Minneapolis: Fortress, 2008.

————. "Prefaces to the New Testament." In *Luther's Works: Word and Sacrament 1*, edited by E. Theodore Bachmann, 35: 355–411. Philadelphia: Fortress, 1960.

Lutheran World Federation Department for Theology and Studies. "Nairobi Statement on Worship and Culture: Contemporary Challenges and Opportunities." Geneva: Lutheran World Federation, 1996. http://download.elca.org/ELCA%20Resource%20Repository/LWF_Nairobi_Statement_1994.pdf.

Lyotard, Jean-Francois. *The Postmodern Condition: A Report on Knowledge.* Translated by Geoff Bennington and Brian Massumi. Minneapolis: University of Minnesota, 1993.

Matthias, Ronald. Still *on the Move: Wartburg College, 1852–2002. A Sesquicentennial Celebration.* Cedar Rapids: WDG, 2002.

Maves, David. *How Firm a Foundation: The Founding of the St. Lorenz Lutheran Church and the Community of Frankenmuth.* Frankenmuth, MI: Frankenmuth Historical Association, 1995.

McBrien, Richard P. "The Hierarchy of Truths." *Essays in Theology* (March 9, 2012). http://www.votf-li.org/McBrien-%20Hierarchy%20of%20Truths%203-9-12.pdf.

McGrath, Alister E. *The Twilight of Atheism: The Rise and Fall of Disbelief in the Modern World.* New York: Random House, 2004.

Mineo, Liz. "Good Genes Are Nice, But Joy Is Better." *Harvard Gazette* (April 11, 2017). https://news.harvard.edu/gazette/story/2017/04/over-nearly-80-years-harvard-study-has-been-showing-how-to-live-a-healthy-and-happy-life/.

Muenich, George R. "The Victory of Restorationism: The Common Service, 1888–1958." Chapter in a Manuscript Textbook on Liturgics. Edited by Patrick R. Kiefert. St. Paul: Luther Northwestern Theological Seminary, 1984.

Nessan, Craig L. *The Air I Breathe Is Wartburg Air: The Legacy of William H. Weiblen.* Eugene, OR: Wipf & Stock, 2003.

———. *Beyond Maintenance to Mission: A Theology of the Congregation.* Second Edition. Minneapolis: Fortress, 2010.

———. "Friedrich Bauer zum 200. Geburtstag: Genealogie eines vergessenen Vorfahren." In *Friedrich Bauer (1812–1874): Pionier in der Weltmission, Wegbereiter des Duden,* edited by Claudia Jahnel and Hermann Vorländer, 245–64. Neuendettelsau: Erlanger, 2014.

———. "Interpreting the Bible Lutheranly: Between the Undertow and a Tsunami." In *Lutheran Perspectives on Biblical Interpretation: The 2009 Hein-Fry Lectures,* edited by Laurie Jungling, 11–35. Minneapolis: Lutheran University Press, 2010.

———. "Lernendes Begleiten: Die Arbeit der Iowa-Synode unter Indianern im 19. Jahrhundert." *Confessio Augustana.* 2008 Special Edition for Loehe Anniversary, 36–38.

———. "Loehe and His Coworkers in the Iowa Synod." *Currents in Theology and Mission* 33 (April 2006) 140–44.

———. "Mission and Theological Education—Berlin, Athens, and Tranquebar: A North American Perspective." *Mission Studies* 27 (2010) 176–93.

———. "The Neighborliness (*Diakonia*) of All Believers: Toward Reimagining the Universal Priesthood." In *Together by Grace: Introducing the Lutherans,* edited by Kathryn A. Kleinhans, 143–46. Minneapolis: Augsburg Fortress, 2016.

———. *Shalom Church: The Body of Christ as Ministering Community.* Minneapolis: Fortress, 2010.

———. "Universal Priesthood of All Believers: Unfulfilled Promise of the Reformation." *Currents in Theology and Mission* 46 (January 2019) 8–15.

Neve, J. L. *A Brief History of the Lutheran Church in America.* Burlington, IA: German Literary Board, 1916.

O'Meara, Thomas F. "Times of Change: 1515–2015. Wittenberg, Rome, Dubuque." In *Celebration of the 15th Anniversary of the Signing of the Lutheran-Roman Catholic Joint Declaration on the Doctrine of Justification,* edited by Janine Marie Idziak and Winston D. Persaud, 11–19. Dubuque, IA: Loras College Press, 2015.

Olson, Jeannine E. *Deacons and Deaconesses through the Centuries.* Revised Edition. St. Louis: Concordia, 2007.

Olson, Roger E., and Christian T. Collins Winn. *Reclaiming Pietism: Retrieving an Evangelical Tradition.* Grand Rapids: Eerdmans, 2015.

Ottersberg, Gerhard. *The Brothers Fritschel.* Waverly, IA: Wartburg College, n.d.

———. "Wilhelm Loehe." *Lutheran Quarterly* 4 (1952) 170–90.

———. "The Evangelical Lutheran Synod of Iowa and Other States, 1854–1904." PhD diss., University of Nebraska, 1949.

Packard, Josh and Ashleigh Hope. *Church Refugees: Sociologists Reveal Why People Are Done with the Church.* Loveland, CO: Group, 2015.

Panikkar, Raimundo. *The Unknown Christ of Hinduism.* Maryknoll, NY: Orbis, 1981.

Pless, John T. "Wilhelm Loehe als seelsorgerlicher Theologe." In *Wilhelm Loehe: Theology and History,* edited by Dietrich Blaufuss, 255–76. Neuendettelsau: Freimund, 2013.

———. "Wilhelm Loehe and the Missouri Synod: Forgotten Paternity or Living Legacy?" *Currents in Theology and Mission* 33 (April 2006) 126–27.

Ratke, David. *Confession and Mission, Word and Sacrament: The Ecclesial Theology of Wilhelm Loehe.* St. Louis: Concordia, 2001.

Reed, Luther D. *The Lutheran Liturgy: A Study of the Common Liturgy of the Lutheran Church in America.* Philadelphia: Muhlenberg, 1947.

Reiner, Hermann. "Nachhaltige Wirkung: Zum 200. Geburtstag von Friedrich Bauer Grümder der Missionsanstalt Neuendettelsau." In *Naher Osten: Christen in der Minderheit. Jahrbuch Mission 2012,* edited by Bettina von Clausewitz. Hamburg: Missionshilfe Verlag, 2012.

Reu, J. Michael. *Catechetics or Theory and Practice of Religious Instruction.* Chicago: Wartburg, 1927.

———. *An Explanation of Dr. Martin Luther's Small Catechism. Together with Four Supplements.* Columbus: Wartburg, 1947.

———. *Homiletics: A Manual of the Theory and Practice of Preaching.* Chicago: Wartburg, 1927.

———. *How I Tell the Bible Stories to My Sunday School.* Chicago: Wartburg, 1918.

———. *Lutheran Dogmatics.* Dubuque: Wartburg Seminary, 1941–1942.

Rössler, Hans, ed. *Friedrich Bauer: Begegnungen.* Neuendettelsau: Freimund Verlag, 2012.

Rössler, Hans. "Friedrich Bauer: Ein fränkischer Theologe und Schulmann mit weltweiter Wirkung." *Neuendettelsauer Heft* 6, Special Edition of *Zeitschrift für Kirchengeschichte* 80 (2011) 39–48.

———. "Neuendettelsauer Missionare bei den Chippewas in Michigan und den Crows in Montana/USA: Vier Modelle missionarischer Aktivität." *Zeitschrift für Bayerische Kirchengeschichte* 77 (2008) 227–34.

Salzmann, S. F. "The Theology of Wartburg Seminary." *Wartburg Seminary Quarterly* 17 (November 1954)11–23.

Sasse, Herman. "Walther and Loehe: On the Church." *The Springfielder* (December 1971) 176–82.

Schaaf, James L. "The Controversy about *Kirche* and *Amt*." In "Wilhelm Loehe's Relation to the American Church: A Study in the History of Lutheran Mission," 121–62. PhD diss., University of Heidelberg, 1961.

————. "Wilhelm Loehe and the Missouri Synod." *Concordia Historical Institute Quarterly* 45 (May 1972) 54–59.

————. "Wilhelm Loehe's Relation to the American Church: A Study in the History of Lutheran Mission." ThD diss., Ruprecht-Karl-University, Heidelberg, 1961.

Schalk, Carl F. "Sketches of Lutheran Worship." In *A Handbook of Church Music*, edited by Carl Halter and Carl Schalk, chapter 2. St. Louis: Concordia, 1978.

Schattauer, Thomas H. "Liturgical Assembly as Locus of Mission." In *Inside Out: Worship in an Age of Mission*, edited by Thomas H. Schattauer, chapter 1. Minneapolis: Augsburg Fortress, 1999.

————. "Reclaiming the Christian Assembly as *Communio*: The Significance of the Lord's Supper in the Work of Wilhelm Loehe." In *Wilhelm Loehe: Erbe und Vision*, edited by Dietrich Blaufuss, 50–66. Gütersloh: Gütersloher, 2009.

————. "The Reconstruction of Rite: The Liturgical Legacy of Wilhelm Loehe." In *Rule of Prayer, Rule of Faith: Essays in Honor of Aidan Kavanaugh, O.S.B*, edited by Nathan Mitchell and John F. Baldovin, 243–77. Collegeville, MN: Liturgical, 1996.

————. "'Sung, Spoken, Lived': Worship as Communion and Mission in the Work of Wilhelm Loehe." *Currents in Theology and Mission* 33 (April 2006) 113–21.

Schmid, Heinrich. *The Doctrinal Theology of the Evangelical Lutheran Church*. 3rd edition. Translated by Charles A. Hay and Henry E. Jacobs. Minneapolis: Augsburg, 1961.

Schmutterer, Gerhard M. and Charles P. Lutz. "Mission Martyr on the Western Frontier: Can Cross-cultural Mission Be Achieved?" In *Church Roots: Stories of Nine Immigrant Groups That Became the American Lutheran Church*, edited by Charles P. Lutz, 117–42 Minneapolis: Augsburg, 1985.

Schoenfuhs, Walter P. "The Story of the 'German Lutheran Chippewa Indian Mission' in the Saginaw Valley." Reprint. *Concordia Historical Institute Quarterly* 37 (October 1964).

Schwarz, Hans. "Wilhelm Loehe zu sozialen Fragen seiner Zeit." In *Wilhelm Loehe: Erbe und Vision*, edited by Dietrich Blaufuss, 239–47. Gütersloh: Gütersloher Verlashaus, 2009.

Seitz, Manfred. "Gottesdienst und liturgische Sprache bei Wilhelm Loehe." Translated by Craig L. Nessan. In *Wilhelm Loehe: Erbe und Vision*, edited by Dietrich Blaufuss, 33–49. Gütersloh: Gütersloher, 2009.

Shantz, Douglas H. *An Introduction to German Pietism: Protestant Renewal at the Dawn of Modern Europe*. Baltimore: Johns Hopkins University Press, 2013.

Spener, Philipp Jakob. *Pia Desideria (1675)*. Translated by Theodore G. Tappert. Philadelphia: Fortress, 1964.

Stache, Kristine and Craig L. Nessan. "Adventures into Digital Teaching, Learning, and Formation: A Case Study from Wartburg Theological Seminary." *Journal of Religious Leadership* 17 (Fall 2018) 20–45.

Strohm, Theodor. "Wilhelm Loehes Verständnis der Diakonie der Kirche und die Wirklichkeit der Diakonie heute." In *Wilhelm Loehe: Erbe und Vision*, edited by Dietrich Blaufuss, 259–81. Gütersloh: Gütersloher Verlashaus, 2009.

Thomasius, Gottfried. *Christi Person und Werk: Darstellung der evangelisch-lutherischen Dogmatik von ihrem Mittelpunkte der Christologie aus.* 3 vols. Erlangen: Blaesing, 1856–62.

Thompson, Deanna A. *The Virtual Body of Christ in a Suffering World.* Nashville: Abingdon, 2016.

Tickle, Phyllis. *The Great Emergence: How Christianity Is Changing and Why.* Grand Rapids: Baker, 2012.

Tietjen, John H. "The Ecclesiology of Wilhelm Loehe." STM thesis, Union Theological Seminary, New York, 1954.

Vicedom, George. *The Mission of God: An Introduction to a Theology of Mission.* Translated by Gilbert A. Thiele and Dennis Hilgendorf. St. Louis: Concordia, 1965.

von Hoffman, Johann Christian Konrad. *Der Schriftbeweis: Ein theologischer Versuch.* 4 Volumes. Nördlingen: Beck, 1857.

Wartburg Kalendar der Evangelisch-Lutherische Synode von Iowa und anderen Staaten. Chicago: Wartburg, 1904.

Wartburg Theological Seminary. "Mission Statement." (September 3, 2019). https://www.wartburgseminary.edu/mission-and-vision/.

Was lehrt die Iowa-Synode von der Inspiration der Heiligen Schrift? Aus ihren eigenen Publikationen und anderen Quellen Dargestellt. Twin City Local Conference, n.d.

Weber, Christian. "Die Anfänge der Neuendettelsauer Mission unter Johann Konrad Wilhelm Loehe aus der Retrospektive nach 25 Jahren." In *Franken und die Weltmission im 19. und 20. Jahrhundert.* Edited by Wolfgang Weiß, et al. Quellen und Forschungen zur Geschichte des Bistums und Hochstifts Würzburg 65. Würzburg: Schöningh, 2011.

———. "The Future of Loehe's Legacy." *Currents in Theology and Mission* 31 (April 2004) 96–102.

———. "Loehe in the Congo: Missionary Perspectives against Pessimism." In *Wilhelm Loehe: Erbe und Vision,* edited by Dietrich Blaufuss, 67–79. Gütersloh: Gütersloher, 2009.

———. *Missionstheologie bei Wilhelm Loehe: Aufbruch zur Kirche der Zukunft.* Gütersloh: Gütersloher, 1996.

———. "Weitblickend, konzentriert und ehrlich: Das missionarische Bildungskonzept Friedrich Bauers (1812–74)." In *Friedrich Bauer (1812–1874): Pionier in der Weltmission, Wegbereiter des Duden,* edied by Claudia Jahnel and Hermann Vorländer, 135–88. Neuendettelsau: Erlanger, 2014.

Weiblen, William H. *Life Together at Wartburg Theological Seminary: 1854–2004.* Sesquicentennial Edition. Edited by Craig L. Nessan. Dubuque, IA: Union Hoermann, 2006.

Williams, Rowan. *Being Disciples: Essentials of the Christian Life.* Grand Rapids: Eerdmans, 2016.

Zehnder, Herman F. *Teach My People the Truth: The Story of Frankenmuth, Michigan.* Bay City, MI: Zehnder, 1970.

Zeilinger, G. J. *A Missionary Synod with a Mission: A Memoir for the Seventy-fifth Anniversary of the Evangelical Lutheran Synod of Iowa and Other States 1854–1929.* Chicago: Wartburg, 1929.

Zelman, Elizabeth Crouch. *Our Beleaguered Species: Beyond Tribalism.* North Charleston: CreateSpace, 2015.

Zizioulas, John D. *Being as Communion: Studies in Personhood and the Church.* New York: St. Vladimir's Seminary Press, 1997.

Index of Names

Index of Subjects